EVERYTHING YOU WANTED TO KNOW ABOUT HAPPINESS AND WELLBEING

But Were Too Miserable To Ask

A R Arnold

Copyright © 2024 A R Arnold

Everything You Wanted To Know About Happiness And Wellbeing

All Rights Reserved. No part of this book may be reproduced in any form or by any electronic or mechanical means including information storage and retrieval systems, without permission in writing from the author. The only exception is by a reviewer, who may quote short excerpts in a review.

This is a work of non-fiction. The events and conversations in this book have been set down to the best of the author's ability, although some names and details may have been changed to protect the privacy of individuals. Every effort has been made to trace or contact all copyright holders. The publishers will be pleased to make good any omissions or rectify any mistakes brought to their attention at the earliest opportunity.

Cover by A R Arnold
First edition: June 2024
Second edition: November 2024
Paperback ISBN 978-1-7637945-0-4
eBook ISBN 978-1-7637945-1-1

Originally published as WEALTH & Wellbeing

*To my beautiful wife, Megan and our beautiful daughters, Emma and Cassie. I love you. You are my joy.
Also, to every middle-aged person who wonders what the hell happened and can't afford a midlife crisis saying, "I'll be happy when..."
Well, the answer is hopefully now or at least after you've read this book.*

CONTENTS

Title Page
Copyright
Dedication
INTRODUCTION
PART I	1
BEYOND BILLBOARD HAPPINESS	2
THIS IS HAPPINESS AND WELLBEING	5
THE WEALTH MINDSET	17
FAILURE TO LAUNCH	29
WELLBEING AND THE BRAIN	39
YOU ARE A CHICKEN	51
THE CHEMICAL BROTHERS	59
YOU ARE A DODO	73
EMOTIONS	76
MENTAL HEALTH	82
IT AIN'T SO BAD	106
PART II	112
INGREDIENTS FOR WELLBEING	114
KNOW YOURSELF	116
MONEY, JOBS, AND STUFF	134
Money	136

PERSPECTIVE	164
Control	175
ROCK	190
HAVING A VISION AND MEANING IN YOUR LIFE	192
SAVOURING LIFE'S JOYS AND LIVING IN THE MOMENT	205
MEDITATION	216
SIGNATURE STRENGTHS	229
LEARNING	235
GROWTH MINDSET	243
KINDNESS	254
GRATITUDE	261
SOCIAL CONNECTION	267
EXERCISE	282
SLEEP	289
FOOD AND DRINKS	298
SETTING AND COMMITING TO GOALS	309
PRACTICING SPIRITUALITY AND RELIGION	323
AVOID OVERTHINKING AND SOCIAL COMPARISON	331
ACTING LIKE A HAPPY PERSON	339
PART III	350
IT IS TIME TO GO FROM WELL NOW TO WELL ALWAYS	351
PROCRASTINATION	354
SELF-DISCIPLINE	360
MOTIVATION	366
BUILDING GOOD HABITS AND BREAKING BAD	378
NEXT STEPS	396
BIBLIOGRAPHY	400
ENDNOTES	404

About The Author

INTRODUCTION

Have you ever seen one of those memes where someone has attempted to bake a cake, intending it to look as good as the one in the recipe, only to have it turn out absolutely terrible, with the tagline: 'Nailed it'? That's life. Society sells us the beautiful cake – the dream of wealth and fortune, health and vitality, an amazing life of happiness and wellbeing – only to end up with a spongy mess that's never as good, or even close to what we expected. Yet, and here's the stinger, we continue to do the same things, use the same ingredients, follow the same recipe, process, and routines. We still hope to get that perfect cake and wonder why we keep getting a monstrosity instead. We're achieving the same temporal, ultimately unsatisfying, results. What is going wrong?

Many people are unhappy (read: miserable, anxious, depressed) and it stems from, amongst other things, the fact that they don't have any real purpose or meaning in their lives. I use the word "real" because many believe that they do have purpose and meaning in their lives, but our society has created these artificial reasons in the pursuit of prosperity at the expense of our mental health.

We live in an age of leisure and pleasure, where everything we want is a click away except that what we really want (and need) isn't a quick fix. What we really need is a purpose, a reason to get up every morning beyond going to work to pay bills and buying stuff that doesn't bring us any long-term joy. In many cases, the stuff simply makes us feel even more unhappy as we compare and despair with those around us who seem, unlike us, to have it all together.

It really sucks.

There are certain inalienable truths that need to be addressed. One. Yes, it really sucks, but two, you are not alone. Not many, if any, people have it truly all together. Think of someone you know. How well do you really know them? Truthfully. How well do people really know you? In fact, how well do you really know yourself?

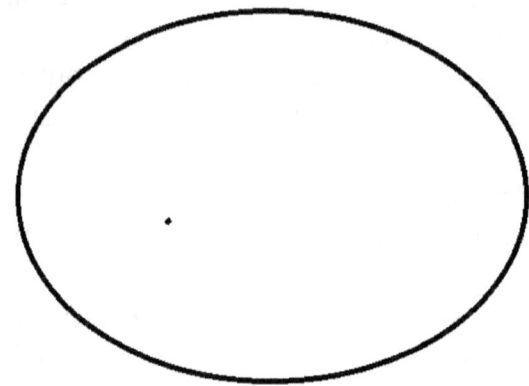

This circle is someone's life, and that dot is what you know really about them. It's not much so just realise that as much as you may be struggling in certain areas of your life, so too is everyone else.

We live in a world of information overload where we are more aware than ever before of what is happening around us. Yes, as a consequence we can compare and despair but we also have greater awareness of the environment, of our collective past, and our inclusiveness or lack thereof. It can make us want to be better people but the media, television, and Internet overload us with things we do and don't need to know. It can become overwhelming for our primitive brains, which want to provide a sanctuary of safety for us, and we can become anxious and stressed, far from the happiness and wellbeing we all crave.

This book will not change your life. Only you can do that. This book looks at the happiness and wellbeing we all strive for and provides a reality check on why, like most things in life, it is fleeting and unfulfilling. It will then look at some of the many ways you can feel happiness and wellbeing, dissecting them to understand what they are. We'll look at what is involved, what lasts (and what doesn't), and the things you need to do if you want to incorporate them into your life in order to have a better sense of overall positive wellbeing.

Why is this important? Because too many of us keep doing the same thing, hoping for a different result. Others simply give up and think the problem lies with them, or worse, everything and everyone else.

In order to make the journey easier, I have split the book into three distinct parts.

Part One

Most of what you are about to read is the result of exhaustive research done by countless professionals in their respective fields of expertise. I have compiled this research into easily digestible chunks so that you can get a better understanding of the subjects presented and make informed decisions based on that information. I don't pretend to be an expert in the subject matter of wellness, however through many hours, days, months and even years of interest and research in this field of study I have concluded that there are certain themes that recur and are key to ensuring long-term, positive wellbeing in your life.

It should also be noted that I am not a specialist or professional in the field of psychology or psychiatry. The information gathered is presented to you so that you are informed. When dealing with such topics as anxiety and depression, the information is not advice and you should seek professional help.

In this book you will be introduced to the concept of WEALTH. WEALTH is an acronym that stands for: Will, Experience, Action, Learning, Time, and Habits. These are the foundation of happiness and wellbeing, underpinning all of the 'ingredients' necessary for a life of wellbeing. I will explain how each of these are at the root of everything you need for a life of wellbeing.

> *The reason people find it so hard to be*
> *happy is that they always see*
> *the past better than it was, the present worse than it is, and the*
> *future less resolved than it will be.*
> *– Marcel Pagnol*

My aim with this book is to show you simple ingredients, things that you can mix together to find a recipe that works for you, that will guide you to a happier, more fulfilled, and meaningful life instead of one spent in idleness and wanton pursuit of billboard happiness.

Together we will explore wellbeing for the modern world, offering a realistic and attainable grasp of what brings positive wellbeing and happiness, why it is hard to keep, and what you can do to build it into your everyday life and make it a part of your lifestyle. We will acknowledge the realities of the world we live in and the difficulties of being happy and doing what is good for you.

Ultimately, I want you to unlock a better version of yourself for the rest of your life.

That is a tall ask and certainly not easy! Maybe you feel lost, unable to find a sense of true wellbeing and feel you're alone in feeling this way. The fact is, there are literally millions of people who feel lost in this world. We have created a world where everyone feels everyone else is happier, better, and more together than they are. It is a place where the midlife crisis has just become a life crisis, moving from one crisis of thought to another, hidden behind a façade of smiling faces and fancy cars.

Many of us live lives of inaction and only exist, caught in the expectation trap, the hole that is consumerism, money, cars, big houses, toys, and gadgets, all the throw away things. We have chosen, for the majority of our lives, to go through the motions and to live without actually achieving anything real, anything that has any meaning to us as individuals. This leaves us feeling hollow and down, and we wonder if something is wrong with us - if we are the problem.

We will look at why we are like this, why our primitive brain seems so determined to make us anything but happy, and its complicity in determining why we are the way we are. We explore the multitude of emotions and biases that influence the way the think and act, look at our mental health, and the chemical brothers (not the music act), the chemicals that make our brain work, and okay, not all are chemicals (some are hormones) but they explain a lot about human nature and our propensity to let fear and failure get the better of what we know is good for us. All of this needs some context as what good is wellbeing if we don't have a clear definition of what it is? Don't worry, you will, and we will also differentiate happiness and wellbeing, why this is important, and why sometimes, you have to let go of the picture of what you thought your life would be like and find the wow in the story that you are living.

Part Two

Decades of research by professionals and specialists in the

field of psychology have determined the nineteen ingredients I have selected that you can incorporate into your life to provide you with an overall sense of positive wellbeing. I call these nineteen things ingredients because like the 'Nailed it' cake analogy, by putting them together, whichever work for you, you are creating for yourself a unique recipe for wellbeing in your life. Not all ingredients will work for you, but many will, whether it is setting goals, changing your perspective, exercising, having a growth mindset, or simply acting like a happy person, you can work to become the person you always wanted to be.

Part Three

This part is the glue that binds everything before it together. If we are continuing the cake analogy, it is the flour providing the basic structure and solidity, binding everything together and stopping it falling into a blobby mess.

There are lots of books on *what* makes you happy and barely any on *how* you can be happy, aside from glib statements, such as 'practice this daily' or with little guidance beyond, 'get into the habit of doing this every day using our free chart, which you can download from 'givemeyouremailaddress.com'. In this part, we look at overcoming procrastination, enacting self-discipline, and finding what motivates you so you can both break bad habits and build good habits. Habit is therefore the flour to our cake, the final of the WEALTH foundations and the thing that ensures wellbeing is long-lasting and forever present within your life, and hopefully turning this book from a simple self-help book you read once into one you refer back to many times in order to build a sustainable sense of positive wellbeing in your life.

At the end of it all, happiness and wellbeing can be achieved by only about five and a half inches.

Before you start considering other things, that is the width of your brain. In the end, that is all that matters. Ultimately, it is through your brain, the little grey cells, that your wellbeing is determined.

This book pulls together, in an easy to read and follow format, what you need to know on the topics of happiness and wellbeing and what can be done to make you feel happier, what you can do to live a better life, and how you can maintain it through the building of good habits. It is my aim for you to be able to pick and choose what works for you, and end this book equipped to enjoy a positive sense of wellbeing.

'Brace yourself. This could be fun.'

MacGyver

PART I

BEYOND BILLBOARD HAPPINESS

Happy. It is the first word many of us say at the start of each year: Happy New Year!

We wish each other a happy year ahead and enter each year with hope and renewed positivity, armed with resolutions to do things we think will make us happier. But what does that mean, and why do we tend to fail to accomplish what we have resolved to do? Why do we end up feeling like we are on a treadmill moving ever faster but going nowhere?

The start of the 21st century has seen an explosion of interest and research into the fields of happiness and wellbeing as our society continues to evolve. This change has been incredibly fast with advancements in nearly every sphere of life. Yet, as much as our lives have become easier, they don't appear to have made us feel happier or more fulfilled. Social media has made many of us feel socially isolated and inadequate, while the pursuit of billboard happiness and to be everything to everyone has left us wanting.

We are led to believe that happiness comes with a price tag, but find it is always temporary and elusive. Despite massive economic growth and technological advancements over the past century, people, especially those living in Western countries, are unhappy, unfulfilled, and unsatisfied. If you take nearly any measure, you will see that we should be happier than ever, but we are not. The prevalence of mental illness, particularly depression and anxiety, alongside increased loneliness and social isolation, and the breakdown of communities, has led to a disillusionment with society. Stress, meaningless jobs, and debt compound the problem.

What is to be done? The obvious thing is to consider what makes us feel happy, safe, comfortable, and healthy. This is, in essence, what wellbeing is. If we have a sense of wellbeing, then we aren't limited to survival but will instead thrive in the world. Wellbeing is the elixir to modern living, but at the same time it is also the antithesis. As such, this causes conflict as the two continually vie for domination. The key is to find a happy medium or balance. This is difficult to achieve because of their contradictory natures. It is hard to make positive wellbeing a natural part of your life because quite simply our brain does not do what is good for us or even what we want it to do, but what makes us comfortable. And what makes us comfortable is not always what is good for us.

Our brain has a lot to answer for and essentially what we need to do is reprogram it. That is no simple task, however knowledge is power, and to use the ingredients in Part Two to their full potential, it is good to understand why you find yourself stuck in a loop of starting and stopping, taking two steps forward and if you're lucky, only one step back. Knowing how your brain works will help you to overcome its incessant desire to stay in its happy place, the comfort zone that prevents you from moving forward, and push out of it, building new neural pathways that open you up to new experiences and long-lasting happiness and wellbeing.

When I was five years old, my mother always told me that happiness was the key to life. When I went to school, they asked me what I wanted to be when I grew up. I wrote down 'happy'. They told me I didn't understand the assignment, and I told them they didn't understand life.

The above quote, often attributed to John Lennon, needs to be updated for this book, because as much as I want you to be happy, I also want you to know that even when you are not, you are still okay. Happiness, like the tide, comes and goes and then comes again. I want to encourage you through it all, with the help of this book, to seek a life of overall positive wellbeing and to be the best version of yourself, no matter the circumstances.

THIS IS HAPPINESS AND WELLBEING

An American executive was taking a much-needed vacation in a Mexican coastal village when a small boat with just one fisherman docked. Inside the small boat were several large yellow fin tuna. The American complimented the Mexican fisherman on the quality of his fish and asked how long it took him to catch them.

'Not very long,' answered the Mexican.

'But then, why didn't you stay out longer and catch more?' asked the American.

The Mexican explained that his small catch sufficed to meet his needs and those of his family.

The American asked, 'But what do you do with the rest of your time?'

'I sleep late, fish a little, play with my children, and take a siesta with my wife. In the evenings, I go into the village to see my friends, have a few drinks, play the guitar, and sing a few songs… I have a busy and full life.'

The American interrupted, 'I have an MBA from Harvard and I can help you! You should start by fishing longer every day. You can then sell the extra fish you catch. With the extra revenue, you can buy a bigger boat.'

'And after that?' asked the Mexican.

'With the extra money the larger boat will bring, you can

buy a second one and a third one and so on until you have an entire fleet of trawlers. Instead of selling your fish to a middleman, you can then negotiate directly with the processing plants and maybe even open your own plant. You can then leave this little village and move to Mexico City, Los Angeles, or even New York City! From there you can direct your huge new enterprise.'

'How long would that take?' asked the Mexican.

'Twenty, perhaps twenty-five years,' replied the American.

'And after that?' the Mexican asked.

'Afterwards? That's when it gets really interesting,' answered the American, laughing. 'When your business gets really big, you can start selling stocks and make millions!'

'Millions? Really? And after that?'

'After that you'll be able to retire, live in a tiny village near the coast, sleep late, play with your children, catch a few fish, take a siesta with your wife and spend your evenings drinking and enjoying your friends.'

As the story above tells, happiness is subjective but at the end of the day, we all want the same thing. No-one can really agree on what happiness means as it means different things to different people. Defining what happiness is becomes an exercise in frustration. Much like Pluto was originally a defined as a planet and then it wasn't because the definition of what a planet is was never clear. It was demoted to a dwarf planet, so is technically still a planet, but not really. It is the same with happiness — a consequence of a badly defined meaning.

So, what exactly is that meaning and how does it differ from wellbeing?

Happiness and wellbeing are like two threads that weave their way through our daily experiences in the grand tapestry we call life. Both terms are often used interchangeably yet there are subtle yet significant differences between them.

Happiness

happiness, n.
The quality or condition of being happy.[1]

Being happy is an emotion, albeit a positive one, and all emotions are temporary – they don't last. That is a major problem with how people see happiness. Many assume it is a long-term emotion, whereas it is a transient emotional state. It comes and goes, but it never stays. It's the joy we feel when we accomplish a goal, share a laugh with friends, or indulge in a favourite treat. The pursuit of happiness often involves external validation, material gains, or momentary pleasures. Happiness is beautiful. It leaves us with a warm glow but fades away like an ember, as quickly as it has appeared.

Happiness is the consequence of personal effort. You fight for it, strive for it, insist upon it, and sometimes even travel around the world looking for it. You have to participate relentlessly in the manifestations of your own blessings. And once you have achieved a state of happiness, you must never become lax about maintaining it. You must make a mighty effort to keep swimming upward into that happiness forever, to stay afloat on top of it.

- Elizabeth Gilbert, Eat, Pray, Love

One of the issues with happiness is that many people see it as the end goal, something to be obtained. The irony is that, in fact, it isn't the end or the goal at all, it is what happens on the way to achieving our goals or any other number of things. Most of the time, people don't even recognise happiness until after the fact, and sometimes not at all. Here is an important thing to learn and remember – we are the product of the stories we tell, and those stories become who we are. With a positive sense of wellbeing we can more easily find the happy moments that we may have missed in the moment. For example, you may have hated the holiday you had, but afterwards, in the quiet when you have time to reflect, you remember the little things that happened, and see the big picture of your experience and find happiness. Another example of this is raising children. Lots of studies have been done on children and happiness, and what you get is a lot of conflicting information.

In the act of raising children, the day-to-day stuff, parents aren't very happy but when you ask them what it is like having kids, they will say it is one of the most enjoyable things they have done in their lives. We seem to forget the details and see the overall picture, remembering the good and closeting the not so good. Such is happiness in your life.

As Nicolas Chamfort, the French writer, once said, 'Happiness is not easy to find. It's very difficult to find it in yourself – and impossible to find anywhere else.' Happiness is a major component of wellbeing and for that reason, we need not necessarily find it, as it is not something to be pursued, but to be allowed it into our lives through the best means that work for us. Those means are, like ourselves, unique to each of us.

Happiness is a butterfly, which when pursued, is always just beyond

your grasp, but which, if you will sit down

quietly, may alight upon

you.

– Nathaniel Hawthorne

Wellbeing

> *well-being, n.*
>
> *With reference to a person or community: the state of being healthy, happy, or prosperous; physical, psychological, or moral welfare.*[2]

Wellbeing (or well-being or wellness) is a term that even if you don't fully understand it, you've likely have heard it many times in recent years. It has become a staple of modern Western life, lending itself to a host of health and wellness initiatives, trends, and even political goals.[3] However, wellbeing is not an elixir for all the ills and issues in your life but aims to provide some balance and an overall sense of comfort and contentment in your life.

Wellbeing is the overall state of being comfortable, healthy, and content in life. Wellbeing is a broader concept that encompasses physical health, mental and emotional stability, and a sense of purpose. It's the foundation upon which we build our lives, providing resilience in the face of challenges and the strength to navigate the twists and turns of our journey. Physical wellbeing involves maintaining a healthy lifestyle through regular exercise, proper nutrition, and sufficient rest. Mental and emotional wellbeing delve into the realms of mindfulness, stress management, and fostering positive relationships. Imagine wellbeing as the roots of a tree—anchored, deep, and essential for the tree's longevity. It provides stability and resilience, allowing individuals to weather life's storms with grace and navigate the complexities of their journey.

Let's also be clear that wellbeing, like happiness, is subjective. Wellbeing is unique to every individual; what is wellbeing to you will be different to what is wellbeing to someone else. We all have different expectations and aspirations for ourselves which will affect our wellbeing. Cultural influences on wellbeing can bring a sense of belonging socially, even if it is at the expense of our individuality. Equally, the opposite may apply, where the need to conform to social norms can bring a sense of dissonance and negative wellbeing.

Wellbeing is a term that can be either positive or negative. Even positive wellbeing varies depending on perception; it is more like a sliding scale. Negative wellbeing or ill-being, as defined in the Casual Networks Model of Wellbeing[4], often has its seeds in early childhood and comes from feelings of worth. Self-worth and self-acceptance are essential to wellbeing. You, the individual, should determine your self-worth, not someone else, even if it is a parent or caregiver. You should have your basic emotional needs met. These include feeling safe, accepted, and appreciated, having autonomy in your life, a sense of achievement and purpose, and feeling socially connected.

Refuse to remain stagnant; harness your curiosity and strike out in

life - seek the unknown territory that lies beyond your comfort zone

to discover your ever-unfolding, remarkable potential.

- Patricia Furness-Smith, Introducing Well-being: A Practical Guide

Wellbeing is more than your health or happiness. It is a term that encompasses the physical, emotional, social, and mental health of yourself, others, the groups we are a part of, and all of us as a whole. It looks at the activities and choices people make that will aid their wellbeing. Wellbeing is a state of being comfortable, healthy, or happy and there are many models and components that have been developed to explain and define what wellbeing is. These include but are not limited to:

- Positive psychology with its emphasis on eudaimonia.
- The biopsychosocial model of wellbeing, which focuses on what it sees as the modifiable components needed by a person to have a sense of wellbeing.
- Flourishing[5], which says mental wellbeing has three main components:
  1. Emotional wellbeing
  2. Psychological wellbeing
  3. Social wellbeing
- The six-factor Model of Psychological Wellbeing[6], which is based on Aristotle's Nicomachean Ethics[7], where the goal of life is to live virtuously, with the model consisting of six factors: –

1. Self-acceptance

2. Personal Growth

3. Purpose in Life

4. Environmental mastery

5. Autonomy

6. Positive relationships with others

Looking at positive psychology's view of wellbeing, you need to live a happy, engaged and meaningful life. Martin Seligman, in his book *Flourish*[8], identified five elements of wellbeing using the mnemonic PERMA.

- Positive emotions:

All positive emotions, not just happiness, as all positive emotions are related to positive outcomes.

- Engagement:

What activities draw and build up your interests?. True engagement is called flow. It needs skill and is challenging but still possible, absorbing you completely to the point where you lose all sense of space and time.

- Relationships:

Other people are important in your life. They fuel positive emotions and give, receive, and share emotions with you.

- Meaning:

This is your purpose and what gives meaning to your life.

- Accomplishments:

This is not only what you accomplish but the pursuit of your goals, the journey you take to attaining your goals and accomplishments.

Wellbeing is an umbrella term of which happiness is just one component but one that is often confused for the whole. The American Declaration of Independence talks of the pursuit of happiness. However, in the modern context, we should perhaps see it as the pursuit of wellbeing. The foundations of wellbeing mentioned are: emotional, mental, physical, and social. They do not include financial wellbeing. However, to achieve a true sense of wellbeing, your finances are just as important, If you want to have a healthy balance of the other foundations, being financially healthy enables you to remove monetary stressors detrimental in your life.

In differentiating happiness and wellbeing, it essentially comes down to short-term versus long-term. Hedonic and eudaimonia are the words used to define the differences between the short-term and long-term definitions.

Hedonic happiness focuses on the outcome or 'the intense but brief feelings of pleasure for pleasure's sake,'[9] examples of which are having sex, a bottle of wine, getting likes on your Instagram or Facebook post, or watching a favourite television show. In other words, what we define as happiness.

Eudaimonia focuses 'on the content of your life and the process involved in living well.[10]' This is more about living a more meaningful life, being kind, having good relationships with others, choosing a fulfilling job, and living to your potential by doing what makes you better. This what we have defined as wellbeing.

We need to be aware of not only the differences between hedonic and eudaimonia, but how they mix. Hedonic pursuits, although valid, have the potential to be detrimental to the happiness of yourself and others around you, as they can be selfish and have an unhealthy focus on present experiences as opposed to the bigger picture. Long-term building of a healthier and more socially connected you is preferable. In other words, you need to work on the deep and meaningful you too. Instead of waiting for someone to say something nice about your new dress or shoes in order to make you feel happy, flip it 180 degrees, say something nice to someone else, and bring them happiness. The funny thing is that being nice will also elicit a sense of happiness in you. Win-win.

It would also be remiss not to mention stoicism at this point, which is a philosophy based on two fundamental beliefs: eudaimonia and emotional resilience. It sees eudaimonia as a happy and smooth flowing life, which comes about from thriving at bringing our actions into harmony with the best version of ourselves or our higher selves. Stoics see eudaimonia as being made of three key ideas:

> Take responsibility for your life. After all, you are ultimately responsible for it.

> Focus on what you can control, not what you cannot.

> Live with virtue or excellence; what stoics call arete. In other words, to close the gap between who we are and who we can be, we should use arete[11].

Stoicism sees strong emotions as our weakness, especially

when we allow them to dictate our behaviour. Emotional resilience is about taming our negative emotions, not suppressing them, acknowledging they exist, determining what has caused them, and then redirecting them for our own good. Stoicism believes that if you are good to your inner spirit and live in harmony with your higher self, you will flourish in life.

At the end of the day, your sense of wellbeing is in your hands. Choosing to have a positive sense of wellbeing, just like choosing to be happy, takes courage. As you will discover, the things that don't give you a sense of wellbeing or don't make you happy aren't always what you thought they were and in fact, you may not want to change and remove them from your life.

Happiness is simply one piece of what wellbeing is. It also includes your state of physical and mental health and level of satisfaction with life. It considers physical, mental (including emotional), and social health, as well as personal fulfilment and a sense of accomplishment. Happiness is literally and figuratively a state of mind.

By focusing on wellbeing as opposed to short-term happiness, we should be looking at things that bring us value and meaning. By focusing on them, happiness then happens as a consequence. Instead of torturing ourselves through the internal dialogue we have with ourselves as we compare and despair, failing to live up to the expectations of ourselves as we chase the spectre of a happy life, we should aim not to be happy but to have a sense of overall positive wellbeing in our lives.

This means accepting that life is like a tide. You will feel the ups and downs, get smashed by the occasional wave, but have the sense of mind to know that this is normal and through certain actions and mindsets, see the light more than the dark, and know that all will be right with the world.

So, what have we learned? Much like defining time, everyone knows what happiness is until they have to describe it. It also depends on the context in which you look at it. Generally defined, happiness and wellbeing are subjective. In other words, it all starts within you.

Happiness, like a spark, is a flicker of light that come and is soon gone. Wellbeing on the other hand is like a long, slow burn that keeps on going. You think you want happiness but what you really want in your life is wellbeing.

Like all good things, achieving a sense of positive wellbeing isn't easy. It takes effort and a WEALTH mindset for it is your current mindset that is preventing you from achieving your full potential and wellbeing. This isn't your fault; it is the result of millennia of conditioning on your brain and its need to protect you above all else.

THE WEALTH MINDSET

Choosing to be happy isn't easy. Happiness and wellbeing doesn't come from all the trappings of modern living but the definitions we've looked at don't offer a balance between the two – modern living and wellbeing – instead making it difficult to consistently live a life of wellbeing and a life in the modern world. It is hard to find wellbeing while still doing a job you dislike, the financial stress of daily life, and the pressure to be happy in a world that isn't.

What wellbeing is and the difficulty of living a life with it, when it contradicts so many things that we promote in our society, can create many stresses and confusion. It can at times seem pointless and too difficult to embrace wellbeing on a day-to-day basis, especially while we live in a capitalist, consumerist and liberal society. Not to mention trying to grow as a person.

Life can be a shitshow. Everyone is unique. One size does not fit all. People need to grow and learn and ultimately feel not just better but more in control of their lives, that life is pretty good, amazing in fact.

True wellbeing is about being honest with yourself, identifying who you are (and who you are not), understanding what makes you tick, what motivates you, and gives you zest, and then trying different things to see what works for you and brings you joy and a sense of wellbeing over the long-term. It is about accepting that not every day can be a good day and that not every bad day is definitive of your life. It ebbs and flows. As long as you can understand and accept the vagaries of life and still see the good and the light ahead, ignoring the fluff and static that surrounds you then you are good and on the path to true wellbeing.

True wellbeing comes from being a better version of yourself. We must acknowledge that we need to make an effort to be a better version of ourselves. It won't just happen because we've read about it and want it to happen.

Wellbeing comes from taking action and having experiences, which you learn from and then, over time, through the experiences and the building of habits in your daily life, you reach a state of true wellbeing.

To experience long-term happiness and wellbeing, there are six pillars that underpin the WEALTH mindset:

Will

Experience

Action

Learning

Time

Habits

WEALTH is an appropriate acronym because the true value of your life is the positive wellbeing you have in it.

As you read Parts II and III, you will see how this mindset is embedded in each of the ingredients. Here are a brief summary of what each means.

Will

Will power is but the unflinching purpose to carry a task you set for yourself to fulfilment. If I set for myself a task, be it ever so trifling, I shall see it through.

George S Clason, The Richest Man in Babylon

Willpower, often referred to as our 'inner strength' or 'self-discipline', is critical in steering our lives towards positive wellbeing, success, and achieving our goals. It is like a compass, serving as a guiding force, steering us in the right direction and keeping us on course, empowering us to make choices aligned with our long-term aspirations, even in the face of challenges, distractions, or temptations.

If we have strong willpower, we are better equipped to overcome and stay motivated during setbacks and adapt to changing circumstances. We are less likely to succumb to instant gratification and instead make choices that align with our long-term goals, ultimately increasing our chances of success.

Willpower is the linchpin of personal development and accomplishment. It propels us forward, allowing us to conquer challenges and embrace opportunities that align with our aspirations. Developing and nurturing our willpower through consistent practice and self-awareness empowers us to make intentional choices, resist short-term temptations, and navigate the complex journey towards achieving positive wellbeing. You need to be committed to following though, and being determined as it is your will and determination that binds the pillars of WEALTH together.

In a nutshell, you have to want positive wellbeing in your life. More than just want, you have to be willing and able to make the effort required to allow this to happen. It takes desire, discipline and commitment. Like the achievement of any goal, you have to be invested in making it happen. Happiness may be like a butterfly that is always just out of reach when pursued but wellbeing is like learning to ride a bike. You have to keep at it, committed to learning the new skill and persevering even after you have fallen and hurt yourself. It is about figuring out how to balance, pedal and break until you have mastered the skill and it becomes something you do without even thinking about it any longer.

Experience

Experience is the teacher of all things.

–Julius Caesar

The word 'experience' comes from the Latin word, 'experientia', meaning *trial, proof, or[i] experiment.*[12] The experience can be good or bad, it doesn't matter – all experiences are valuable and something we learn from. From our experiences, we perceive the world around us. These experiences do not even have to be conscious; many are subconscious but have a huge impact on who we are as individuals. The greater and broader the experiences we have, the greater understanding we have of ourselves and the world. Those with greater experiences tend to balance better emotions and reasoning; they have more empathy; know how to temper their expectations and are therefore more likely to achieve goals; are better at anticipating future events; have a better understanding of 'the big picture'; and through their experience, are able to better gauge or grasp a situation more quickly than someone with little or no experience.

Experience is the sauce of life. We have experiences every day, but it is those who pursue life experiences and opportunities to better themselves that learn and grow. Many of us are too scared to experience life as we would like to. We fear making mistakes and failing. We then live with regret and 'what if' scenarios for the rest of our lives. Wellbeing is about identifying what you love and pursuing it, not at the cost of your security, finances, relationships or otherwise, but because experience is the seed of growth and a life worth living.

Making mistakes is scary, especially when you have responsibilities, but sometimes mistakes can be the best part. There is no surer way to know who you are and to grow and mature as a person than from making mistakes.

The story you build with your experiences, the journey you take, is the key to being your authentic self. When you look back on your life, it is at the experiences you have had, some good and some bad, which make up the story of you, not the stuff you have purchased or money you have accumulated. You can't go through your life afraid to be yourself forever. At some point, you have to be true to yourself and do what is right for you, even if you do it with small steps. The recipe you choose for happiness and wellbeing will help you experience life, face the fear and find purpose and meaning in your life.

The only source of knowledge is experience.
– Albert Einstein

Action

Experience comes from action. For anything to happen, for any experience to occur, you need to act. You need to take action to achieve anything, be it happiness, success, or a cheese and ham sandwich. If you want to be a better person, you need to be prepared to act. Nothing will come to you.

If the mountain will not come to Muhammad,
then Muhammad must go to the mountain.
– Francis Bacon, Essays

If you do nothing, nothing will happen. If you want to make changes in your life, you need to make it happen. No-one else will. It is one thing to want to do something, to read this book or a dozen others, but until you actually move and act, you are procrastinating and achieving nothing. This is why Action is a pillar of the recipe for happiness and wellbeing. It is great that you purchased and then read this book, but if you do nothing about it, then what was the point? Steve Jobs, founder of Apple, said, 'You have got to act and you have got to be willing to fail; you have got to be willing to crash and burn... if you are afraid of failing you won't get very far.'

Happiness is a state of activity.
- Aristotle

What action you take doesn't have to be big or grandiose. It can be the proverbial one small step, but one small step is still better than one big plan. You can plan all you like and analyse all the possible outcomes but you will become bogged down with doubt and fear, paralysis by analysis, and be no further forward. Action will help you find what motivates you and build your self-confidence and self-discipline. It will help you find your passion and show you how to develop a growth mindset as well as turn your values into committed action.

Action is the foundational key to all success.
– Pablo Picasso

Learning

The more that you read, the more things you will know. The more that you learn, the more places you'll go.
– Dr. Seuss

Life is full of lessons. Everyone you meet in your life and everything you do is a chance to learn. Intelligence doesn't make a better person, choice does. Live a life where you choose to be a better person. Be someone who seeks new experiences and learns from them. Don't continue to do the things that don't make you a better person or don't make you happy. Learn from your mistakes and build on this to be a better version of yourself.

The first word revealed to the Prophet Muhammed by Allah was 'Iqra', which means to read. It is to seek knowledge, to educate yourself and learn.

*Education's purpose is to replace an
empty mind with an open one.*
— *Malcolm Forbes*

Lifelong learning improves your cognitive ability because you are continuously using the grey matter. You are more likely to be socially connected, earn more, and have depression less often. The value of lifelong learning is huge and gives you a broader and better understanding, not just of the world but the people in it. You have a better perspective, more confidence and resilience.

Without learning, you will stay stagnant and never move forward. Learning is a lifelong opportunity. School teaches you what you need to learn to thrive in society. You then choose what you want to lean to thrive in your life.

*Never let formal education get in the way of your
learning.*
– Mark Twain

Time

*They always say time changes things, but you
actually have to change them yourself.*
- Andy Warhol, The Philosophy of Andy Warhol

Saint Augustine wrote, 'What then is time? If no-one asks me, I know what it is. If I wish to explain it to him who asks, I do not know.' There are many philosophical and scientific debates about the answer to this question, but one thing is for sure – we only have a limited amount of it in which to live. Unfortunately, many of us live as if there is no tomorrow and the rest as if there will always be a tomorrow. Your time perspective helps to determine whether you are usually living in and focused on the past, the present, or the future. Research done on the subject of time perspective by psychologists Philip Zimbardo and Ilona Boniwell found that it could affect your wellbeing. They deduced that there are five time perspectives:

Future: Able to delay gratification and work towards future goals.
Present Positive: Live and enjoy life in the here and now with little thought about the consequences of your actions
Present Negative: Have a sense of hopelessness, believing external forces, rather than you, control life.
Past Positive: Get pleasure from looking back on your life and reminiscing, finding family traditions important.
Past Negative: Focussed on what you should have done differently in the past, with many regrets.
The research found that a balanced time perspective was best and those who had one were:

- Happier
- More satisfied with life
- More positive with their emotions
- Had a stronger sense of purpose in their life
- More self-efficacious
- More optimistic

You can see where you sit by taking the test[13]

> *Time is the coin of your life. It is the only coin you have, and only you can determine how it will be spent. Be careful lest you let other people spend it for you.*
> – Carl Sandburg, American Poet

Whatever your perspective of time, we are all prone to wasting it, especially the opportunities that it presents to us. A good way to look at time, particularly regarding wellbeing, is to measure it in opportunities as opposed to seconds, minutes, and hours. This will give you a better appreciation of time.

Take for example, your parents. Let's say you are middle-aged, and they are in their early seventies. As the average life expectancy is about eighty years of age, you can see them for another ten years, right? But you live in another city and only get to see them twice a year, which means that even though they have about another ten years to live, you will only see them about 20 more times. Ever.

When you look at time this way, based on the opportunities time offers, how many opportunities are you taking advantage of and how many are you wasting? The same can be said for any opportunities that come into your life. How many are passed up because you are giving your time away to someone or something else? The television may have cost you $1,000 but how much is it costing you in lost opportunities?

Putting it another way, how much is your time worth? Maybe you think it is worth $100 per hour, maybe $50. Maybe you have low expectations of yourself and think your time is only worth $10 per hour. It doesn't really matter what it is. Obviously, you won't earn that every hour, but when you put a value on your time, you are putting a value on how you are spending that time and whether it is worth it. The true test to determine if you are spending your time wisely is to answer this simple question: Would you pay someone what you think your time is worth, for example $50, to do what you are doing?

If the answer is 'No', then why are you doing it?

> *No, Mr Bond. I expect you to die.*
> *- Auric Goldfinger, Goldfinger (1964)*

You are going to die. No matter what else happens in your life, you will end up dead. Time is your biggest asset because you don't know how much of it you have. What's gone is gone and there is nothing you can do to get it back. What you have done is done and you cannot change it.

You may have hurt someone; someone may have hurt you. You may have had your heart broken, got divorced, lost the love of your life, had any number of bad things happen to you, but it's done. It's not like a pencil drawing that you can erase and change to fix up to be better. What's gone is gone. It is in the past. Focusing on the past will ensure only one thing and that is the wasting of your greatest asset because it is all you've got and to spend it focused on the past instead guarantees one thing: your future will be the same as your past.

Another aspect of time is timing. Not everything can be done now, sometimes you have to have the right timing. Now, that isn't an excuse to do nothing and delay indefinitely, it just means that you aren't ready to do this or that at this time. For example, practicing spirituality may not feel right to you as a tool for wellbeing with your current mindset. You may have had experiences in the past that need to be addressed first.

So, with time, it is limited, we need to make use of the opportunities and experiences when they are presented to us but with the awareness that what we are doing needs to be right for us as the individual at this time and place in our lives.

Habits

Critical to all the other pillars of wellbeing are habits, for without habits everything is just a one off or a phase like going on a diet – it works for a while, but the temptation and desire to return to the status quo overrides all else. Without the right mindset, fixed ways of thinking and repetition, wellbeing becomes a diet instead of a way of life.

For any of the ingredients to have a lasting effect, you will need to develop positive habits around the actions you take to make them work for you. For that reason, Part III is dedicated entirely to understanding why you don't do things and choose to procrastinate, through to building self-discipline and good habits and of course, breaking bad habits.

All the pillars of wellbeing are intrinsically linked, which makes them stronger. Throughout the book, you will see the themes of WEALTH and how they bind all the ingredients into one cohesive piece, making wellbeing accessible and achievable for everyone. There are nineteen things you can choose from to build yourself a life of true happiness and wellbeing. They are called ingredients because just like all ingredients, some of the items you will like and some you won't. What you need to do is look at the ingredients; see how they work, what is good about them, and what is not. Based on the information, then make a choice about what ingredients will work for you. Just as you are unique, come up with a recipe that is unique and works for you.

Here's to your wellbeing!

Success comes from continually expanding your

frontiers in every direction—creatively, financially, spiritually, and physically. Always ask yourself, what can I improve? Who else can I talk to? Where else can I look.
- James Altucher, Choose Yourself!

FAILURE TO LAUNCH

Success has many fathers, but failure is an orphan.

John F. Kennedy

Many people look back on their lives with a sense of disappointment, seeing all the things they wanted to do and achieve in life and lamenting that they have barely done any of them (of course, forgetting all the things that they have done and achieved). Maybe you don't even know what it is you want to achieve, but know that there is something, that there has to be something more than the life you are living now. Maybe you have been told that your expectations are too high; that you should lower your expectations and accept what life gives you. Maybe they have a point. Low expectations mean you won't be disappointed, whereas unrealistic expectations will only lead to disappointment. The balance is to find where expectations and reality cross and aim for that juncture. Expectations are dreams, they are goals; they are a desired reality. You shouldn't have to accept the proverbial lemons.

The problem is, for many of us, our fear has always held us back. Fear of failure, of success, change, and ultimately a fear of the unknown, and all for what? Staying where it feels safe in our comfort zone but going nowhere.

Someone once said, 'There is no such thing as being shy, it just means you have no guts!' It's true. Ample opportunities are lost because we didn't have the guts. We have let fear and self-doubt get the better of us.

Why does wisdom come with age? Why can't you be taught the keys to a good life? Why does it take years to work out who you are, what you stand for, and what your values are? We are not all some cookie cutter clones of each other, and each have our own identities, needs and wants. That 'stuff' doesn't make us happier, just poorer. Happiness is like a rainbow: when you chase it, the closer you get to it, the further away it becomes. The thing is, most of us know this stuff, but at the same time we don't. The reality we live is like cement – it weighs us down, whereas the reality we want is like an ember simmering in the back of our mind, waiting for a spark to light our fire.

Our brains are like a helicopter parent, always there, stopping us from doing anything that might have the slightest risk (or bit of fun). Our brains are curbing our ability to live a full life through a desire to ensure we have a life. Like a fly on the windowpane trying to get out and find its freedom, our brains hold us prisoner. An invisible shield preventing us from being our best selves and achieving what we know we are capable of. The same brain that wants us to shoot for the stars is also the same brain that is holding us on a short leash, so we don't stray too far. It's frustrating!

Before looking at the brain and its massive effect on the way we behave, let's have a quick look at the fear of failure and the full stop it puts on our efforts to moving forward and finding success.

We will forever be stuck in the cycle of procrastination, never finding self-discipline and motivation if we don't know why we fail or are reluctant to even start on our journey to finding wellbeing. It is easy to say that failure is a teacher, not a disaster, but if you don't know why you fail or worse, even why you never start, it can be hard to believe this and remove the concrete blocks from around your feet.

It is sometimes easier never to start than to fail. After all, how can you fail if you never start? Even when pressured to start, how many come up with excuses like, 'I'll do it when...', or 'The time isn't for me right now'? The problem is, the timing is never right. At some point, you just have to say, 'Screw it, let's do it'[14].

> *The best time to plant a tree was 20 years ago. The second best time is now.*
>
> *- Chinese proverb*

There are multitudes of reasons we stop at the gates instead of roaring full bore towards our future. Here are some. How many do you identify with?

1. You focus on your weaknesses. This is the classic caveman brain at work, focused on negative thinking, filling your head with what can go wrong, and that you are not up to it because of A, B, and C weaknesses. You need to work out your signature strengths, what you are passionate about and want, and then you need to take what you have learned and push through the negative thoughts, gaining confidence and experience through action. Set a growth mindset with a positive mental image of who you are and where you want to be. Practice 'as if' thought exercises where you act as if you are the person you want to be. How would you act and what would you do? Try it now. Practice for where you want to be.

2. You fear rejection. Research has shown that there is a correlation between those with high levels of social anxiety about rejection and lower levels of oxytocin in the body. The reason you fear rejection may be from childhood or something that has happened in the past and so you look for the cause, but it doesn't really help. Focusing on negativity won't

bring positive results, it will just bring more negativity into your head. You may be told to embrace rejection to overcome it. That just hurts. Rejection means coming out of your comfort zone and that is hard, but it is where happiness lies. The only thing to do is accept that rejection is one of the possible outcomes. Be prepared, and practice being rejected by doing it over and over again. It sucks and is not easy, but it is the only way to move forward and away from the 'what if' and 'if only' scenarios of what might have been that plague your mind.

3. You keep listening to others. Everyone is a critic. Friends and family are the worst because their opinions matter to us. If there is something you really want, and I mean *really* want, you need to let go of the opinions of others and use their doubts as drivers for your success so you can say, 'I told you so.' The problem with others' opinions is that they tend to mirror the internal voice we all have that says you can't do it, it's too risky, you've failed before and you'll fail again, it's better to stick with what you already have. If you want to succeed, you need to push past the voice and through your doubts.

If you end up with a boring miserable life because you listened to your mom, your dad, your teacher, your priest, or some guy on television telling you how to do your shit, then you deserve it.

Frank Zappa

4. You won't take feedback. It is one thing to ignore people who tell you you cannot do it, but it is an-

other to ignore people who are trying to help you by giving you advice. Just don't fall into the trap of taking on-board all the advice you are given.

Advice is a form of nostalgia.
Dispensing it is a way of fishing the past from the
disposal, wiping it off,
painting over the ugly parts and recycling
it for more than it's worth.[15]

It is not wise to be too stubborn to take advice. Being stubbornly driven has its advantages but can still steer you towards failure because you refuse to listen. It is possible that you are too confident or lacking in humility; that is, believing you know more than you actually do. There is always more to learn. Believe it or not, lots of people want you to succeed, so listening and considering that maybe they have a point, that you might be wrong, can put you on the fast track to success and open up your mindset.

Building and nurturing strong relationships and a network with like-minded people can help you achieve your goals. Social connection is a great alternative to the isolation and loneliness that pursuing goals can create. You are more likely to succeed with support than by powering on alone.

5. You don't believe you deserve it. This can come from your upbringing or something that may have happened when you were young. Maybe someone teased, bullied, or told you that you were a failure when you were young, and you have grown up believing it, feeling unworthy of success. The whole idea of being successful and achieving your goals,

even if solely for your own personal benefit, makes you feel uneasy and like a fraud. Doubts plague you. Unfortunately, the only way to get over it is to get over yourself. Your lack of self-esteem will ruin you (harsh words, but true) and keep you in a mediocre existence, well below where you want and deserve to be unless you resolve why you feel as you do and work hard to overcome and change those beliefs.

6. You fear standing out from the crowd. To change, which is what setting goals and personal growth are all about, means being different from the rest and standing out. People don't like change and won't like you changing. Tall Poppy Syndrome comes into effect. People will look at you and wonder what you are doing. They will wonder why you want to change. They may become toxic to you and your desire to better yourself. If you have a weak opinion of yourself or don't really believe in your goals and ideas, you are going to fail pretty quickly. Is it such a big deal to stand out? Heck, yes, people will look at you and you will probably feel pressure to succeed because if you don't, your supposed friends will be there to catch you when you fall, but tell you they 'told you so' at the same time. With that thought, not even trying seems like a pretty good option. Ultimately, you need to find your new comfort zone because not standing out from the crowd means not changing or not growing except in resentment to those who are holding you back, including yourself.

7. You focus on status. Not all that is worth doing has worth. At least not monetarily, but that doesn't mean it is not worth doing. If you persist in seeing value only in things that will give you status,

including money, jobs, and stuff, you will never achieve personal development and growth. The value in these are intrinsic and only of value to you. Wellbeing is about you being your best self, in all aspects of your life.

8. You lack persistence. It is too easy to quit. We discuss the building of habits in Part III. To build success, you need to keep going. It is so easy to quit when things don't go according to plan and you can see failure coming straight at you. Quitting is easy when you lack the faith and courage within yourself to keep going. Keep trying, repeating what has worked, even when you encounter resistance. Keep it simple. Don't over complicate what you want to achieve. Copy others. If they are doing well, don't reinvent the wheel. Use theirs. It is easy to say but stay positive. Look at your perception and mindset and adjust as appropriate.

9. You are a doer, not a thinker. Do you find yourself busy doing stuff but not achieving anything? There is a difference between *motion* and *action.* If you are doing without achieving, you are only in motion. You need to stop, think, and review what you are doing and see what is bringing results and what isn't, and then stop what isn't.

10. You are an over-thinker. You think about what needs to be done and then think about it again and again and again. You come up with scenarios that become blocks, reasons to not even bother starting. Paralysis by analysis allows you to come up with all the reasons not to do something when really, you just need to start.

11. You have the wrong mindset. A fixed mindset keeps you fixed in your current position and way

of thinking. You need to adopt a growth mindset. You need to believe in yourself and that you will succeed. If you believe you will succeed, the chances are a lot higher that you will. Sometimes a little delusion can go a long way to creating success. And if you do fail, you have learned from it, pushing you that little bit further towards your goal. Aside from a growth mindset, you will need a plan to succeed, echoing the famous saying, 'If you fail to plan, you plan to fail.' You need to believe not only in yourself and have a strong self-image, but also to believe in your idea and what it is you are trying to achieve. If you are not invested in your idea or goal, it is a doorway to failure.

12. You have no purpose. If you don't know where you are going, you will never get there. You waste time, doing but not achieving, distracting yourself, and postponing through procrastination on the slippery slope to failure.

13. You play the blame game. 'It's my work's fault.' 'The government changed the rules and now it's too hard.' 'My family needs me to spend more time with them.' The blame game can go on forever but, in the end, it comes to down to taking control and responsibility for yourself and to understand that blaming others is just an excuse, preventing you from being your best self.

How many reasons stopping you from starting, and instead failing, do you identify with? It all comes down to being ill prepared and fear – fear of failure, fear of change, and fear of success. According to Brianna Wiest in her book, *The Mountain is You: Transforming Self-Sabotage into Self-Mastery*, we all have mountains to climb, things to overcome. The biggest mountain of all is ourselves: our fears, our self-doubts, and self-sabotage. To climb the mountain, you first need to know what it is.

Our self-sabotage comes from irrational fear. Irrational, because we refuse to believe we are capable of doing what we subconsciously know we need to do and so we do all we can to sabotage ourselves. We self-sabotage because we have negative associations with what we want to achieve. Weird as that sounds, we sabotage our efforts to achieve our goals because, consciously or not, we believe negative things about the kind of people who have achieved the goals we want for ourselves.

Think of the goal of being rich, for example. Do you find yourself sabotaging your own efforts to achieve this goal? Take a look at your perspective on money and those that have lots of it. What did your parents have to say about it? Did they struggle to make enough and give up, saying the rich are the problem? They are bad people. If so, this has likely influenced your opinion of rich people. Who wants to be rich if it means they will be terrible, be part of the problem? Hence the self-sabotage and fear of success.

Of course, fear is another way of saying anxious. We are, for the most part, suffering from high functioning anxiety – still able to manage day-to-day but not able to move ourselves forward. Once we know what is holding us back, we can work on overcoming it. The challenge is turning failure into a learning opportunity and ultimately into success. That is the journey, that is the experience, and that is the pay-off to a life lived, and a life of true wellbeing. The mountain that is your self-sabotage is really not a mountain at all, but a puzzle. It is a challenge, even a gift or opportunity for you to become your best self by presenting to you, in no uncertain terms, the opportunity for self-improvement because your present is no longer sustainable, and if you keep choosing to accept it, then you are denying yourself the opportunity to be better.

You cannot get rid of fear. Fear is inbred in all of us. It is your brain's protective mechanism. Because of this, some fears you will overcome once you have faced them but most you just have to master. Once you do this, you will see that fear isn't a wall to your happiness but the key to your growth and wellbeing. The key is to see fear as an opportunity, not a barrier as your brain wants you to see it. Your brain wants you to behave in a certain way and to be happy, but sometimes you have to do the opposite.

Failure is action. Failure is experience. Failure is learning. Failure is growth. Failure is an essential part of wellbeing.

> *I learned that courage was not the absence of fear, but the triumph over it. The brave man is not he who does not feel afraid, but he who conquers that fear.*
>
> *– Nelson Mandela.*

WELLBEING AND THE BRAIN

So, we know what happiness and wellbeing is. We know we want it. It seems so simple, so why is it so hard? We know that fear and anxiety are holding us back from being our true selves but why? Why is our brain sabotaging our happiness? How does the brain work? How does it fill us with dreams and then create seemingly impenetrable barriers to achieve them?

Much like Beauty and the Beast, wellbeing and the brain is a story of hope and despair, where what you see is not always as it seems. The trusty servants (serotonin, oxytocin, dopamine and cortisol) both aid and hinder the Beast (our brain) in order to make sense of and allow Beauty (or wellbeing) into our lives. However, the brain has doubts and fears, and dislikes change, preferring everything to stay the way it is, the safe and predictable way, even if it is at the detriment of its long-term prospects and success. The brain knows comfortable and uncomfortable. Good and bad are arbitrary and foreign to the brain.

We don't know what we want, often sticking to what we know because the brain cannot predict the outcome of an event we haven't experienced before. This is the sad irony and why we settle for the comfort of the known, even if it really isn't that comfortable. It is why we stick with bad relationships, get stuck in ruts, and choose the security of the comfortable known instead of exploring the unknown, going with the flow of transition, which is the passing of time and evolution.

Do you ever feel like you are being left behind, that life is moving on without you?

It is.

Life moves, and you need to as well. It is our brain that stops us, throwing fear and discomfort at us, enticing us to settle, to do what everyone else does to feel safe and happy. No wonder so many of us are messed up. The brain is derailing our desire for happiness and wellbeing. Honestly, when you learn about the brain and how it works, you can see how so many of us are messed up in the head and why not giving a fuck[16] is probably the smartest piece of advice you could get.

Your brain is the product of millions of years of evolution. Over that time, the human brain has been programmed to ensure your survival. Until recently, this was very important. We had to ensure we had enough food, shelter, and clothing to survive. We had to be aware of the many dangers that were inherent in our environment, as we were not only the hunter, but also the hunted. We had to be prepared to run and hide or fight to survive at a moment's notice, hence the expression, fight-or-flight. Our brain was always 'on', ready to do either of these options, and this has continued to be the case for thousands of years.

Times may have changed, and we may no longer be as concerned with having enough food to eat (in fact, often it's quite the opposite) or having clothing to keep warm, but our brain still acts in this manner. Your brain will allow change, but whenever it can, will revert to the tried and tested – what it knows to keep you safe. This is all well and good, but also a hindrance for the growth and wellbeing of you as a person. It is for this reason that happiness is short-lived as your brain is designed to ensure your survival so goes back to fight-or-flight mode, making sure there are no threats. You can't always be happy. You need bad feelings to have good feelings. As long as you are alive, no matter how well your needs are met, there is a perceived threat to your survival and your brain needs these feelings to help keep you alive. Your brain has been set to help you survive, not thrive.

Memories

> *It is a poor type of memory that only works backwards.*
>
> *– The Queen of Hearts, Lewis Carroll's Through the Looking Glass*

Your brain is like a sponge soaking up millions of bits of information every minute, and although it only makes you aware of a tiny percentage of that information, everything is still stored. Your memories are built using neural pathways and the more you do something, the stronger those memories become until those behaviours become habits, things you do on autopilot. In fact, habits run about 40% of your day. The problem is your brain doesn't know a good habit from a bad one, and the more you follow one pathway, the more engrained that behaviour becomes, making it a neural highway – something that is hard to change. Later in the book, we will discuss habits and how to both build and break them.

Why do you follow these pathways, anyway? A lot of your behaviours are associated with things that happened to you in your youth, usually before the age of seven. As a sponge, your brain stores experiences; it won't delete them. Whether, consciously or not, our brain will influence and guide us towards or away from experiences. This is known as learned experiences.

Imagine you were, as a child, bitten by a dog. That experience may put you off dogs for the rest of your life. Even if you don't remember the event at all, you will likely always be wary around dogs. As individuals, our experiences and feelings are unique. These experiences have created neural pathways unique to each of us and explain why we react differently to the same situations.

As much as we use our memories to remember the past, that is not their purpose. As Jordan Peterson so aptly said, 'The purpose of memories is to extract out from the past, lessons to structure the future.' All animals, whether they be human, cat, dog, horse, or elephant, create memories, and as much as your pet cat or dog likes to think back on their time as a kitten or puppy chasing balls of string, *oh, good times,* memories are not there to reminisce over, they are there to help you learn and survive. It is why we create neural pathways through repetition, to engrain the memory, such as how to ride a bike or learning a mathematics equation. How these will enable our survival or structure our future isn't always made clear when learning these things. Maybe this is something the education system needs to consider in order to enable teaching and learning to be a coordinated effort that suits all. On the other hand, some learning doesn't need repetition to be engrained. One experience will be enough, such as putting your hand on a hot element and being burned. You are unlikely to repeat that behaviour.

What were the best years of your life? Many of us consider our teenage years and early twenties to be the pinnacle of our lives and there is a good reason for this. As mentioned in Bill Bryson's The Brain[17], 'The nucleus accumbens, a region of the forebrain associated with pleasure, grows to its largest size in one's teenage years. At the same time, the body produces more dopamine, the neurotransmitter that conveys pleasure, than it ever will again. That is why the sensations you feel as a teenager are more intense than at any other time of life.' Another study[18] showed that a 70-year-old remembers more from their teens and twenties than their 30s and 40s because they experienced more momentous occasions and change moments that defined them as they were the first and most memorable.

Think of your own teens and twenties. You probably got your first job, had your first romantic partner and sexual encounter, earned your first pay cheque, travelled without your parents, moved out of home, and many other things that were firsts and helped define who you are. You had the freedom and lack of responsibility to be and do what you wanted before having to settle down and take on responsibilities like a career, marriage, family, and a mortgage.

In fact, it is these responsibilities that are likely responsible for much of the unhappiness and depression felt by so many, but we'll get onto that in a moment. So, just as many of our behaviours are set in early life, so too are our best memories set in our teens and twenties. Our brain saves happy chemicals for new information. That is why the first time is always the best and subsequent times can make you happy, but not to the same degree. The best summers were always when you were younger because they were new. The same with the worst events too.

When we are young we are full of messy potential, much like many of our bedrooms at the time. Things could go anywhere, any way, but we liked that. We liked that we had potential that could take us in any direction. It gave us the vitality that only youth can. Becoming older, we become more structured and responsible. Many don't like that and so they try to stay young, to retain their potential. They want to be the proverbial Peter Pan with Captain Hook as the piratical adult trying to take away their potential. He is facing death, signified by the crocodile (and ticking clock) who has had a taste (when he ate Hook's hand) and wants more. No-one wants that and so they fight it while they can, denying responsibility and growing up, fearing loss of their potential, but that is the crux. Unrealised potential is nothing. You need discipline to turn your potential into actuality.

Lack of discipline leads to living in the past and the glory days of potential, but growing up turns that potential into something real. Living in the past stifles your growth and you become like a coiled-up ball of potential, which with no outlet for growth, you either explode or wither and die. You become depressed and withdrawn, unable to let go of the past and seize the future.

> *Inside every older person is a younger person*
> *wondering what happened?*
>
> *–Jennifer Yane*

When you get nostalgic is it usually in response to transformative events in your life such as marriage, a job, or death. Memories offer you comfort through their predictability and recollection of stability, when life was not so stressful. Funnily enough, nostalgia was initially thought of as a mental disorder as defined by Swiss physician Johannes Hoffer in the 17th century and it stayed as such until the mid-20th century. In fact, the American Psychological Association still defines nostalgia as a subset of depression because when it invites negative thoughts, it can become bitter-sweet and detrimental to health, potentially causing anxiety, insomnia, and depression. We can look back at the past with longing for a simpler time and feel melancholy because things are not the same as they used to be, seeking solace in the comfort of selective memory of what it was like.

Dillon Thomas in his poem *Should Lanterns Shine*, a poem about looking back at his youth, encapsulated this feeling well when he said, 'The ball I threw when playing in the park has not yet reached the ground.' He is looking back at his childhood and playing in the park, the ball not having touched the ground referring to his not having let go of his youth and the past.

We have a tendency to look at the past through rose-tinted glasses, remembering the past for what we wanted it to have been and not necessarily what it was. There is a belief that things were better and you were happier than you actually were. This is understandable when you consider that in many cases happiness is retrospective and take into account that our memories are not the most reliable of things. Indeed, we alter memories to suit our circumstances. When looking at people with depression or anxiety, however, this is not a good thing as it only seeks to emphasise the chasm of feelings within them as they look towards a future with little hope.

> *There is no greater sorrow*
> *Than to recall a happy time*
> *When miserable.*
>
> *- Dante*

Nostalgia is now considered to have positive effects on your mental health, as it emotes good feelings for the most part. A 2008 study[19] found that nostalgia increases people's perception of social support, while a 2013 study[20] found positive effects. 'Nostalgia is experienced frequently and virtually by everyone and we know that it can maintain psychological comfort. For example, nostalgic reverie can combat loneliness,' commented Dr Tim Wildschut, co-author of the study. He also added, 'Nostalgia raises self-esteem, which in turn heightens optimism…nostalgia does have the capacity to facilitate perceptions of a more positive future. Memories of the past can help to maintain current feelings of self-worth and can contribute to a brighter outlook on the future…nostalgia, by promoting optimism, could help individuals cope with psychological adversity.'[21]

There is a possibility of being over-saturated with the past, which isn't hard to imagine given the plethora of media content including social media always reminding us of what has passed. Consequently we become desensitised to it[22] and it loses its effect, much like habituation (something we will look at shortly). Like a good diet, anything in moderation is best, otherwise we get fed up with it very quickly.

> *Nostalgia is denial – denial of the painful present...*
> *the name of this denial is golden age thinking –*
> *the erroneous notion that a different time period*
> *is better than the one one's living in – it's a flaw*
> *in the romantic imagination of those people*
> *who find it difficult to cope with the present.*
>
> *- Paul, Midnight in Paris (2011)*

Stories strengthen our memories. Think of popular childhood stories such as Hansel and Gretel, Beauty and the Beast, or Peter Pan. We remember them because we know the story. It is the same with song lyrics. Through oral tradition, ancient cultures used to pass on their history through stories for thousands of years. It is for this reason that we know the stories of Gilgamesh, the origin stories of the Australian First Nations and Torres Strait Islander peoples, the New Zealand Maori and many more.

In a study, people were asked to remember twelve lists of ten words. Thirteen per cent remembered without stories, whereas those that turned them into stories remembered 93% of the words. For the mathematicians out there, that is about twelve out of the thirteen words, on average.

To improve your memory and build new neural pathways, the easiest and best thing to do is give yourself new experiences and stories to tell. This is especially important in today's digital world where the need to remember things has become less important because we can store information on our phones or computers. If we need to research something, we can just look it up on a search engine. No longer do we need to go to the library, lookup microfiche for research of old newspapers or historical records.

Do you know your partner's or best friend's phone number? Chances are that you don't. Your phone stores it and when you need to make a call, you simply look up their name or ask your phone to call them. Jim Kwik in his book, *Limitless*, describes this as Digital Dementia. Later in the book, we will look at this further.

When looking at yourself, consider yourself as two versions of the same thing. There is the experience version and the memory version of yourself. The experience version of yourself lives in the moment, experiencing the event as it happens. The memory version of yourself sees it upon reflection. Of the two versions, memory is the strongest as it interprets your view of the past or experiences and how you remember them. Think about it, most of the time we do not experience happiness in the moment but see it upon reflection. Think also of your old relative who tells you the same stories over and over again as if you haven't heard them a million times before. As people get older, the memories remembered are those that stood out in their unique brain make up, coupled with what we have just discussed.

Both remembering and imagining use the same parts of the brain. The brain doesn't distinguish between the two. Our memories are fickle things, and we are only likely to accurately remember half of something that happened a year ago. Over years, our memories become 'no better than expected by chance' according to a study published in the year 2000 in the *Journal of the American Academy of Child and Adolescent Psych-*

iatry.[23] This is important to understand because most of what we remember from an event, especially one that happened years ago, didn't happen at all. It is clouded by our bias and the inconsistency of our memories. With this knowledge, it is important to be able to imagine a future and not simply live in the past.

Human brains are predictors. They like life to be easy, so base much of what we do on expected outcomes based on certain cues and triggers, much like with the development of behaviours when we are younger. Our pre-frontal cortex enables self-reflection and abstract thought. Our brain has trouble envisioning the future, simulating it by reconstructing the past, and this is seldom accurate. Based also on our brain's primary directive to ensure our survival, it sees threats that have not yet occurred and will therefore predict things that probably won't happen. We have what is called a negative bias. Expectations are determined by our life experiences. We watch the news, see bad things and project what will happen but can't see the positive. It is why the news in newspapers and on television is negatively biased. The media know our brains are genetically focused on danger for survival and the negative instinct associated with that, which is why they report as they do. Negative emotions like anger, fear and disgust can be understood as an evolutionary adaptation to the threats our ancestors faced. This was great when we wanted to remember we didn't want to go up to the sabre-toothed tiger and pet it, but not so helpful in today's world. It is why we remember the insults but forget the compliment. 'Nice shoes, Fatso!'

Our neurons and cortex can construct scenarios and as we are negatively biased, we can take an event that happens infrequently, for example, not getting a job promotion, and the fact that it may have happened more than once builds the neural pathway that it will happen every time. The pattern seeking brains can create a bad future even if the evidence says otherwise. This negative bias can blind us to the opportunities of experiencing positive emotions. Alternately, our self-serving bias allows for the tendency to attribute positive events to our own character, but attribute negative events to external factors. This colouring of our internal narrative conflicts with reality and can lead to mental issues.

An example is winning a running race and putting it down to all the training you did but if you lose, blaming the track for being too soft, too hard, or not having enough support from your peers, anything that removes blame from yourself. To counter this, we can look at setting up competing narratives where we can look at the future and see results that are both good and bad. It seems like a risky suggestion given our negative bias, but if we are displaying a self-serving bias and cannot see anything beyond our positive future scenario, it is a worthwhile activity.

Failure is a distinct possibility. Not everyone can win the race, so allowing for looking beyond the self-serving bias will provide balance and grounding. Even though the focus will be on working towards success, both possibilities should be recognised. The same applies to our natural inclination for negative bias. We anticipate the worst thing happening, but just as validly we should look at the possible positive outcomes. To increase our memories, we need to imagine a future as well, not just live in the past.

What makes your brain happy isn't necessarily what makes you happy. Hundreds of irrational biases guide and often *misguide* our thinking. The brain desires stability, clarity, and consistency, and like a machine, predicts and detects patterns. It needs certainty over ambiguity. Making sense of the world makes our brain happy. We like to know why things happened even if there was no why. Random things happen, but our brain likes a pattern, a cause and effect.

We say 'everything happens for a reason' even if we know it doesn't. As mentioned, our brain is a prediction and pattern detection machine that desires stability, clarity, and consistency. Random things throw it. For example, on top of the biases already discussed, we have selective bias[24], which demonstrates how selective our attention is. We only see what we want to see or are told to see. For example, take the Eriksen Flanker task[25], made famous by the *Gorillas in our Midst* study by Daniel Simon's and Christopher Chabris. In it, observers are asked to focus on the number of times a basketball is passed between a group of people. The observers are so focused on performing this task that more than half, usually much more, don't notice a person dressed in gorilla suit wandering around in the background. What this demonstrates is that we find it very hard to focus our attention and have to choose what we take in and what we ignore. This can result in the brain ignoring important information because it doesn't fit with the stability, clarity, and consistency the brain desires. This bias can increase the influence of other bias such as the self-serving and negative bias.

Even though we are by default negatively biased, it is important to remember that we all have positive things that happen to us each day. We do experience happiness, but many of these things are not remembered in the normal memory process, by which I mean they don't stick or become long-term memories. This is because we haven't experienced them for long enough, no more than a few seconds, or they haven't been million dollar moments, and the memory simply gets pushed out by the influx of new experiences or just information flooding the brain.

So how can we make these positive experiences stick? To start with, you can stop and experience the present moment, such as smelling the roses or feeling the sun shining on your face. Pay attention to the positive things around you. When you do these simple things, the neurons in your brain will start to fuse together to create positive memories.

YOU ARE A CHICKEN

Once upon a time, a man found an eagle's egg and placed it under a brooding hen. The eaglet hatched with the chickens and grew to be like them. He clucked and cackled; scratched the earth for worms; flapped his wings and managed to fly a few feet in the air.

Years passed. One day, the eagle, now grown old, saw a magnificent bird above him in the sky. It glided in graceful majesty against the powerful wind, with scarcely a movement of its golden wings.

Spellbound, the eagle asked, 'Who's that?'

'That's the king of the birds, the eagle,' said his neighbour. 'He belongs to the sky. We belong to earth—we're chickens.'
So the eagle lived as a chicken for that's what he thought he was.[26]

This chapter identifies what most of us do, the road we travel, that makes the achievement of wellbeing that much harder, as well as addressing why we are all eagles, but choose to peck in the dirt every day like chickens.

Lifelong wellbeing can be achieved by anyone but first they must recognise the chicken, address why they are a chicken, discover the eagle within them and then soar.

Why is it that so many of us can identify with the chicken in the parable above? And how many more of us think, what can I do about it? Someone has to be the chicken and be grounded, do the things that still need to be done. Not everyone can be the eagle and be at the top. True, except that being the eagle doesn't mean being at the top, it means being the best version of yourself and we can all be that.

What makes a chicken a chicken? What are the chick magnets?

Do you buy lottery tickets, always hoping that one day your numbers will come up and you will be rich? Perhaps your parents buy one each week too and like you, have yet to win big. What is their response to another loss?

'Oh well, we're not destined to be rich. The only way we will ever get any money is to work for it.' As you grow up, this kind of language seeps into your being and subconsciously leaves an impression on your psyche. *We will always be chickens; we will never be eagles.*

We are all subject to the environment and upbringing of our childhood and though we may have been told positive things, it is the negative things we remember. We touched on negative bias earlier, but of all the things that keep us as chickens, it is our tendency to pay more attention to, and give more emphasis to, negative emotions, experiences, and information instead of those that are positive.

So why is it that some people seem happier than others do? Why are some people always happy, no matter what, and others just seem like sad sacks all the time? There must be a balance somewhere. The sobering fact is, research around the world suggests that about 50%, yes half, of your happiness is predetermined by your genes. This includes personality traits, emotional states and excitability. That's right – blame your parents, who can blame their parents and so on and so on. It is all part of your genetic make-up. You really are a sad sack or full of beans and there's nothing you can do about it! This is fascinating stuff, so take it in.

Imagine a scale from one to ten with one being truly miserable and ten being incredibly happy. Like a thermostat, you sit most of the time at a set point. Your mood swings may change by maybe two points each side of your set point but never go higher or lower. So, if your standing mood level is at a six, you could go as high as an eight or as low as a four, whereas someone else may sit at eight and go as high as a ten and as low as a six. What is fascinating is that you and each and every person is incapable of going outside these boundaries no matter what happens. If you were a six and won the lottery, you couldn't feel happier than say, an eight. If your dog died, you couldn't feel sadder than say, a four. You would never feel truly miserable, relatively speaking.

So, how does this help? It may seem quite discouraging to know that half of your happiness is genetic but having this knowledge and knowing the truth about yourself and understanding who you are, helps make you a happier person, even if you are not capable of being overly enthusiastic about it. Knowing why you are never over the top happy or feel any exhilaration is not because you are depressed, probably, but because you were born this way. You are normal. We are genetically negatively geared and unlike the housing market, we can't use our negative gearing as a tax deduction, however, knowledge of this can help us change our attitudes and outlook.

So, if 50% of your happiness is genetic, what about the rest? An additional 10% of your happiness is determined by life circumstances such as where you grew up, what kind of family life you had and have, your schooling or lack thereof, health, wealth, and so on. That leaves 40% unaccounted for. That 40% is determined by you and is where you can use the ingredients that follow in this book to create a life of wellbeing.

Don't be dismayed by these figures. As much as they are accepted by many experts and as much as you may have a predisposition to being less happy relative to other people, experts are increasingly coming to the view that happiness is a talent and not an inborn trait. In other words, happiness is like a muscle, which with repetition can be flexed to grow stronger and last longer. Whether genetic or a talent that can be honed and perfected, either way, the nurturing of happiness does emphasis the value that the ingredients of wellbeing can have on your future happiness and wellbeing as well as the importance of building good habits to flex your happiness muscles.

Before that, let's continue to look at what makes us chickens. On top of negative bias, our minds are very adaptive, they get used to things. This is known as habituation, which in turn leads to what is called impact bias[27], that is, we tend to overestimate the emotional impact of a future event both in terms of intensity and its duration. In other words, 'we think they're going to be better than they're going to be at the moment we get it,' says Laurie Santos in her course on the Science of Wellbeing, 'and we think that it's going to last longer than it really does.'[28]

Take any number of examples. Getting a new phone, a new car, job, house, even just a chocolate bar. We think it will be better and have a longer lasting impact on us than it actually does. We know this, but how many of us keep buying the latest iPhone or car? Impact bias is also true for negative emotions as well, in that they too are only finite, don't last as long or are as intense as we think they will be. This is linked to duration neglect, which is when we evaluate our experiences, both positive and negative; the duration of them barely matters as long as some conditions are met. The first is the intensity of the peak positive or negative emotion and the second is how the experience ends. As long as the end is better than during the experience, we will see it as a positive experience whereas even if the experience is over a shorter timeframe, if the end is worse than during the experience, we will remember it as a negative experience. Take for example, going to the dentist and having a root canal. Even if the procedure takes two hours and causes a lot of pain, as long as it is not painful at the end of the process and it ends on a high note, we will see it as a positive experience. Contrary to this, even if the root canal is done in only thirty minutes, if it ends with pain and on a negative note, that is how you will remember the event.

Additional chick magnets include our inability to just be content with what we have. We compare ourselves to others, the old 'keeping up with the Joneses' mentality. We want more: more money; better jobs; more stuff like televisions, cars, and houses; love; a good body; and good grades. People feel happy when they think they are better off than their neighbours are, but these feelings are temporary. They provide insecurity in the competitive nature of its inherent one-upmanship. These short-term happiness boosters contribute to life circumstances (the ten per cent we mentioned earlier) that makes us happier. The happiness derived from these pursuits are called hedonic, focusing on the outcome, 'the intense but brief feelings of pleasure for pleasure's sake.'[29]

The thing with hedonic pursuits, although important, is that they undermine the happiness of yourself and others, as they can be selfish and an unhealthy focus on present experiences. They focus on quantity as opposed to quality because the happiness is so fleeting, and to maintain that sense of happiness we pursue more and more, only to need more and more. As Lucretius[30] said, 'Mankind is perpetually the victim of a pointless and futile martyrdom, fretting life away in fruitless worries through failure to realise what limit is set to acquisition and to the growth of genuine pleasure.'

Remember, in the definition of happiness, it was summarised as 'subjective wellbeing', a correlation between objective conditions and subjective expectations. If this is the case, then the basis for our modern society is inadvertently making us miserable. How? Consumerism requires us to buy-in order to keep the wheels of capitalism turning and to buy, we need to know about what is available and then want it for ourselves. Advertising and mass media fulfil this function but inadvertently at the cost of our contentment. Does an advertisement on TV, social media or a billboard showing someone happier, more popular and richer than you make you happier or believe that you could be happier if you had their advertised product?

We live in a world with the self-fulfilling belief that consumption will fill us, complete us, but which has instead left a void. For all the possessions we accumulate, the luxuries we have, we are left empty and wanting, but for what, many of us do not know. According to Sonja Lyubomirsky, author of *The How of Happiness*, materialistic people seem to hold unrealistically high expectations of what material things can do for them.

In his book, *The Five Thieves of Happiness*, author John Izzo notes that we think happiness comes from consumption, but it doesn't and always leads us to wanting more. We covet what our neighbours have, becoming jealous and envious. Social comparison is ridiculous, in part because much of what we compare is beyond our control. Ironically, we like to control as much as we can around us but lack the ability to regulate our self-control, choosing to give into our natural desires, whereas psychological studies show that higher self-control is linked to higher wellbeing,

Another of Izzo's thieves is Comfort, the comfort zone we all like to sit in but which makes us idle and lazy. We don't like it but we feel unable to move and change and then something happens, such as the COVID-19 pandemic, where we are forced to change and none of us are ready for it and are thrown into disarray, leading to anxiety and uncertainty.

This brings to mind the story, *Who Moved My Cheese*[31] by Dr Spencer Johnson, where Hem and Haw, two characters, metaphors for indecision, never change, stuck in their comfort zone. Eventually their circumstances compel them to change but even then, they refuse to come out of their comfort zone, believing things will be okay and it is only when they are nearing death and forced to confront their new circumstances that they force themselves to act. It is easy to see why we behave like this. When we do try to come out of comfort zone, it can feel very uncomfortable. We try to be confident, but it feels like arrogance. We try to be assertive, but it feels like aggression. We try to be kind to ourselves and put ourselves first, but it feels like selfishness. It feels easy to stay where we feel comfortable and that is the problem.

> *The side that stays within its own fortifications is beaten.*
> – Military Maxim of Napoleon

We live our lives in the pursuit of luxury, which is, in essence, the pursuit of boredom. How can our lives have any possible reason or purpose when we pursue nothing? How can we expect to live fulfilled and meaningful lives when our primary goal is the pursuit of an idle tedium? Where is the wonder at the beauty and miracle of nature? Instead, we wonder at the science behind it. We no longer see miracles at all, just a question that has yet to be answered. For all that science and enlightenment have given, it has also taken away. Many of us seem to be so caught up in our own self-importance and materialism that we have forgotten the greater, simpler things and beliefs that we used to live by generations ago. We are reactive instead of proactive, choosing the easy path even if it is the wrong path because we focus on now instead of tomorrow.

What can we do? Maybe we can continue to seek solace in the fact that we have more than our neighbours, that even if we are poor, there are millions more still poorer. It is, after all, within our genes to be selfish and do what is best for us, for our own survival. But why, if we have it all, is it not enough? Why is something still missing? Why are we more depressed and anxious, more unhappy and alone than we have ever been in the past? Have we been pursuing the wrong thing?

It is easy to find blame for why you don't feel in control of your life, happy, fulfilled, or with a sense of wellbeing or purpose, but there are other things that need to be taken into consideration. These can have an incredible impact on you and your sense of identity and self-worth, and it is all of these things that we will go through and digest.

For all that we are and pretend to be, human beings are essentially apes with a bigger brain. A lot of what dictates our behaviour is still very primal. What helps set us apart from other animals is our ability to practice metacognition, which is basically being able to think about thinking. Being able to ask 'why' helps make us human, to be self-reflective and have abstract thought.

This behaviour sets us apart, but it is double-edged sword. While it allows us to assess what we think about, it also allows us to ask bigger questions like: 'Why am I here?', 'Is there a God?', 'Why does toast always land butter side down?', 'What if this or that happens?', 'Why did that happen?' and of course, 'How can I be happy?' These questions and many others can become obsessive for people, to the detriment of themselves and those around them. We are all unique and accordingly, what allows you to discover your eagle will be different to anyone else. These questions need to be asked. They allow you to identify and find peace with who you are, who your best self is, and ultimately what your sense of wellbeing is.

THE CHEMICAL BROTHERS

We have talked about happiness; we know what it is and its importance to our mental health and wellbeing, but biologically, what is it? How can we use our brain to feel happier more often?

Feelings of happiness come from four chemicals or hormones. They evolved because good feelings get us to do things that promote our survival. The brain turns these chemicals and hormones on when it sees something good for survival. It then turns them off again until something else good comes along. The chemicals and hormones are:

- Dopamine
- Endorphins
- Oxytocin
- Serotonin

Additionally, there is cortisol. Cortisol is the primary mover of the fight-or-flight part of your brain. It is the hormone related to stress that tells you something isn't right. It tells you there is pain or the expectation of pain and 'motivates you to do whatever it takes to make the bad feeling stop.'[32] It doesn't have to be physical pain either. Your brain struggles to tell the difference between physical and emotional pain, so when your partner won't stop talking and you just want quiet, it really does feel like your head will explode and you want to scream. Alternatively, when you haven't been invited to a party or there is the possibility that you may lose your job, the feelings you get of anxiety, stress and panic are all examples of your cortisol being let loose.

Imagine being alone in a house at night and the power goes out. You are in complete darkness. This may start the cortisol seeping a little. You then hear a tapping noise on the window and other unknown noises around the house. You may start feeling a little anxious or stressed. You go to the window where the tapping is coming from and draw back the curtains. On the other side of the window, dressed in black and wearing a clown mask, is a person with a knife. Now you feel fear. Your cortisol is now gushing.

There is now an uncontrollable urge to remove this feeling so you can either run away or fight. Either way you brain wants to get back to status quo. To take another less extreme example, you are waiting for your friends to call and ask you out as they said they would, but they don't call, so you feel down and rejected. Your brain has motivated you to get away from this feeling as soon as you can, so you go to the kitchen, get some ice-cream and do a Bridget Jones on the couch. This releases some happy chemicals, and you feel good. A neural pathway is being created and if you have done this before in this situation, it is reinforcing the behaviour. Your cortisol has gone down but what you have done to make you happy is very temporary and something you will likely regret later, especially if you do this often.

When cortisol surges, we call it pain, and when it seeps out in smaller doses, it varies from stress, fear, and anxiety to panic. Your brain hates pain and remembers this and the cues and triggers that caused it and will release cortisol as a warning to you when any of these cues are presented again. As with the example of Bridget Jones above, your brain doesn't recognise a real threat from a perceived one, only what has happened in the past, so will release cortisol in the situation.

How many times do you slow down on a stretch of road where previously you had received a speeding ticket or avoid walking past a specific tree in the springtime because previously you had been swooped by a magpie, or avoid hard sweets because you chipped a tooth? You will be able to think of a multitude of scenarios that relate to you.

Looking at your brain from a physical standpoint, two parts work together like circuits to trigger and control the release of cortisol. They are the hippocampus and amygdala. The hippocampus is involved in storing and retrieving explicit memories. It registers the context of an experience based on memories and the context of a situation. The amygdala is like a decoder, determining what the emotion is, and if it is a threat, it sounds an alarm bell that sends signals to other parts of the brain about what kind of experience it is, for example, a threat, and releases chemicals like cortisol and adrenaline. As we are under more stress in our daily lives with all the things we need to do and experience such as deadlines, commitments, and traffic jams, the little stresses in our lives are overworking the amygdala and it is always on alert.

When you are stressed, you are in fight-or-flight mode and on edge. This means your amygdala is on and being overworked. Coupled with cortisol continually being released, which is sensitising the amygdala, it is also weakening and eating away at the hippocampus. This is bad as the hippocampus becomes unable to keep the amygdala calm and we end up more stressed and wired, and over the long-term it could possibly affect our memory as it is being eaten away by the cortisol hormone. So, what does this mean? We have to practice and train ourselves not to get upset at the small things. If we don't, all we are doing is regulating our body to be constantly in stress mode and chronic stress leads to a multitude of problems, including death.

As an aside, within you are what are called mirror neurons. Mirror neurons allow you to feel empathy for other's pain, which is a great attribute to have, but if you spend too much time around them, you can start to suffer as you start to mirror their feelings. Additionally, in social situations, as we have seen, exclusion makes you feel unhappy, but inclusion can also make you feel the same way as you start to compare yourself to others. Social comparison raises cortisol levels. When you see someone with something you want, a new mobile phone, for example, your cortisol levels are raised as you become aware of their increased social status in relation to you. You don't have what you feel you need to be appreciated, respected and even envied, so you go and get a phone – hopefully not by stealing it but by purchasing one yourself. You may have gone into debt to do so but your cortisol has been calmed and you are happy... for now.

To stop cortisol and its control over your life, you can start by focusing on something else to remove the anxiety or fear. Most of the bad things you think will happen never do. Look at how you react in situations where your cortisol is raised. Stand back and look at your reactions objectively. Is a stressed reaction the best response? Sometimes it is, as in the example with the knife-wielding clown, but sometimes you need to change your responses and consequently build new neural pathways and reactions to cortisol. You can go for a walk, chat to a friend, or start a hobby. Again, the ball is in your court as to what you choose to do. We will be discussing more on social comparison later in the book, but for now let's look at the other chemicals and hormones of happiness: Dopamine, Endorphin, Oxytocin, and Serotonin.

Dopamine

The first sip of a drink is the best, just as is the first bite of a burger, or getting to the next level in a video game. The reason for this is the dopamine release. Dopamine is a feel-good chemical. It is the reward for getting what you want. Dopamine provides an incredibly strong feeling, but unfortunately, the feeling dopamine gives you is temporary and does not last long. It is the victim of a thing called habituation. Habituation is a psychological terms, referring to the decrease in response to a stimulus after being exposed to it repeatedly. In other words, you get used to stuff and don't like it as much as you did.

Take, for example, a burger. The first few bites are delicious, but you quickly get used to it and each additional bite offers less pleasure and by the end of the burger you barely registering the taste of it. Think too of an expensive restaurant and the meal you get. You've paid a lot of money for your food and when it is presented to you, there is barely anything on the plate. It seems like a rip-off, but in fact, it is very smart. The restaurant is not selling you a filling meal; it is selling you the experience of taste. Offering you wonderful, tasty food but only a little of it, ensures that habituation does not set in and you savour every part of the meal.

Our brains remember both the intensity of an experience and how the experience ends. If the experience at the end was pleasurable, then we are likely to remember it favourably. Having a small meal fits the bill as it has not allowed habituation to take place and you will leave the restaurant with a feeling of satisfaction (unless you are a tightwad and feel ripped off by the exorbitant price of the meal!).

In another scenario, because dopamine does not last long, do what you dislike first, the hard tasks, so you can look forward to those you enjoy. The same goes for when you are eating. Eat what you dislike first and then what you do like. In all things, if you want to increase your sense of wellbeing, as mentioned in the previous chapter, always look for ways to end experiences on a positive note. As William Shakespeare said, 'All's well that ends well.'

Dopamine is a like a two-edged sword. It gives you the greatest feelings of joy and satisfaction, but its lasting effects are short and consequently you are always looking for the next way to get dopamine. It requires you to keep looking for a new release of dopamine and the next hit has to be bigger than the last in order to release enough dopamine because of the effects of habituation.

Consider the gambler who keeps putting money into the slot machines. They are no longer doing it for the money, they are doing it to get out of the dopamine dip and get the dopamine hit from winning, but to get it they need to win bigger and bigger as the brain wants a new experience and to overcome what it has become used to – the habituation. Here is where the risk is – the pursuit of dopamine release can lead to addiction and addiction can lead to many personal and social issues.

Dopamine and cortisol go hand in hand and the bigger the dopamine hit the bigger the cortisol hit. Remember, dopamine is all about the chase. Once it is achieved, it is no longer needed and cortisol has the opportunity to settle in. Anxiety builds up as the addict convinces themselves the only way to get the dopamine hit they need to is gamble more often and with more money in order to get a bigger win and a bigger dopamine rush. It becomes a vicious cycle.

Dopamine is part of your brain's survival mechanism. Without it, our ancestors would not have had the enthusiasm to go and hunt or mate with one another and would have essentially died out. Dopamine gives the motivation for the chase and once a goal is reached the dopamine goes away, but your brain is always looking for the next way to get dopamine.

Think of a child with a new toy or playing a game. They have been doing it for five minutes and are then always looking for what they are going to do next, never satisfied with what they are doing in the moment. Good dopamine hits come from collecting, planning a project such as a holiday, or travel. The same occurs in normal life. Take for example, meeting a new partner. When you are first going out and doing new things together, the dopamine is flowing, and life is good. You are truly happy. But once that wears off, routine kicks in and the cortisol takes over. You start to see holes and flaws both in your life and in your partner and may blame them for things that were probably always there but didn't bother you when you were wearing the rose-tinted glasses, now lying crushed on the ground of your dreams and aspirations.

How do you overcome habituation and get the most of out the dopamine release?

Dopamine is the joy of finding what you need and getting what you want, but the more we have it, the less we appreciate it. Contemplate the times you have said to yourself, 'I'll be happy when...' It could be getting a new car, a new house, a new job, a new phone. The reality is habituation will make sure you are never happy if you believe this, as you will get used to anything and want more and more. Instead, before buying a new non-essential object, ask yourself how long it will keep you happy. Do you remember your best holiday and have then gone back to the same location expecting it to be just as good and it hasn't? Again, this is habituation. Instead, vary it up, go with someone new, go somewhere different, try something different and experience new things. Variety really is the best defence against habituation. Step outside your comfort zone, try something new, meet new people, go somewhere different, and grow as a person because of it. Instead of changing things around you, change the focus to yourself.

Dopamine is the reward chemical. In summary, it comes from eating food, achieving goals, getting enough sleep or something as simple as having a bath.

Perhaps, when all is said and done, we can learn from dopamine and habituation. Maybe life is limited because if it went on for too long, we would not appreciate it. Therefore, a limited amount of time to live is a blessing, the limitation giving the possibility to lead your best life.

Endorphins

Endorphins are hormones that the body releases when in pain or under emotional stress. There are actually over 20 types of endorphins in humans, but those we know most about are called beta-endorphins. Their role is to block pain and when released, can cause a feeling of euphoria with the pain relief being greater than that of morphine. It does this as part of our ancient survival mechanism. When a sabre-toothed tiger was chasing you and you sprained your ankle, you still needed to get away. Endorphins gave you that chance by hiding the pain.

Traditionally, we associate endorphins with exercise and their release when you are under stress because you are pushing yourself to your limit, commonly known as the runner's high, but they can also be released when doing things like acupuncture, massage therapy, eating spicy food, and having sex. As the saying goes, there's a fine line between pleasure and pain. The *Fifty Shades of Grey* franchise has shown us that pleasure really can come from pain, in a controlled environment. But there are situations where things can get wildly out of hand.

Opium derivatives can simulate endorphins and become addictive simply because, while hiding pain, they give us pleasure, but due again to habituation, we need more and more to feel the same feeling of euphoria. This increases the downs and lows and creates a loop that gets worse.

To activate endorphins, there are simple, natural things you can do such as laugh, cry, vary your exercise, make it fun and stretch, and even listen to music. In fact, crying is your body's way of releasing intense emotions. Crying actually releases stress hormones contained in your tears from your body. The act of crying can also stimulate the production of endorphins and the release of happy hormones such as oxytocin[33], the next of our chemical brothers to look at. No wonder they call it a 'good cry'.

Oxytocin

Do you remember when you were in a new relationship with someone and you got that warm feeling inside when you thought about them or saw them, and being with them was the best feeling in the world? You wanted to be with that person always because of the way they made you feel – they were your favourite. You might call it love and you might be partly right.

Oxytocin is commonly known as the love hormone because of the higher levels of the hormone in couples in the early stages of their relationship when compared to unattached people. It assists with bonding such as when you're attracted to another person. This causes your brain to do three things: release dopamine, increase your serotonin levels, and produce oxytocin. As a consequence, you to feel a gush of positive emotion. This is especially prevalent in mothers with their newborn children and why skin-to-skin contact and bonding immediately after birth is seen as so important.

Oxytocin makes you feel safe with others, which is why it is good for building social alliances, and why we like people with whom we have things in common. Think of social groups you belong to, such as sports teams and group fitness groups or when you go to a concert, nightclub or hobby event. We feel good in groups we can relate to and who share the same interests and values as we do. This is especially so for family units, as they traditionally supply the greatest feelings of safety within a group. Oxytocin makes you feel safe, secure, and happy within a group but can also make you feel suspicious of others based on the environment.

As an illustration, oxytocin can intensify memories of good bonding in youth with family but can also have the opposite effect, for example, in cases where men have had poor interactions and bonding with their mothers. Subsequently, people can become less accepting of people and see them as outsiders. In a related example, oxytocin drops when there is conflict within a group or romantic couple. We try to stay with groups, whether family, friends or lovers, because they relate to us but over time, you, them or the environment can change, and you need to decide whether you should stay or go and what is best for you. Your survival instinct, the fight-or-flight mode, kicks in and you have to choose to stick with the status quo, the devil you know, or move on. Think of those in destructive and abusive relationships and the difficult decision that has to be made, to go into the unknown or stay in an existing relationship that they know is not good for them.

Oxytocin affects males and females differently, especially in the context of social interaction. This is possibly because of the way the hormone acts in the female and male amygdala, which is responsible for emotion, reward, and motivation. In females, oxytocin may help them in identifying whom to befriend as well as how to behave and nurture in those relationships, whereas in males, oxytocin may be a factor in the way they recognise competitive relationships and manage the fight-or-flight response. Indeed, oxytocin may help our bodies adapt to a number of different emotional and social situations, and research[34] suggests that it has a positive impact on social behaviours related to relaxation, trust, and overall psychological stability. Additionally, it has been shown that oxytocin decreases stress and anxiety levels when released in certain parts of the brain. Summing up, oxytocin is the love hormone. It is stimulated by socialising, physical touch and helping others. Even simple things like petting animals can stimulate it.

Serotonin

Serotonin is a last of the chemical brothers. It is a chemical that nerve cells produce and it sends signals between the nerve cells. It is found mostly in the digestive system and as such, is made from the essential amino acid called tryptophan, which gets into your body through what you eat, primarily foods like nuts, cheese, and red meat. Every part of your body is affected by serotonin including your mood and motor skills. Additionally, it helps with sleeping, eating, digestion, healing of wounds, reduction of depression and regulation of anxiety, among others.

In regard to your mental health, serotonin helps you feel happier, calmer, more focused, less anxious and more emotionally stable. Low levels of serotonin have been linked to memory problems, feeling low, and depression, trouble sleeping and craving of sweet foods. Drugs such as MDMA, also commonly known as ecstasy, cause large amounts of serotonin to be released into the body and levels to skyrocket with symptoms including, when levels are very high, restlessness and agitation, a fast heartbeat, high temperature, headaches, dilated pupils, and goose bumps. Once the drug wears off, it can lead to the opposite – low serotonin levels, and trouble sleeping, anxiety, loss of sex drive (low libido) and exhaustion. If taken regularly, ecstasy can, in addition, cause high blood pressure and damaged nerves.

Aside from foods and drugs, serotonin can be gained through exercise, with many research studies demonstrating that 'exercise is at least equally effective at increasing available serotonin as serotonin-enhancing medications are, and in some cases, exercise is more effective.'[35] As much of the serotonin is produced in your gut – about ten times more than we have in our brains – ensuring you have good gut health is important. Bright light or being out in the sunshine is also a natural way to get your serotonin fix, especially important when you consider how much time is spent indoors by people compared to that of our ancestors who spent a lot more time outside in what was more of an agricultural society compared to today.[36] In other words, get out from behind that computer or TV and get outside more often!

Interestingly, serotonin also comes from being respected by others. This comes from our ancestors, where there was a more obvious pecking order with your alphas at the top and the rest underneath. The alphas had access to food and sexual partners first, ensuring their survival and dominance. But the others, those non-alphas, still needed to live and survive. They needed, as we do now, to get food and partners to pass on their DNA to the next generation. To do so, the body rewards you with good feelings for taking a chance. 'Dopamine rewards you for stepping towards rewards; oxytocin rewards you for sustaining social support; and serotonin rewards you for taking the social risks essential to survival.'[37] Again, the feeling doesn't last, much like dopamine, and consequently you have to do more to get more.

In our modern society, serotonin releases not just for reasons of survival but also when others respect us, when we are in power, or even being noticed by someone in power, or who has respect themselves. 'Seeking recognition is part of human life,' says Loretta Graziano Breuning, author of *Habits of a Healthy Brain*, 'despite the potential for disappointment.'[38]

Let's face it, we cannot all be the alpha of the group and have serotonin coursing through our veins, so we have to take opportunities as they present themselves. To build serotonin levels you can look for reasons to express pride in what you do, enjoy your social position in the moment, take notice of what influence you do have, and accept what you can control and ultimately what you cannot. You can get more sun exposure, practice mindfulness and be out in nature. Finally, accept that you will not always be the best. Teach yourself and your children, if you have any, to keep trying as trying is good too.

So those are the chemicals that keep us happy, but what about happy drugs? Based on what you've just read, you could easily conclude that all we need are drugs to manipulate the chemical brothers so that we feel happy all the time. With our understanding of the brain and its function, we now have the ability to manipulate the biochemical processes in the brain and can use drugs to feel good all the time.

Prozac, among other drugs, both legal and illegal, can cause the brain to release the chemicals mentioned and consequently we feel happy and content. This is a simple solution to wellbeing, right? It makes complete sense when you stop and think about it. If we all took drugs and felt good, there would theoretically be less crime as we would feel happy, less wars, less discontentment, and less misery – at least in our minds.

This idea is looked at in Aldous Huxley's 1932 novel, *Brave New World*, in which people are given a drug called 'soma', which makes them happy without affecting their productivity or efficiency. There is no need for police or elections, there is no war, revolutions, or strikes because everyone feels happy. The problem with this interpretation of happiness and wellbeing is that it sees that the sole goal of happiness as pleasure and that once we have that, our mind will want for nothing more and we will be content. It will override our need for food and water, our drive, willpower, and desire to grow as a person.

We need to factor in habituation and the need for more as we get used to what we feel. You can see in the way drugs such as heroin can turn its users into zombies, only concerned with getting their next hit. Their own sense of self is lost in the pursuit of the feeling the drug gives them. It also doesn't consider another factor of the human mind: it doesn't always associate happiness and contentment with the moment in which it is happening, it is usually after the fact, in looking back, that happiness is determined.

Humans gain wellbeing from having meaning in their lives, something to believe in and live for. Drugs alone don't provide that. It comes from the experience of living, identifying who you are as an individual, and of creating moments and aligning with people who share the same ideals and vision as you do.

YOU ARE A DODO

So far, we have seen just how much we are slaves to our primal brain. We have changed as the world has changed, but our brains haven't. It still behaves as it did thousands of year ago and hasn't adapted to the changed conditions in which we now live.

This is much like the Dodo, a flightless bird that lived on the island of Mauritius, off the coast of Madagascar in the Indian Ocean. It had no natural predators and flourished for thousands of years until humans arrived. Within eighty years, the bird was extinct. It knew no fear, so went willingly to its death. There was no hunting required. The dodo didn't adapt to the human threat and went willingly to their human killers. Whereas they are famously considered dumb for doing so, we suffer from the same inability to adapt. However, instead of having no fear, it appears that our lives are directed by fear, led by a desire to survive but in a world that no longer needs that degree of emotion. Consequently, our fear and anxiety are directed by feelings of inadequacy, longing for things we don't need, greed, and the need for a quick hit of dopamine.

Our default to feel negatively inclined leaves us thinking that bad things will come true, but good things unlikely will. Hope, it would seem, was left in Pandora's box for a reason, lest everything would seem hopeless. Thought-action fusion is a peculiar yet common psychological phenomenon in which we believe the worst in things. For example, just by thinking something bad will happen, you believe that it will.

An experiment was done with a bunch of psychologists at a workshop where the presenter asked them to imagine a person they loved and then to write out the following sentence with their name in place of XXX: 'I hope XXX is in a car accident.' How would you feel in that situation? Would you feel comfortable writing down the name of someone you love, or even just saying it? Not many of us would, yet the same psychologists were then asked to do the same thing again with the same loved one's name but with the following sentence 'I hope XXX wins the lottery.' Everyone laughed at this because no-one believed it would come true. So, why was it ridiculous to believe someone could win the lottery simply by writing it down but not so, when we hoped they would be in a car crash? It's because we are all crazy in the head.

Our survivor brains are programmed to give more credence to things that will hurt us rather than will help us, more likely to believe something bad will happen than something good. Feel for the person who has obsessive-compulsive disorder (OCD) and how they must feel with thought-action fusion, but don't despair too much. We do have a belief that good can happen, for example, in the form of prayer. Why do we wish people good luck if we don't believe it? So, next time, when you are worrying, think about what you are letting your brain do and move to overcome it.

> *Negative thoughts stick around because we believe them, not because we want them or choose them.*
>
> *– Andrew Bernstein, Philosopher*

Conversely, when it comes to us personally, we are more likely to think that something good will happen to us rather than something bad. In 1998, American psychologist, Scott Plous[39], did an experiment where students were given a list of 42 positive and negative events, such as getting an illness, getting a raise at work, or buying a house. Each student was then asked to estimate the chances that these things would happen in their lives and not happen to others.

Results showed that people thought the likelihood of the good events happening to them was 15% higher than the bad events, and 20% lower than for others. This is known as the Irwin Effect, in which we think that something good is more likely to happen to us as opposed to something bad. Looking deeper into this, it means that for many of us, when it comes to making decisions, we don't look at the big picture. How many people have enough savings put aside for the proverbial rainy day? Consider those that still drink and drive, believing that they will be okay and won't get caught, won't cause an accident or worse, kill themselves or someone else. The same goes for those in bad relationships and thinking they will be okay, and their partner will change.

What would it be like if we lived in a world with no happiness? It is after all much like a mirage that always disappears as soon as you get close to it. We would not waste our lives in search of it. We would not see it where it does not exist and pursue it only to make ourselves unhappy in its quest. Happiness is, at its base level, a tool of the brain that encourages us to act in order to protect and preserve our lives and create new life. It is simply an emotion, much like all of the other emotions we feel. Think of our emotions like String theory. Nerd alert! String theory attempts to unify the four forces in the universe – electromagnetic force, the strong nuclear force, the weak nuclear force, and gravity – together into one unified theory. It replaces all matter and force particles with strings that vibrate at different frequencies to create everything. Everything is connected. This is how we should look at emotions. They are the same thing but resonate at different frequencies to give us anger, hate, love, joy and happiness. Depending on where a guitarist holds their fingers, different sounds come from the strings. The different chords are the different emotions. All emotions are linked; we just need to learn how to play them to get what we want.

EMOTIONS

*Those are your emotions acting
without the benefit of intellect.*

Charles Rane, Passenger 57 (1992)

Wellbeing is both enhanced and diminished by emotions. Life is a juxtaposition of everything and to say you have experienced life fully is to say you have experienced all the emotions that come with it. And there are a multitude of emotions to feel and there are multitudes of experiences to be had.

Great experiences come to those who put themselves out there and especially to those who live a life with meaning, but too many of us experience the mediocrity of a life with no meaning. It is a simple thing to do, but it can also be the hardest – to let go of life and let it do with you what it will. We spend so much time trying to control our lives, that we lose what life we had. We lose the ability to experience what life has to offer, instead trying to get it to give us what we want, in the process making ourselves unhappy, feeling unfulfilled and empty. So much so, in fact, that we live vacant hollow existences, not lives at all.

The air of melancholy hangs over us day after day, only broken now and then by bursts of happiness that have come from the simplest of things: a walk in the park, birds singing in the trees, or our children laughing. Despite this, we still pursue gratification through the means we know to be wrong.

Happiness does not come in a $100,000 car with all the bells and whistles that are supposed to make us look cool or important. The same goes for promotions, where we are piled with even more work than we had earlier and consequently get even less time to spend doing the things we enjoy with the people that make us happy – if only so momentarily. Herein is the experience. From this experience, this emotion, we can learn what we want and can know where it is we can get it but first we have to savour the experience and emotion to appreciate what we really want, what we really need to lead self-fulfilled lives. It is hard work but if we can wallow in our own rollercoaster of emotions and experiences, we can come out as complete human beings, able to be the people we always meant to be, finding real happiness and contentment in our lives.

'Emotions,' summarises the Merriam Webster dictionary[40], 'are 'a conscious mental reaction (such as anger or fear) subjectively experienced as strong feeling usually directed toward a specific object and typically accompanied by physiological and behavioural changes in the body.' We can relate this back to the Chemical Brothers already discussed.

What is of interest is that there is no scientific consensus on what emotions are. This has been compounded by the inclusion of other components, such as mood, temperament, feelings, personality, traits, perceptions, and beliefs among others. At its base level, an emotion can be positive or negative, evolved in response to the challenges faced by our ancestors, therefore hardwired into us with the intention of having us survive. Emotions for that reason are not something that have adapted well to modern life. They tend to lead to short-term bias, which in turn leads to the disregard of long-term pleasure. This worked well thousands of years ago, but not so much now.

Emotions are chemicals and the glue that holds our body, memories, and identity together. They are physical and physiological, not abstract and mental. In his book, *Personality Isn't Permanent,* Benjamin Hardy, Ph.D, says, 'We need to reframe how we see our body and look at it as an emotional system.'

Our bodies get used to these chemicals, for example, dopamine, and having certain levels of it in our system and so we do what we can, usually sub-consciously through habit or addiction, to maintain these levels, these emotions. Our bodies become addicted to certain emotional levels and alter our behaviour to fulfil that need. This is why it is so hard to overcome addiction; it is not solely a mental disorder, but one in which you literally need to change your biology.

> *I've got a bad feeling about this.*
> *Star Wars (1977)*

It is important to distinguish between an emotion and a feeling. An emotional experience is by default a feeling because feeling is a conscious experience, such as feeling pain, whereas an emotion by itself 'can only ever be felt...through the emotional experiences it gives rise to, even though it might be discovered through its associated thoughts, beliefs, desires, and actions.'[41] Emotions are not conscious, but manifest in the unconscious mind.

We are such complicated creatures and the emotional spectrum we have is so long and layered that it is a surprise, when you look into it deeper and see the interdependencies, cues, and triggers, that we are as highly functioning as we are – most of the time.

Our beliefs are what we hold to be true. These beliefs can be influenced by our culture, upbringing, and experiences. A belief is not a feeling. You can believe something but not feel it. For example, you can believe that something is scary but not be scared. Additionally, a belief is either right or wrong, whereas an emotion is not so black and white. Our beliefs can be influenced by our perceptions, which 'aim to reflect objective reality whereas emotions aim to reflect subjective reality; not reality itself, but our reality.'[42] Our emotions are also able to motivate us into action, acting upon decisions we have made – think fight-or-flight – and interestingly, those with reduced emotions find it hard to make decisions and act upon them. Examples of these people might be those who have had brain injuries, mental disorder, or severe depression.

Our basic emotions, including happiness, sadness, fear, disgust, anger, and surprise are supported or at least able to be extracted in a multitude of other emotions. This is too in-depth for this book but which include loneliness, depression, gratitude and anxiety. One of the reasons we are fascinated with such characters as Star Trek's Spock is because he does not feel emotion.

As emotionally driven creatures, the thought of dealing with situations and experiences without the hindrance or benefit of emotions, depending on your point of view, fascinates us even though as mentioned above, those with reduced emotions find it harder to make decisions and act upon them. Yet, in the same breath, maybe what fascinates us most is that we are brought up to be like Spock. Especially among males, held to such standards in our society where we are not only encouraged but expected to suppress and ignore our emotions.

The obvious problem is that we are human beings, led by our emotions. It seems like an oxymoron to behave this way, but it has been an expectation of our society for millennia. Only now is society seeing that it is important to express and talk about emotions as opposed to suppressing them, regardless of gender.

The 'man myth' extolling the apparent virtues of what it means to be a man has persisted for far too long. Expressing emotions is considered by many to be counterintuitive to reason and logical decision-making. How can you make a good decision if you let emotions get in the way? That is weakness. Being a man is showing no emotion, bottling it up. 'Don't be a pussy.' 'Man up!' 'Get over it.' 'She'll be right.' These are all messages repeatedly drilled into boys and men. Men do not show emotion unless that emotion is anger. That is the only acceptable emotion. Other emotions can therefore only be expressed as anger, so when a man feels scared, it is okay for him to express this as anger. It is pretty messed up and rightly so.

Slowly, this is being addressed as it has been identified and appreciated that expressing emotions is good and the emotional expectations put on men are having a devastating toll on their lives. Emotions are an amazing part of the human experience. Emotions help us to survive and thrive.

Societal views on emotions aren't just negatively gendered for men. If a man feels sad or scared, he is a wimp or a loser. If he expresses anger, hey, he's a man, but if a woman expresses anger, she is a bitch. If a woman expresses any emotions that shows their vulnerability, they are just 'being emotional.' Women are expected to be emotional but to an extreme where, when they show emotion, they are not taken seriously, and everyone just rolls their eyes. 'There she goes, crying again!' If a man shows any such emotions and cries, for example, he is told to stop crying like a girl.

At some point, something has to give. Is it any wonder that suicide rates are so high when there is so much expectation and stereotyping around gender roles and emotional expectations? A lot of societal deconditioning needs to take place and people need to be open to all emotions in order to overcome this programming that has eroded the value of our life's expectations to date. To reiterate, emotions are an important and integral part of the human condition. To deny or suppress your emotions is to supress your humanity.

Emotions are said to have either a positive or negative aspect. 'Positive emotions like joy, happiness, contentment and love,' says psychologist Barbara Fredrickson, allow you to 'see more possibilities in your life.' Negative emotions do the exact opposite. How you allow your emotions to dictate your life is up to you. It is up to you how you perceive an event, situation, or experience. You determine your emotional resilience. The word 'resilience' is an overused blanket term assigned to anyone having to cope with adverse conditions, whether or not they are coping. However, when it is self-determined, it is okay.

Strong emotions, both negative and positive, are our greatest weakness. Remember, this is what Stoicism believes, especially when we allow emotions to dictate our behaviour. This doesn't mean that we should suppress or hide our emotions. In fact, as has been discussed, it is quite the opposite. Acknowledgment is key. Once we recognise our emotions, we can then consider what has caused them and learn how to redirect them for our own good. Through this process, we can learn how to calm and train our negative emotions, recognising at the same time what we can and cannot control, reflecting on how we react to situations, experiences, and the emotions they produce.

MENTAL HEALTH

*No great genius has existed without
a strain of madness.*

Aristotle

Sometimes the colours of life are swept away and our mind paints a canvas of a hundred shades of misery. Winston Churchill, former politician and British Prime Minister during World War 2, suffered from depression, calling it his 'black dog' and was relieved when his depressive episodes had gone away, once penning, 'He [the black dog] seems quite away from me now – it is such a relief. All the colours come back into the picture.' We all want a life of colour and brightness but for the majority of us, at some point, we will experience mental health issues, feeling the weight of life drain away the colour of life, our desire and in some cases, our ability to live life as we would like.

> *I have found that one must try and teach people that there's no top limit to disaster – that, so long as breath remains in your body, you've got to accept the miseries of life. They will often seem infinite, insupportable. They are part of the human condition.*
>
> *– Ian Fleming, You Only Live Twice*

For our own mental health, we need to accept that happiness is just one emotion, one that is overrated and unable to be sustained for any period. Everybody's mood and emotions fluctuate – no-one is happy all the time. They even made a movie about it![43]

Nevertheless, we have internalised that we should and need to be happy all the time, and of course when we are not, we feel sad, anxious, angry, frustrated and a mix of numerous other emotions. Because we see them as bad, we fixate on trying to rid them from within us and in the process, feel even worse because we cannot. It is like when you decide you will not have any more alcohol or chocolate, but you then start obsessing over the alcohol or chocolate and you want it even more than before. You then feel bad because you feel you are failing and then give up and have more alcohol or chocolate.

Trying to stop negative emotions is hard. You focus on it and that focus makes you feel that emotion even more acutely. It is a loop that keeps on spiralling downwards and out of control. Erich Fromm, in his book, *To Have Or To Be*, noted that, 'We are a society of notoriously unhappy people: lonely, anxious, depressed, destructive, dependent—people who are glad when we have killed the time we are trying so hard to save.' He wasn't wrong.

It doesn't help when we turn to social media as a default escape from reality, only to see the perceived reality of other people being so much better than our own. This leads people to have Facebook Envy, which can lead to depression[44] and for those who spend more than two hours a day on social media, poor mental health, and psychological distress. They are also at greater risk of obesity, heart disease, and early death.[45]

When people realise that life is responsibility and we are each responsible for our own life, the devil-may-care attitude of youth evaporates, causing for some great grief at the loss of the carefree childhood.

David Attenborough, English broadcaster and natural historian, noted, 'In moments of great grief, that's where you look and immerse yourself. You realise you are not immortal, you are not a god, you are part of the natural world and you come to accept that.' The transition from child to adult is a difficult one at the best of times, but even more so in today's society with the pressures and expectation of success, whether realistic, warranted, or even wanted.

The expression, 'Youth is wasted on the young', never rings truer than when you have lost your youth. Not because you want to be young again but because the experience of youth, the potential, the possibility, and the opportunity that lay ahead of you, is never to be had again. This carries on through life into the midlife crisis, which happens several times throughout your adult life. No longer able to go out and buy a Harley-Davidson motorcycle because you cannot afford one, still paying off a massive mortgage, sufferers now have to look at themselves and find ways to get out of their rut or fall further into the recesses of their mind.

> *Stress is nothing more than a socially acceptable form of mental illness.*
> *– Richard Carlson*

The worst part about having mental health issues is that no-one sees them, and you basically have to have a breakdown for people even to know you are struggling and just how hard you have been trying to hold yourself together. In their book, *F*ck Feelings*, authors Dr Michael Bennett and Sarah Bennett say that people read self-help books and see specialists such as psychologists and psychiatrists to fix and heal them. The thing is, that in many cases, you cannot be cured. We are all f*cked up in our own special way (in the same way that we are all crazy in our own special way) and need to identify and accept what we cannot change and manage what we can. The key is how to manage the shit in our lives as opposed to trying to change it.

Some Stats

So how big is the mental health issue? We hear about the mental health epidemic all the time, but what is happening, what are the numbers, and how much of a problem is it, really? Here are some statistics to give you an idea of the issue at hand and why we need to do something about it.

If you have chosen to read this book, then you are at least on the right pathway to learning what and how to be a better you, but this is a worldwide problem and as much as you can help yourself, more needs to be done by governments, workplaces, schools, and even families to make wellbeing a major focus. Bear in mind, this is just a small sample of information on a much bigger problem, but is here to give you an idea of what is going on in the wider world.

Mental Illness

Mental illness affects everyone to a degree at some point in their lives.

Mental illness includes:

- Anxiety disorders
- Mood disorders such as depression and bipolar disorder
- Personality disorders
- Psychotic disorders such as schizophrenia
- Eating disorders
- Trauma related disorders such post-traumatic stress disorder

According to the *Institute for Mental Health Metric and Evaluation* and reported in their *Global Burden of Disease* study, 792 million people live with a mental health disorder, which is 10.7% of the world's population (at the time of the study in

2017)[46]. Broken down, a disproportionately large percentage of the 792 million are in Western countries like Australia and the United States. As of 2016, about 7.1% of American adults aged 18 and over, or 17.3 million people, have depressive symptoms in any one year.

The World Health Organization estimates that on any given day, more than one in 20 Americans are depressed.[47] For anxiety, it is double that. Anxiety is the most common form of mental illness in the United States with 40 million adults, approximately 19.1% of the population with a disorder. On top of this, seven per cent of children aged three to 17 have issues with anxiety each year.[48] In Australia, about one million people experience depression – one in six women and one in eight men. For anxiety, the number doubles to two million in any one year.[49] In the United Kingdom, based on 2014 data, 19.7% of people aged 16 and over showed symptoms of anxiety or depression, an increase of 1.5% from the year before.[50] Only 17 per cent of American adults are considered to be in a state of 'optimal mental health' according to the U.S. Department of Health and Human Services. One American adult in ten is on some kind of medication to cope with depression. That number jumps to one in four in American women aged in their forties and fifties. When it comes to death because of mental illness, the numbers are quite alarming. In 2017, over 47,000 Americans died by suicide[51] and over 67,000 died from drug overdoses[52] including illicit drugs and prescription drugs, an increase of over 56% since 2010. With instability in the economy and society and employment, these number will likely only get worse, and the numbers say it all. There is a mental health issue.

Loneliness

Loneliness becomes a lover. Solitude a darling sin.
- Ian Fleming, The Spy who Loved Me

The feeling of loneliness is increasingly common, and it is not just about more people living alone, although 30% of people now do compared to 10% in 1950.[53] It is about feelings of isolation and the inability to connect with those around you. Nearly half of Americans feel lonely[54] and 35% of those over the age of 45 feel chronically lonely. Only half (53%) say they have meaningful, daily face-to-face interactions with other people[55] and less than 92% report having important conversations with their neighbours in any given year![56] Meanwhile, members of Generation Z (adults aged 18-22) claim to be the loneliest generation despite the social engagement tools we have at our disposal including the so-called social media.

Loneliness really is a big issue, and we will discuss this further later on in the book.

Drugs

We are a sad lot, with consumption of antidepressants in Australia having more than doubled since the year 2000. This equates to three million people or nearly one in eight on antidepressants, including 100,000 children, up nearly 100% since 2011/2012[57].

On top of the deaths from accidental drug overdoses in the United States, in Australia it has risen to 142 Australians dying each month, overtaking car fatalities, while suicide is now the leading cause of death in males aged 15 – 44 years of age.

In a survey of American adults, more than half said they regularly take prescription medication and the number of prescriptions filled out for adults and children has increased by 85% between 1997 and 2016, despite the population only increasing by 21% in the same period.

Overall, these numbers give us an idea of the depth of the issue out there and why your mental health is important. We all, at some point in time, will suffer from mental health issues and have negative thoughts. The key is understanding when we are having the issues and knowing what to do about them.

Negative Thoughts

As discussed, people are, generally speaking, negatively geared. Negative thoughts are normal and healthy; they are there to promote our survival. What we tend to do, however, is see negative thoughts as the enemy. This kind of thinking leads to the downward spiral of despair. You are simply fighting with yourself. Thoughts aren't real, they are just words, ideas, sounds, and symbols. If you find yourself with negative thoughts, don't believe them. They are just thoughts. You have chosen to make them negative. Question them. Look at them for what they are and move on. How do you question them?

Ask if the thoughts are useful. How do they behave? Determine if the negative thoughts are real or just noise you can ignore. Other options to explore with questioning include asking if the original negative thought is true. Can you be sure that it is true? How do you react to a negative thought and what happens when you believe that thought?[58] What would happen if you didn't react?

Ask, 'Why, why, why' to determine what you are really feeling. For example, you may be thinking, I hate my job. Why? There is too much work to do. Why? Because my colleague doesn't pull their weight. Why? Because my colleague doesn't have the skills and experience to do the job as quickly as I do. With this kind of questioning, you need to be completely honest to get to a solution. In this case, the colleague could have some training, the workload could be spread, and you will be happier at work. You need to keep asking 'why' until you get to the root cause of your feelings. Once you know the root cause, it is easier to change your feelings and your mood.

Emotional pain is the same as physical pain. Our brain cannot tell the difference, and just like physical pain, emotional pain is your mind's way of telling you that something is not right, and you need to address the cause and have time to heal.

There will be occasions where your negative thinking can be caught, like a virus, from those around you. Anxiety, happiness, blame, fear, and apathy are all well researched contagions, and you need to have an awareness of the influence of what are called psychosocial contagions. In a group setting, emotions can easily be spread. The COVID-19 pandemic presented several examples of this, from fear causing panic buying at the supermarket to blaming the pandemic on 5G Wi-Fi transmission and minority groups, forcing logic and common sense to fly out the window. Confirmation Bias, noticing things that confirm your bias and ignoring those that don't, seeks to amplify this and affirm your story and what you believe your life to be. When negatively inclined, this can lead to long-term mental health issues.

Because our brains love us so much (note the sarcasm!), our 'negativity bias', which means we remember bad things more than good, requires up to five positive things to outweigh a single negative so that we feel balanced. That is a lot!

Try to be active instead of reactive. Practice having strong emotional health and intelligence. This means taking control of the way that you feel and not letting events dictate your feelings. It is about being positive, which is not always possible but with the intent to be so, and with practice, you can control your emotions and not let them control you. Although it may feel like it sometimes, the world is not out to get you. It is important to practice this because negative emotions such as stress and bad moods can manifest into physical symptoms like headaches, stomach ulcers, high blood pressure, sexual problems, and sleep loss. Negative emotions can also affect your immune system. You become more susceptible to getting colds and other infections and because you are not in a good place emotionally, you are more likely to take less care of your health, choosing to eat unhealthy food instead of healthy food, or blobbing in front of the TV instead of doing some exercise.

What we need to remember is that negative emotions are a natural part of life. They are part of your neurological and genetic make-up. We are obsessed with getting rid of bad feeling or what we see as the cause of them, but that won't always work. You can't always avoid people or circumstances that make you feel bad, such as a work colleague, or your job. You could make things worse and become irresponsible; but you generally need a job to live.

What you need to do is block, control or manage feelings to stop them from ruining your life. Remember also that feelings are subjective, both good and bad, so don't stigmatise bad feelings as negative, just learn to deal with them. Don't judge yourself by how you feel, but by what you are doing to change the way you feel. Everyone is an arsehole to someone. As much as you have negative feelings towards someone, someone else will have negative feelings towards you and in the same way, just as you think someone is awesome, someone else will not, but will think that you are.

Be aware of how you feel about yourself and try not to surround yourself with people who hate you as much as you hate yourself. That is a downward spiral for sure. Where you can, focus on and appreciate what you do with your feelings, not what they do to you. 'You can't always control feeling negatively, but you can keep it from controlling you.'[59]

Regret

The last thing we want in life is to regret what we didn't do with our lives. At least if you try something, even if you fail, you know, whereas the regret from not having even tried gnaws at you until the very end. Regret is a form of loss because of what could have been and as such, our brain tries to avoid regret wherever it can so it can remain in its stable comfort zone. Regret, however, is actually a very important emotion because even though it is perceived as negative, it is a function that enables us to learn.

Using counterfactual thinking, we can reflect on decisions made and consider alternatives 'counter' to those that actually happened and how they may have affected the outcome. For example, if you had driven to work that way, instead of this way, then you wouldn't be stuck in this traffic and late for work. Of course, it is in our genetic make up to blame ourselves or others and focus on what went wrong, overshadowing the learning we can take from the experience. Blaming is easy too. It makes us feel good but takes away our sense of control and need for a solution. Your brain will keep revisiting bad decisions made as it wants a solution, a learning from the error so it can go back to its happy place, something that regret and counterfactual thinking provides us. If you have depression, the regret over decisions made and the counterfactual thinking can go on indefinitely, as you berate yourself over 'what if' scenarios and learnings. In order to stop the brain overthinking and over-analysing decisions made, take a step back, become partially detached, and see the situation from a metacognitive point of view, without becoming entangled in it. You can consider different ways of looking at the issue while at the same time keeping a focus on present realities, not 'what ifs', through a constructive inner dialogue that doesn't include self-destructive or self-demeaning thoughts about yourself.

> *Twenty years from now you will be more disappointed by the things that you didn't do than by the ones you did do. So throw off the bowlines. Sail away from the safe harbour. Catch the trade winds in your sails. Explore. Dream. Discover.*
>
> – *Mark Twain*

When you have the knowledge to look at regret as a learning

experience, it allows you to move on and start living your life. This is incredibly important, as we have a propensity to dwell on past mistakes. As much as this affects you, it also affects those around you, especially if you have children. Carl Jung, founder of analytical psychology, nailed it when he said, 'the greatest burden a child must bear is the unlived life of the parents.' Stop and consider that statement. It is certainly something all parents should think about. Are you living your life or merely existing? What effect is this having on the people around you, especially those that look up to you for guidance and as a role model?

Depression

In the middle of the journey of our life
I found myself astray in a dark wood
where the straight road had been lost sight of...

How I got into it I cannot clearly say
for I was moving like a sleepwalker
the moment I stepped out of the right way...
- Dante's Inferno

Among all the mental health issues affecting people today, both depression and anxiety top the list. Seen by many as a chemical imbalance in the brain, sales of anti-depressant medication grow every year. According to Britain's NHS Digital, the number of prescriptions for antidepressants in England almost doubled over a decade, from 36 million in 2008 to over 70 million in 2018. Anti-depressants and anti-anxiety medication even out the levels of serotonin and other brain chemicals.

The number of prescriptions shows the extent to which medication is being used to treat depressive disorders. What the diagnosis of depression is now extends beyond depression, the mental disorder, treated by psychiatrists. Using medication to treat what are, for the majority, mild and short-term cases is damaging to those people whose causes are likely the result of life circumstances, psychological, or life problems.

Anxious people have a reduced risk of early death, most probably because they are more likely to take better care of themselves, paying attention to their health, and seeking medical advice when required. On the other hand, research from Norway shows that depression is roughly the equivalent to smoking in terms of increasing the risk of early death.

Our brains are happy in their comfort zone. They are protective, predictive, and conservative, the opposite of what our modern society offers — a place of unpredictability, speed, and consumption. Our modern society has changed exponentially with the value of the individual being favoured over that of the traditional family. Traditional structures and values have also changed, with religious grounding being replaced by individualist pursuits.

Do you find pressure to conform to this ideal and to believe you have to be happy all time, unable to express conflicting emotions? This can result in feelings of isolation and loneliness even among the throng of people occupying the cities and the planet. Identifying the resulting distress, anguish and suffering as a mental disorder, fixable by popping some pills to fix a chemical imbalance, takes away the opportunity to identify and work on the underlying psychological problems that are causing the distress in the first place. More than that, popping pills takes away the chance for the individual to lead a full life, a life of true wellbeing. Instead, people rely on prescriptions and repeats to keep them balanced and happy, never confronting the underlying problem or problems.

They don't take the opportunity to find a life for themselves where they can find true balance, with an honest and more refined understanding of themselves, the world around them and their place in it, one where they are comfortable and able to reach their highest potential.

In his book, *Psycho-Cybernetics*,[60] Dr Maxwell Maltz studied the dynamics of self-image and discovered an internal self-corrective process he dubbed the psycho-cybernetic mechanism . Essentially, if we go outside our comfort zone, the brain sends a danger signal to the rest of the nervous system to make adjustments to get us back to our usual state.

We are already aware of this tendency of the brain, however, this relates to depression, which as described in *The Road Less Travelled*[61], dictates that you cannot move on unless you face the fear of change and move on to the next level or chapter in your life. In a nutshell, depression is in the inability to move on from a state that is no longer viable or, in other words, you are going to be stuck in a depressive state until you confront the position you are in and the causes for it, enabling you to move on to a more viable, workable state. For many though, this doesn't happen. They continue to use their former selves, the self they cannot move on from, to try and protect their current selves. Life is change, and so must we.

When we have a physical injury, our body tells us through the feeling of pain. We then seek to remedy the pain by going to its source and fixing it. In the same way, our brain puts us in a state of depression or anxiety to signal to us that something isn't quite right internally, that our current situation has become unsustainable and needs working on or to be changed and at the very least, made conscious so we can process and understand it. It is easy to see why we might not realise this as we are so embedded in the societal expectations of us that we fail to notice or appreciate that what society expects of us is not what we want or expect of ourselves, which is obviously more important.

We forget and perhaps don't even know how to use perspective to see ourselves for who we are or how we really think and feel about ourselves. God knows, we do it for everyone else! Taking this step back and looking at ourselves for who we really are without the rose-tinted glasses can help us evaluate not just who we really are, but what we really need and want, and give us a much clearer understanding of ourselves and our lives. Depression can allow us to see ourselves for who we truly are and actually be a door to opportunity and possibility when it is addressed and dealt with. But what we choose to do far too often is seek to remove the psychological pain and sadness with medication, suppressing our own body's cry for help, ignoring it instead of addressing it.

There is an old story of a boy who uses his finger to plug a hole in a leaking dike in the Netherlands. The boy stays there all night in the freezing cold, never removing his finger because the water would leak and flood the country. He waits until adults come to his aid the following morning and make repairs to the hole in the dike. Taking medication for depression (excluding severe depressions) is like sticking your finger in the dike. It is like putting a Band-Aid on the problem, but not actually fixing it.

Whereas adults came and fixed the leak, most people with depression are simply given more anti-depressants and left to their own devices. 'Fixing the dike' requires understanding what caused the depression in the first place. Metacognition and talking to others, such as psychiatrists and psychologists, can help. In fact for the majority of people, talking to someone you can trust, such as a councillor or friend, will be of help. Chances are that the way you feel is not unique to you, but something many are facing on their journey of growth and wellbeing. Ultimately, what you want to do is work out the why, as discussed under *Negative Thoughts*.

Depression doesn't have to be a detriment to leading a life of wellbeing. In fact, many notable people from history have experienced depression and instead of it being a hindrance to their life, it has been a crutch, giving them the oomph to make something of their lives. Many people who suffer from bipolar disorder say they would choose to have the condition instead of having a cure because the highs are worth having to go through the lows. Churchill, as mentioned, suffered from the black dog of depression, and wrote prolifically, some speculate to keep himself busy and out of depressive episodes. Vincent Van Gogh, Edvard Munch, and Ludwig Von Beethoven, all great in their chosen arts, kept busy too and are said to have produced their best works while depressed. Other notable people who have admitted to feeling depressed include authors Virginian Woolf, Ernest Hemingway, and Leo Tolsky. Even Siddhartha Gautama, the Buddha, was thought to have had depression, seeking wisdom to overcome suffering and despair, and coming up with Buddhism's Four Noble Truths:

1. Suffering is an inherent part of existence.
2. Suffering is caused by attachment and craving, and our ignorance about this.
3. We can reduce suffering by letting go of our attachment and craving.
4. This can be done by following the Noble Eightfold Path of the right understanding, thought, speech, action, livelihood, effort, mindfulness, and concentration.

Understanding why you feel depressed doesn't always mean you will suddenly be cured. Depression, like anxiety, is a condition that likely has no cure but like a bad back or embarrassing uncle, is just something you have to learn to live with, and accept as part of who you are, and live the best life you have in spite of it. Understanding the why is a big part to gaining acceptance.

> *There is, at the very least, something comforting about the strong possibility that our human*

struggles stem from our animalistic selves trying their damndest to protect us.

Seeing Science: An Illustrated Guide to the Wonders of the Universe by Iris Gottlieb

Through the book, many topics will be discussed that will enable people who feel depressed to find ways of dealing with it and taking action to control it in their daily life.

Anxiety

If you are depressed, you are living in the past. If you are anxious, you are living in the future. If you are at peace, you are living in the present.
—Sarah Wilson, First, We Make the Beast Beautiful: A New Journey Through Anxiety

It really sucks that you get anxiety in the 21st century, where it serves no good purpose, whereas if you had been around thousands of years ago, maybe even just a few hundred years ago, it would have been of great benefit to you and your family's survival.

Anxiety and depression are like two sides of the same coin. One can cause or feed off the other, both can keep returning, 'like a bad penny, I always turn up'[62], and both can respond to the same medications. And like depression, there is no real cure. It is a toss of the coin as to if and when it returns.

Because anxiety comes from the fight-or-flight mechanism we evolved hundreds of thousands, if not millions, of years ago, there is little you can do to get rid of it. Whereas depression is the inability to move on from the past, anxiety is fear of the future and unknown, of what might happen to us or in parts of our life that are important.

This fear is a battle between the rational and emotional parts of the brain, including the fear-producing amygdala, which we know is always on alert. 'Fear,' says Brian Sachetta, author of *Get out of your Head: A Toolkit for Living with and Overcoming Anxiety*, 'is a synergy between two forces: our innate fight-or-flight mechanisms and the looping-thinking we engage in, either consciously or subconsciously, over the things that scare us.' The fear of what might happen is found in uncertainty; what might happen as opposed to what will happen. Think of a time you worried about something that might happen. Most of the things we worry about never eventuate. We spend far more time worrying about what may happen than what actually does.

> *There are more things to alarm us than to harm us, and we suffer more often in apprehension than reality.*
> *– Seneca*

As much as we fear the uncertainty of the future, we also feel apprehension and anxiety about missing out on life and what is happening in the here and now, when we are not a part of it. This fear of missing out, famously called FOMO, is amplified by the social connectedness that surrounds us and which we find hard to escape. Ironically, social connection, through social media channels, was supposed to make our lives more connected but has instead made us feel more isolated and anxious as we see the joy others are feeling and the great, got-it-together life they seem to be living. Doubly ironic is the fact that most people who have anxiety are, on the outside, fully functioning, in fact overly functional, in their day-to-day lives, running about doing this and that, keeping busy being busy.

To everyone else, they look like the ideal of what a modern, happy, and functional person is supposed to be like. The mask of competence and 'no worries' they wear becomes a problem unto itself. Appearing to have it all together adds to the problem as the anxiety they feel becomes a personal battle, isolating them in the dark recesses of their bedroom and their minds, trying to cope. When they feel like crying and burying themselves under the blankets, they instead bury themselves in their work, doing what needs doing, whether it is necessary or meaningful at all.

Sarah Wilson, in her book, *First, We Make the Beast Beautiful: A New Journey Through Anxiety*, recommends that we actively practice missing out, forget FOMO, curl up on the couch and order takeaway. With anxiety, the more you delve into it, the worse it becomes. As with all negative thinking, we get stuck in a loop as we feel the emotion more acutely the more we think about it. Our brains are trying to find out what will happen as soon as possible in order to remove the uncertainty, causing our thinking to spiral into a loop of obsessive, endless thinking.

A great anxiety felt by many people is the fear of death itself, and up to that, a life unlived and unfulfilled. As Earnest Becker in his book, *The Denial of Death*,[63] noted, 'The irony of man's condition is that the deepest need is to be free of the anxiety of death and annihilation; but it is life itself which awakens it, and so we must shrink from being fully alive.'

Sarah Wilson supports this when she says of her experience with anxiety, 'We have an original anxiety that stems from feeling we're missing something, that there's more to life, that we need to know where and how we connect with life. But to sit with our true selves causes another anxiety, a lonely, exposed anxiety. Then, if we flee this sitting with ourselves, we encounter the anxiety of, well, knowing that we're fleeing ourselves and truth.'[64] When faced with the prospect of facing multiple anxieties, it is not hard to see why people seek comfort in the known, hiding where they can from uncertainty and the anxiety that accompanies it. For that reason, they stay in unhealthy relationships, jobs they hate, won't change diets, even when they are bad for them, avoid change, and try to justify the way they are with the old mantra, 'Better the Devil you know' instead of admitting they are scared shitless and paralysed with fear of the unknown.

So, what is the solution? There isn't one. It would be easy to say, 'Get over it. Your anxieties are pointless. Most of the time, what you worry about will never happen. Just move on.' This is short-sighted and shows a lack of understanding about what anxiety really is. Sure, medication can help but again, as with depression, except in the most extreme cases, it is a Band-Aid, not addressing the underlying problem. Instead, the way to fight anxiety is not to fight it at all. Like a peaceful protest, just let it go, put it down and walk away, figuratively, not literally, although exercise is a wonderful 'mind aphrodisiac'.

Brian Sachetta, in his book *Get out of your Head: A Toolkit for Living with and Overcoming Anxiety*[65] has come up with the following 10 steps:

1. Breathe.
2. Determine the true importance of what's making you anxious.
3. Evaluate the potential outcomes and reconnect to the one you want.
4. Shift your focus to something positive.
5. Recite a powerful mantra.
6. Stop questioning yourself.
7. Utilise an empowering way to feel good, right now.
8. Get back to the present moment.
9. Remind yourself the worst part of anxiety is the waiting.

10. Remember, this too shall pass.

Many specialists offer different ways to manage anxiety and Sachetta's are just some. Others of note include distraction and forming healthy routines, as well as embracing the unknown.

Alex Korb, in his book, *The Grateful Brain*, recommends focusing on positive things such as gratitude. 'Gratitude can have such a powerful impact on your life,' Korb says, 'because it engages your brain in a virtuous cycle. Your brain only has so much power to focus its attention. It cannot easily focus on both positive and negative stimuli.' Literally, you can't be grateful and anxious at the same time. Once again, the threat system in our amygdala is overridden.' Wilson agrees, saying in her book, *First, We Make the Beast Beautiful*, that we need to create a 'gratitude ritual'. In addition, Wilson says anxiety is something we need to accept.

Simple outer order can create inner calm. For example, making your bed as soon as you get up every day is something you can control, and it sets you up for the day, every day. Creating a positive routine can give you the sense of control and coping mechanisms to take on more areas in your life that would previously have caused anxiety. Additionally, she says we should eat to curb anxiety, not junk food, but real food, food that can give us the nutrients and daily requirements to make us feel healthy and in control. Breathing also helps, as well as the healing power of meditation.

Anxiety has the side effect of limiting your ability to move forward with your life, living up to the true potential of yourself and with a sense of meaning in your life. Gain comes from embracing the unknown, completely counter to what anxiety proffers. There are many possibilities to achieve gain, even with anxiety. Anxiety lies in the unknown, but so does possibility and hope. It is like going on a rollercoaster or having to do public speaking. When you have done it, the relief and elation you feel because you did it, that you conquered your fears, makes it all worthwhile, and most of the time it is never as bad as you expected. You just need to be prepared, know your stuff, know your limits, and embrace the challenge and opportunity to have the experience.

Embracing the unknown can be achieved little by little. Start small; distance yourself as you make decisions so you can be objective and less emotional. If you are anxious around people, do something alone but around people. For example, go to a movie where there will be interaction but it will be minimal. Build from there. Study the behaviour of others who fret and have anxiety to see how they behave and learn from them what you are doing and how you can change. Act like someone you wish you could be. Talk to a stranger. Take on new tasks at work or delegate tasks if you are becoming overwhelmed. Slowly take away the mask you are wearing and let people in. As with depression, talking helps. A problem shared is a problem halved, as the saying goes. Take on new experiences, again small and with minimal anxiety. The unknown is scary, embracing it even scarier, but remember, experiences are one of the pillars of WEALTH.

Throughout this book, there are ingredients you can use, mix together and see what gives you a successful recipe to bring you the life you want, able to cope with any mental issues you have and the optimism to embrace not just the unknown but all that life has to offer as well.

Optimism

A pessimist sees the difficulty in every opportunity; an optimist sees the opportunity in every difficulty.
– Winston Churchill

Optimism is like hope, that last vestal of goodness, left untouched and still within us, while the rest: fear, anger, hate, and so on, escaped and plague the world. Optimism is a way of seeing light in the darkness and changing hate into love by a simple switch of the way things are perceived.

Gratitude is the best attitude, but optimism ensures a positive attitude. The reason optimism is so good for you is the benefits it offers your mental and physical health:[66]

- Research has shown that optimists suffer less anxiety, depression, and distress than pessimists.
- People who are optimistic are better at coping with problems. They will deal with problems instead of avoiding them and be more accepting, using humour and positive reframing.
- Optimism is linked to higher life satisfaction and increased wellbeing.
- Optimists tend to have better health with stronger immune systems, lower cardiac risk, and being able to recover from surgery faster and reportedly experiencing a higher quality of life after surgery.
- Optimists have stick-to-it-ness and will persevere when faced with serious hardship. Pessimists, on the other hand, are more likely to give up.
- Optimists are more likely than pessimists to accept the reality of a bad situation and to do something about a problem by taking action.

Having an optimistic attitude and outlook on life sets you up to deal with whatever happens, positive and negative, adversity or opportunity. Having an optimistic disposition can significantly contribute towards enhancing your wellbeing.

There is one small caveat and that is what is called a 'defensive pessimist'. 'Defensive pessimists,' says Bridget Grenville-Cleave, author of *A Practical Guide to Positive Psychology:*

Achieve Lasting Happiness, 'use the expectation that things will turn out badly as a coping mechanism: they perform better when they're allowed to imagine what could go wrong and keep hold of their low expectations. Defensive pessimism helps anxious people manage their anxiety, and contrary to what you might think, trying to be optimistic actually makes their performance worse!'

Assuming you are not a defensive pessimist, how do you go about becoming more optimistic and seeing the benefits that optimism has to offer? As we have seen, the brain is very conservative and doesn't like change. It is negatively inclined and likely to see and remember the bad things that happen in our lives, more than the good things. Our biases make it is easy to see how we can become despondent and down about what is happening in our lives and the world around us. Regardless of all of this, we have the power to change our perception of everything that happens in our lives. Optimism is a choice. We can all learn to be more optimistic and positive. Research shows that 75% of what causes us to be successful is down to how we process the world.

Try these five simple exercises and see your optimism increase daily:

1. Be grateful. Each day, consider what you are grateful for. Think of new reasons to be grateful each day. Keep a diary so you don't forget, maybe use the notes on your phone. Do this consistently and your brain will start to automatically look for positive things each day. Gratitude will change your outlook, fixating on the positive instead of the negative.

2. Be kind. Make an effort to be kind to people. Don't pick the same people all the time, mix it up. Simply saying 'thank you' makes a huge difference to people; it will increase your social connection and strengthen your relationships network. This is an

easy exercise and will fuel your desire to be more positive, more often.

3. Find meaning. Think of meaningful things that have happened to you recently. Write them down if it makes you remember more details of the experience. The key is to relive the experience, imprinting it in your brain so it remembers the positive event and increases the impact of it, giving meaning to your day, reminding you that you had a meaningful and worthwhile day.

4. Get active. Doing some form of exercise, even if it is just walking, gets the heart pumping, it gives you timeout as you do your activity, and allows your brain to process events up to that point. Your creativity will increase and you will release endorphins, which will make you feel good.

5. Breath. Stop. Breathe. Focus. Meditation allows your brain to rest and reset. By focusing only on your breathing, you switch from multitasking to single tasking. You are in the moment, focused on the here and now. To be effective, practice for a minimum of two minutes a day and listen as your brain resets itself, ready for new positive experiences.

IT AIN'T SO BAD

It is the human condition to find reasons or excuses for why things haven't happened the way we wanted them to. Primary among these excuses is to blame others. It is a classic reaction, but it does no good. By blaming others, you are simply losing any sense of control that you have had.

Bad things happen all the time and many are outside of our control so the only way you can gain control again is over the way you react. By taking responsibility and accepting the situation, no matter how bad it may seem, the sooner you can work on finding a solution. Think of the person who has married and been piled with responsibility and stress to pay bills and support a family and can only see a future that will be just as bad, if not worse. Before marriage, they had ample money, time and few responsibilities and now blame their partner for the relative misery they feel in their life. Is it their partner's fault? Of course not. Life happens and things go beyond our control. Deal with what you can and move forward to a place of happiness.

We actively choose to be chickens and stay with what we know instead of facing the unknown. Our inability to move outside our bubble of comfort and the known is supported by a society that prays on those fears, where there are crises everywhere. But the fact is that there is as much good news out there as there is bad. Everyone today seems to be trying to escape the reality of life. Television, games, gambling, music, drink, and drugs. Everyone has their vice or device to escape and get away. The reality is – you can't. It only catches you and drives home what your reality really is.

The world and everything in it always appear to be on the cusp of catastrophe. We fret about everything and everything demands our attention. Life is the experience of one near calamity after another. If the country is not almost bankrupt, it is almost at war. If a business isn't on the verge of collapse, some other force is attacking it. If the environment isn't almost ready to collapse, another animal has just become extinct – and usually at our own hands. If we aren't coping with an addiction or relationship problem, we are battling with our inner demons. The truth is, things are not always as bad as they appear.

The news we see each night on the television or read in the newspapers very rarely focuses on the positive things happening in the world, but they are happening. Our biases blind us to the good that is happening in the world and that, believe it or not, things are not always as bad as the media and our negatively inclined brains would have us believe.

Let's first look at you. You are a miracle. There is a 1:400,000,000,000,000 chance of you being who you are at this time in history. That is a one in four hundred trillion chance![67] Of all the living things that have been on this earth, 99.9% of them have been and gone.[68] The odds of you being here at this time and this place in history are amazing. Your brain is more powerful than the world's most powerful computer.[69] Your brain is capable of 1,016 processes per second and contains about 86,000,000,000 (that's 86 billion with a B) neurons.[70] You have up to 70,000 thoughts per day or over 48 thoughts per minute.[71] Your brain's pattern of connectivity is as unique as your fingerprints[72], which is not surprising really when you consider we are all unique and our experiences equate to distinctive neural pathways and connectivity.

The cellist, composer and conductor, Pablo Casals, summarised just how unique and amazing you are:

> 'Each second we live in a new and unique moment

> *in the universe, a moment that never was before and never will be again. And what do we teach our children in school? We teach them that two and two make four, and that Paris is the capital of France. When will we teach them what they are? We should say to each of them: Do you know who you are? You are a marvel. You are unique. In all the world, there is no other child exactly like you. In the millions of years that have passed there has never been another child like you... You may become a Shakespeare, a Michelangelo, a Beethoven. You have the capacity for anything. Yes, you are a marvel.'*[73]

We like to think in terms of opposites: us and them, rich and poor. The fact is, these are imagined positions and relative. Saying that Western countries are rich and other countries are poor is an example of this. We lament third world problems such as famine, disease and dying and laugh at first world problems such as not being able to get good Internet access or there is only one toilet in the house, but the reality is that there are no longer such clear lines to define the world in which we live.

The 'third world' is not a term used any longer and the stereotypes we have of this supposed group are erroneous and in a good way. Only 9% of the world lives in low-income countries whereas 200 years ago, it was over 80%[74]. Low-income is the equivalent of living on one dollar or less per day! 75% of the world's population now live in middle-income countries and 16% in high-income countries. Even as recently as 1966, the majority of humans lived on less than one dollar a day. In the last 20 years, the number of people living in extreme poverty has almost halved and the average life expectancy of the world is now 72 years of age.[75] The biggest poverty victories in the past 30 years have been in India and China. 721 million fewer people worldwide lived in extreme poverty in 2010 than in 1981. This is despite the fact that during that time, the world population increased by 2.5 billion from 4.5 billion to 7 billion. China alone was responsible for about 80% of that poverty reduction alone!

What else? According to *Factfulness: Ten Reasons We're Wrong About the World — and Why Things Are Better Than You Think*, by Hans Rosling[76] there is the following:

- The world population is expected to flatten out between 10 – 12 billion by the end of the century. This is because the number of babies being born per woman is decreasing as extreme poverty and child mortality also decreases, just as education and access to contraceptives increase. What does this mean? There are around two billion children now in the world and in the year 2100, there is expected to still be around two billion children, the majority of people will be adults, even though the population has increased.

- The number of people dying due to natural disasters has decreased by 75% to 25% of what it was 100 years ago. Despite a huge population growth, the decrease is because less people live in low-income (less than $1 per day) countries.

- The truth is that 80% - 90% of people living today have their basic needs met. Two hundred years ago, it was the opposite – 80% - 90% did not have their basic needs met.

- Worldwide, on average, men and women have spent ten and nine years respectively of their lives in school by the age of 30.

- Here are some bad things on the decrease:
    - Legal slavery
    - HIV infections

- Child death
- Deaths in war
- Death Penalty
- Deaths from plane crashes
- Child labour
- Nuclear arms
- Smallpox
- Ozone depletion
- Hunger
- Here are some good things on the increase:
- Protected natural habitats
- The right to vote for women
- Harvests
- Literacy
- Democracy
- Girls in school
- Water
- Immunisation

These are but a few of many positives that can be taken from the world right now, but our brains are negatively geared to search for threats, so much of this information doesn't register or even get to us through the media we consume. Much of this information shows our bias and likely you were surprised by a lot of it, expecting it to be a lot worse than it actually is. Things can be good. We can have happiness and wellbeing in our lives and then build on this to create what we ultimately want – lifelong wellbeing. But first, we need to know what the ingredients of happiness and wellbeing are; after all, they are the subject of the book.

PART II

Part I showed us the influence the brain has on everything we do in our lives from the way we think to the actions we take. With that knowledge, we can now move forward, using some of the tools we discovered and create for ourselves a recipe for wellbeing that is as unique to you as you are to everyone else.

Like any recipe, you need ingredients and, so here, in Part II, we will go through each of the ingredients you can select from to create your own recipe for happiness and wellbeing.

Let this be your spark and may the fire within you rage until you are the you, you always meant to be.

INGREDIENTS FOR WELLBEING

- Know Yourself
- Money, Jobs, and Stuff
- Perspective
- Having a Vision and Meaning in Your Life
- Signature Strengths
- Learning
- Savouring Life's Joys and Living in the Moment
- Meditation
- Growth Mindset
- Kindness
- Social Connection
- Exercise
- Sleep
- Gratefulness / Gratitude
- Setting and Committing to Goals
- Foods
- Practicing Religion and Spirituality
- Avoid Overthinking and Social Comparison
- Acting like a Happy Person

Each of the above nineteen ingredients are built on the WEALTH mindset. Many professionals in the health and wellness sector have decided upon these from years of research and experimentation. Each ingredient will bring you closer to a life of wellbeing but not all ingredients are to be used. Not all ingredients will work for you. Some you just won't be comfortable with, and others won't resonate with who you are or where you want to go. This is fine, in fact great, because, as has been reiterated, you are unique and need to choose what will work best for you and push you forward to being a better version of yourself.

Remember the perfect cake we all want our life to be? It doesn't exist. We all have a mess of gooey ingredients that it is up to us make work for ourselves. The following ingredients can be added to the mix and help you make that cake a little closer to the perfect cake you want, although remember, it may look like some inedible mound of sponge, but it is the taste that matters so make it taste as good as it can for you.

You are encouraged to read all the ingredients, see what the science and research says about each, see the positives and negatives with each, try them out, and then see what works for you.

Bon appetite!

KNOW YOURSELF

Knowing yourself is the beginning of all wisdom.
– Aristotle

This is the first ingredient because it is one of the most important. Who are you? How do you identify? Maybe the person you identify as no longer fits into the world you now occupy but you still want to be that person? Times have changed, the people in your life have changed and your responsibilities have changed but you haven't.

In order to move forward you have to address who you were, why that no longer works and why you have to change. Of course, that means mourning the loss of who you were, who you identified as, but when you realise that person, that identity is no longer viable and is instead the cause of your unhappiness and dissatisfaction with life then it becomes not necessarily easier, but accepted, that you need to change. You may see in the other ingredients things that you want to incorporate into your life and into your identity. The key thing to remember is that everything changes, and you have to as well. It is never easy, but it is a crucial step towards true, lifelong wellbeing.

In the United States, the American Declaration of Independence states *the pursuit of happiness is an inalienable right*, but the problem is, the more we pursue it, the more miserable we feel. That is because you cannot pursue happiness. It is like a fly. If you try to catch it, you fail (unless you are the Karate Kid and you can catch it with a pair of chopsticks. 'Beginner's luck.'[77]) but if you stop, it may come and rest on you. We identify ourselves with our feelings and thoughts, the avoidance of those we don't like and the pursuit of those we do, hence the inherent misery.

So how do we attain happiness if we cannot pursue it? Charles Dickens in his book, *The Life and Adventures of Nicholas Nickleby*, said 'Happiness is a gift, and the trick is not to expect it, but to delight in it when it comes.'

Happiness comes not from needing to be happy, but wanting to be happy. The final outcome should not be 'to be happy', it should be to achieve a goal or have an experience, which consequently may make you happy. Instead of always aiming to have our subjective expectations fulfilled, we need to understand ourselves better. As the temple entrance of Apollo at Delphi says, 'Know thyself'. Therefore, instead of trying to achieve happiness, we need to create the conditions necessary so that happiness can come to us.

Before you discover the ingredients of wellbeing that work for you, you first need to look at yourself. This is important as, unless you get an understanding or acceptance of who you are and what qualities make you unique, everything you do is just piecemeal and won't fit together and give you the happiness and wellbeing you want in your life.

Most of us want to be unique, while also conforming and fitting in. It is a juxtaposition of needs that can cause stress and anxiety as we fight the internal conflict to do what we want and be who we want to be versus the expectations of society to behave in a certain way and believe in a certain set of values. It is a big fight too. The expectations put upon us by family, friends, and the wider society are huge and quite subversive, to the point that you don't realise just how much of yourself you sacrifice to conform to social norms.

You can start by looking at the education system, an environment designed to teach people specific subjects in a specific way, neglecting the fact that each of us are unique and learn in different ways. For those who are not academic or low achievers, this model doesn't work as it doesn't offer the flexibility to cater for everyone to develop their potential. 'Once we become part of that environment, our brains begin the work of mapping out the territory so that we can secure a niche,' says Dean Burnett in his book, *The Happy Brain*[78]. 'When that has been achieved, changing things up causes instability, and instability is a threat to the happy brain.' Many people are therefore left thinking they are stupid and failures, which then runs through the rest of their lives and their opinion of themselves. They find it hard to get motivated to achieve anything, which makes it hard to focus at work as it is solely down to willpower to achieve tasks, willpower and the fear of losing your job, and how can that make someone feel happy and satisfied with their life?

Twyla Tharp in her book, *The Creative Habit*, says you need to know yourself, understand your limits and that you cannot do anything about your genes, but you can use your abilities to their fullest potential. If you had no financial or logistical limitations, what would you do? Before you answer this, be honest with yourself and acknowledge all sides of your personality.

- What makes you uncomfortable or insecure?[79]
- What do you love doing?
- What are your dreams?
- What do you want your legacy to be?
- What's your biggest criticism of yourself?
- What mistakes have you made?
- Who is your role model?
- How are you perceived by others?
- What does your inner voice say about you?

- What roles do you play? For example: parent, friend, colleague, boss, emotional support, problem solver?

Do you find you have your own idiosyncrasies, things that maybe you don't even understand, but for whatever reason you are that way? For example, do you find that you are very independent and like to do everything yourself, and don't like to ask for help, even when you know you should? There are extroverts and introverts, people who wear their hearts on their sleeves, and others who are almost robotic and very logical in their thinking. We all have different personalities, and understanding these can really help us. They can become almost like lightbulb moments where we say 'Ah, so that's why I am like that!' Do you find you react to certain situations in certain ways that don't marry with how you see yourself as a person?

Our personalities and the traits we exhibit are influenced by many factors, including our parents, upbringing, events that have happened in our lives, and many more. Trying to understand ourselves better is key to understanding what makes us happy and fulfilled and why *Know Yourself* is the first ingredient in leading a life of wellbeing.

A lot of what defines you is your childhood. The Attachment Theory[80] formulates that a strong emotional and physical bond with your parents or primary caregivers in the early years of your life are critical to your development. It can affect the way you love and how you interact and get along with other people. It states that there are four different attachment styles. On top of temperament, culture and your own self-talk, understanding the different styles is important as it can tell you a lot about how you relate to friends and family, interact with groups of people, and how you handle problems and issues in your life.

Based on research done by John Bowlby and experiments

by Mary Ainsworth with young children, their primary carer and a stranger, in what has been called the Strange Situation experiment, the following four attachment types were determined.

Secure attachment: This reflects about 70% of the population. When young, those who are secure are close to their primary caregiver (usually their mother). They show separation anxiety when away from them and will avoid the stranger when alone with them, but be friendly with them when their caregiver is there. They are happy to see their caregiver when they return and are happy to play, but will check to see that their caregiver is close by. As they grow, they are the type to feel confident that their needs will be met, and are most likely to assert themselves and ask for help.

Insecure avoidant attachment: People with this type of attachment are not as close with their primary caregiver and show no distress when they leave and little interest when they return. They are more likely to play with a stranger and are likely to be comforted by both the primary caregiver and a stranger equally. As they grow older, they are more withdrawn and independent, have trouble making friends, don't believe others will meet their needs, and rarely ask for help. They prefer to talk about intellectual things instead of their feelings.

Insecure ambivalent / resistant attachment: When young, those with this attachment type are very clingy to their primary caregiver and will become very distressed when they leave them. Around 15% have this attachment type. Around strangers, they will feel afraid of the stranger and be upset at the caregiver for leaving them alone, never venturing far from their caregiver, as it makes them feel uncomfortable. This type has been linked to abuse as a child and as this type grows up, they become hard to read. They alternate between being super clingy and pushing people away. They are often insecure and have trouble exploring new situations and can be seen as too sensitive and need constant reassurance by others.

Insecure disorganised attachment: Those with this type of attachment were likely to show relief when the primary caregiver leaves them, are happy to see the stranger and show fear or negativity when the primary caregiver returns. The stranger was also able to comfort the child better than the primary caregiver. People with this type of attachment generally have some kind of child abuse going on, hence the relief when the primary caregiver leaves the room. As they grow older, people with this attachment type view all chances to interact as an opportunity to resolve all traumatic situations from their past. They tend to suffer from anxiety and depression and PTSD and are the most likely to start using drugs and alcohol or start drama with others in order to disconnect from painful feelings. They love to test boundaries, can be aggressive, manipulative and abusive.

The influence of our childhoods on the way we are as adults cannot be underestimated. You may have identified yourself in the descriptions above. Of course, these are just one part of identifying ourselves and why we are the way we are. Another avenue is to look at our personality types.

To understand and find out what your personality type is, go to **www.16personalities.com**. There you can do an eight-minute questionnaire, which will help you to identify your personality type. You may argue that a personality test is useless because we are all unique and cannot be categorised into just one of 16 personality types, and that over time we can change and depending on circumstances, can be, for example, an extrovert and an introvert. Regardless, the test will get you thinking about yourself here and now and asking. 'Who am I? Why do I behave like this?' And in our goal of understanding who we are, these are valuable questions to be asking.

You should start to feel more self-aware once you start

asking yourself such personal questions. Do you react to situations in the same way? Do you confront or avoid unpleasant feelings and thoughts? Are you stuck in a loop?

With personality, it is easy to believe that it is fixed, that you are defined by your experiences, upbringing and genetics. However, your personality isn't fixed, it is a by-product of the decisions you make in your life. Although personality tests can be helpful in understanding your personality type at this specific point in time, don't let them determine who you will always be. Personality isn't permanent and these tests can make you believe the opposite and that you can discover your true self in a flash when in reality your personality is not something to be discovered but determined. Look at what you want to achieve, who you want your future self to be, and then evolve yourself to be that person. That person may be more confident, capable or successful, and so you need to move towards becoming that person through goals, determination, willingness, openness and commitment.

Understanding that your personality isn't fixed opens up opportunities that will transform you, whereas accepting that your personality is fixed means accepting that you can't change and you can't take control of your own life. Don't become rigid to situations and circumstances that feel difficult or outside your comfort zone, applying labels to yourself that give you an out. 'Oh, I'm an introvert, so I don't feel comfortable doing that.' Doing so uses your past as an anchor, never moving forward and at worst becoming emotionally stuck in the past.

Your personality is behaviour based on patterns, often predictable and consistent over time. The reason it remains consistent is because of four reasons, according to Benjamin Hardy, PhD, author of *Personality Isn't Permanent*.[81]

1. We continue to be defined by past traumas that haven't been reframed.

2. We have an identity narrative based on the past, not the future.
3. Our subconscious keeps them consistent with our former self and emotions.
4. We have an environment supporting our current rather than future identity.

These are what Hardy calls 'the levers that drive personality' and these levers can be controlled through change, reframing, and management so that 'your personality and life can change in intentional and remarkable ways', ways that can define your true self.

Take a step back and try to see yourself as others see you. Determine for yourself if the things you do are the things the you you want to be would do. If not, then it is time to change them. Identifying them is the first step. You want to be friends with yourself.

Jordan B Peterson, in his book, *12 Rules for Life*, says you need to treat yourself as if you were someone you were responsible for helping. Why helping? Because we help those who rely on us for help. When we have to look after an elderly parent or a young child, we make sure they are cared for, giving them all the help we can. Think about your pets. When they are unwell, you take them to the vet, make sure they take medication as and when required because you want them to get better. We do this for our pets but are notorious for doing the exact opposite for ourselves. When we are unwell, we start a course of antibiotics but stop halfway through. We forget to take medication or eat a healthy meal, to exercise, or to do what is right for ourselves. Why do we help those who need us but won't help ourselves, whom we need more than anything? It is time to see ourselves as someone responsible for helping.

How to Know Yourself

Do you know who you are? Don't ask. Act! Action will define you.

– Thomas Jefferson

What an awesome quote, and how many of us define ourselves by our actions? Everybody wants to be different, even if it is something small, something that makes them stand out from the rest, something that maybe nobody knows about except them. Among the many surveys that have been done of people who are dying, the number one regret is that they hadn't had the courage to live a life true to themselves. Instead, they'd lived the life others expected of them.

How many of us can say we are living a life true to ourselves? How many of us live a life in service to others, running around helping family and friends and neglecting the needs and wants of ourselves?

An example is a mother who was old. She had Parkinson's disease. Her daughter used to do everything for her – get her groceries, clean her house, take her to appointments and to the shops while also raising her own family and meeting their demands and needs. No matter how much she did for her mother, it was never enough. The daughter's health started to falter, and she fell ill, having spent all her time in the service of others instead of looking after herself first. This is not to say that we shouldn't look after others just not at the expense of our own health and wellbeing.

How many of us are doing a job we don't enjoy, understand, or really care about but which we do because of the status it brings us, because we simply need a job, or we don't know any better? How many are married for similar reasons? How many of us are not living the lives we want because we don't want to stick out and be different, that it is easier just to be like everyone else? It doesn't have to be something big either. It could simply be a hobby that you don't do because it is not common, or you feel you cannot do it because your time needs to be spent with family or others instead of satisfying your own wants and desires.

Ultimately, you have to be true to yourself. Going through the motions of living but either consciously or unconsciously doing what you think you should be doing – for example, getting married, getting a job – instead of what you want to do, will always leave you with an underlying sense of unhappiness. Maybe you don't even know what you want to do or how to be true to yourself, but identifying who you are as a unique individual can help you live your authentic life.

To help yourself, identify your VITALS (a mnemonic for: Values, Interests, Temperament, Around the Clock Activities, Life Mission and Goals, and Strengths).[82]

Values: What is important to you? Your values help to guide you when making decisions and are motivators when you are trying to achieve goals. Values change as your priorities and circumstances change but understanding if you like helping others, physical health, financial security, or family are invaluable in helping you help yourself.

Interests: What do you do in your free time? What fascinates you? What are your hobbies? By identifying your passions and what puts you into a state of flow, you know your happy place and if you can combine that with a career, you will, as the saying goes, never work a day in your life.

Temperament: What is your personality like? Are you an introvert or an extrovert? Do you like to plan things or go with the flow? Do you like the big picture or the little details? Knowing what your temperament is can help you find your strengths in situations and avoid your weaknesses in others.

Around the Clock Activities: What are your daily rituals?

What do you do each day? Are you a morning or night person? When do you feel most energetic? How does this match with your partner? What are the most enjoyable and least enjoyable parts of your day? It is important to identify this as you want to know when you are firing on all cylinders and not pretending to be someone you are not.

Life Mission and Meaningful Goals: What have been the most important events in your life? Why? Where do you see yourself in five- ten years? Knowing this can help you identify what you really get meaning and satisfaction from. It could also lead you to discovering a career that offers you real satisfaction.

Strengths: These are your abilities, skills, and talents as well as your character strength, such as fairness or loyalty. Knowing your strengths brings a deep sense of satisfaction and self-confidence and the opposite is true when you don't so ask around, listen to what people say, take on the compliments and be honest with yourself about your weaknesses and whether you should work to improve them or focus on your strengths.

Once you have a better understanding of who you are and what you stand for, you will be able to feel happier, feel more vitality and pleasure, be less prone to inner conflict and social pressure, make better decisions for yourself, and have more tolerance and understanding of other people.

> *Know your talents and capacity, in judgement and inclination. You cannot master yourself unless you know yourself. There are mirrors for the face but none for the mind. Let careful thought about yourself serve as a substitute. When the outer image is forgotten, keep the inner one to improve and perfect. Learn the force of your intellect and capacity for affairs, test the force of your courage*

in order to apply it, and keep your foundations secure and your head clear for everything.

– Balthasar Gracia, Spanish Jesuit and baroque prose writer and philosopher

Remember that your brain is not designed to challenge the system, it likes the status quo so you are going to have to force yourself to look at who you are and more still, if you want to change. Start by practicing metacognition, thinking about thinking, reflecting on what you have learned about yourself, both the good and the bad, and engaging in some abstract thought. You may not like what you find or be willing to admit it about yourself but be honest with yourself about what you find. Be aware of your pre-existing beliefs and the influence they will have on your thinking. For example, we are full of beliefs that reflect who we are, whether or not we are aware of it. These are preconceived thoughts and opinions.

You may believe certain things about yourself based on past experience, such as that you are bad at mathematics or good at drawing but pre-existing beliefs can extend to stereotypes that have developed around you in regards to drugs, alcohol, sexuality, ethnicity, disabilities and gender. These stereotypes can affect the way you interact with people because of the assumptions you have made about them. By addressing your pre-existing beliefs and the influence they may have on you also allows you to see where you are possibly being influenced and exploited by others.

Biases to be aware of include availability bias, confirmation bias, and self-serving bias. Availability bias is based on things that come to mind easily and given we are negatively inclined, we more readily think of bad things over good. For example, someone won't fly because they can remember an example of a plane crash that happened the previous year and are using this to affect their reasoning. You could argue that only 0.0001% of flights crash and that was simply one example, not reflective of the number of flights that didn't crash and were successful.

Confirmation bias is related to pre-existing beliefs. It looks for and interprets information consistent with these beliefs. You see an article on the news about unemployed beneficiaries being caught doing drugs and this affirms your belief that all unemployed people are drug users and should be in prison. Being able to take a step back and rationally process information requires you to emotionally distance yourself from an issue, which is very hard to do when you have developed an opinion.

Another example of confirmation bias is the belief in conspiracy theories. Many believe in conspiracy theories, even when there is ample evidence to the contrary. They will cling to their beliefs and even use the contrary evidence to corroborate why their belief is correct. For many, this is especially noticeable when they are going through times of uncertainty and anxiety. A loss of control sends them running for theories that can explain the position they find themselves in and give comfort.

Unfortunately, confirmation bias is strong and endemic as it is an efficient way to process information, required for survival. People give credence to information that supports their personal beliefs and protects their self-esteem. No-one likes to admit their beliefs are incorrect, so seek information that supports their existing beliefs. This is linked to self-serving bias, which we discussed earlier when learning about the brain, where we believe that our actions have contributed to success and failure is due to other factors.

We have learned that our brains are amazing things but also amazingly predictive and, therefore, lazy. They don't like change that pulls them out of their comfort zone and when they do come out, they go into crisis mode. Our brains have created mental models of how we see the world around us and how it works. However, just because we believe something doesn't mean that it is correct.

We are all fallible to what is called the Dunning-Kruger effect[83], where we believe things that aren't true. The more objectively bad we are at assessing risk and reward, the more likely we are to make bad decisions. To overcome this effect, we need to increase our objectivity and that can be done simply by taking a step back, especially if we are emotionally involved in a belief or opinion and educate ourselves with facts from reliable sources of information. Alternatively, we can seek feedback from others, do some critical thinking, and question our intuition and beliefs. This is something those who believe all conspiracy theories need to do as failure to do so can result in mental instability as the gap between perception and reality widens.

> *Smallness of imagination, the eye that sees no farther than its own lashes. All things are possible. Who you are is limited only by who you think you are.*
>
> – Egyptian Book of the Dead.

Do you find that when you start a new job, you feel like an imposter and shouldn't really be there, that you don't really know what you are doing, especially with the business having its own little groups, policies, procedures and way of doing things. Some call it the 'dumb fuck stage' of employment where you are new and still getting up to speed with the way things are done. Sometimes it goes further than that and even after months or even years, you still feel like an imposter, that you are winging it each day, not deserving the success you have had, and believing it is only a matter of time before they figure out that you are a fraud and don't have a clue about what the hell you are doing.

This syndrome is not uncommon and not something to be

ashamed of for as much as you feel like an imposter, you feel that way because you are putting yourself out there, displaying some ambition, growing as a person and trying to better yourself. Practice new skills that you need to learn, put time into becoming a master. Stop comparing yourself to others, as that will only bring on more anxiety. Instead, focus on comparing yourself to who you were and how much better you are now than yesterday and the progress you are making.

When you feel less of an imposter and more of a master, make an effort to come out and be seen. People who feel they are imposters tend to be quiet and do not draw attention to themselves in case it highlights their supposed inadequacies. People aren't stupid. If you aren't good enough, people will know and let you know.

You are only limited by who you think you are. Be the master of your experience and the expertise you bring to the table, not just at work but in all life settings, and have a voice. Be the best that you can be. Have an opinion on matters that matter to you. Be authentic in who you are and don't live down to the expectations of others. This will stifle your personal growth towards wellbeing and leave you feeling frustrated and unfulfilled.

> *Go out there and do something remarkable.*
> *Don't live down to expectations.*
>
> *– Wendy Wasserstein, U.S. playwright*

How many people have you seen having issues but said to them, 'You're okay the way you are,' 'You're all good,' or 'You'll be right.' Why do that to them? Maybe someone has said that to you, but you know you're not alright. Inside you're struggling, maybe desperate. Don't tell someone they are okay the way they are. Tell them they can be better. You can be better. Today is today. We have tomorrow and the rest of our lives to improve and be better, to know that we can get better. Sometimes we just need someone to tell us that. If we can get better, we can improve in so many areas of our life and in pursuing that better, we can find meaning in our life too.

If you feel like a failure or too incompetent to live your dream life or to be better for whatever reason, perhaps you don't even know the reason yourself, take heed of what physicist, Stephen Hawking, has to say on the matter, 'There should be no boundaries to human endeavour. We are all different. However bad life may seem, there is always something you can do, and succeed at. While there's life, there is hope.'[84]

Everyone is good at something. You just need to figure out what it is. There are those that weren't the academic type during high school and barely made it through, but come into their own in their working life where they now run their own business, own a big house and have plenty of money in the bank. It doesn't matter how smart you are or how good an education you received, if you don't have the willpower and motivation to do anything, your smarts count for nothing. Doing over brewing gets you ahead. I do over IQ.

Maybe, after all is said and done, you don't really want your dream life, to be fulfilled and happy, and to lead a life of wellbeing? This is why it is important to find out who you are. Perhaps the best way to identify who you are is to identify who you are not. Go through a process of elimination. Remove things that don't resonate with you and stop you from being your true self. Removing the clutter in front of you can then open up pathways to more options that allow you to be you and lead the life you want.

The truth is, however, that most people don't want any of this and they don't even realise it. Maybe this is you? We all have desires that we strive for, and one that is greater than the others. It is possible that the desire you strive for most is one that doesn't require you to put yourself out there and venture into experiences unknown.

Your greatest desire maybe comfort, familiarity, or safety. These feelings don't allow you to grow as a person or to achieve your potential. To be anything close to your true self in life, the future self you see for yourself, you need to take action. Comfort and security will give you the illusion of just that, but it is a choice you need to make to lead a fuller, happier life because happiness and wellbeing are a choice and that choice is your responsibility. Nobody else will come along and change things for you, no matter how much you cry out and lament your lot in life.

You need to live your life closer to the edge of what scares you. It is a relative term too. What scares you may be changing careers, starting your own business, writing a book, getting married, getting divorced, selling it all up and travelling around the world or asking someone on a date. Whatever it is, that is the experience of life, where happiness and wellbeing are made. You need intentional actions that you can commit to and yes, change is scary and not everything will work out as you wanted, but that is all part of the story of your life. Whatever you are doing, get living.

> *Every morning in Africa, a gazelle wakes up. It knows it must run faster than the fastest lion or it will be killed. Every morning a lion wakes up. It knows it must outrun the slowest gazelle or it will starve to death. It doesn't matter whether you are a lion or a gazelle: when the sun comes up, you'd better be running.*[85]

Who are you? Are you up and running, living your life, true to yourself and ideals?

Key Points

- It is important to understand who you are and what you believe.
- You need to understand and accept your limitations, but make use of your abilities to their fullest potential.
- Our childhoods have an immense influence on who we are as adults.
- You can take personality tests, to help you identify traits and characteristics and make you more selfware and ask pertinent questions of yourself in the here and now. But know that your personality should not be defined by your past, but by what you want from the future.
- The number one regret of dying people is that they did not live a life true to themselves.
- In order to understand yourself, you can look at your values, interests, temperament, around the clock activities, life mission and goals, and strengths and skills, as known as by the mnemonic - VITALS.
- Be aware of the bias and pre-existing beliefs you have.
- We are all good at something. You just need to take the time to work out what you are good at.
- Your brain won't want to change, but knowing your true self may require you to step outside of your comfort zone.

MONEY, JOBS, AND STUFF

It's a delusion, it's a bullshit game. All of us are following a toxic dream. What you are sold in this world is a box of rotten goods.
- Florian Homm, former businessperson, and investment banker[86]

For many of us, happiness and prosperity are equated with financial wealth and success. It is difficult to go through each day seeing people with no apparent need or want. If they want something, they just go and get it while the rest of us watch, wondering how the hell they can afford it when we're scrimping and saving to pay bills and get through to the next pay day.

Our society relates status with success and success with wealth. We are, at the heart of it all, still children, seeking the approval and acceptance of others. We all have a burning desire for love from other people, the kind of love no-one ever talks about but spend our lives trying to get. We think that by having a flash car, working hard, and earning a lot of money, it will give us the status, the approval, the acceptance, and the love we all crave. And because we all believe that, it becomes true, but there is no ceiling or at least a glass ceiling on this approval and once we have it, like happiness, it is fleeting and gone again, and we have to continually try and get more and more, something that eventually cannot be done. Therein is the problem with our society. It relies on approval coming without meaning instead of from within.

The expectations we put upon ourselves compound this. We all want to be accepted and we all want the respect and love that status offers but we cannot all have it. Success on merit has been replaced by success by desire. It is no longer thought of as something to be earned, but a God given right. We feel we shouldn't be judged on our merits, but the fact is, merit isn't given, it is deserved. People work hard to succeed.

The desire for status in the 'old days' was not like it is now. People knew where they stood. There was the aristocracy and there were the rest of us. The chances of a serf becoming rich were slim to none, and everyone knew that. The American Constitution introduced the idea of meritocracy, which basically states that people should be successful based on their merits, not on which class they belonged to. This idea has been manipulated to allow anyone to believe and expect that they too can be successful and attain great status and acceptance no matter what their merits are and because this is the case, all of us expect to succeed, not on merit but by default, something that cannot work and never will. Hence, we buy expensive watches and cars, buy gadgets that are the 'latest thing', eat at expensive restaurants and work in jobs that offer no personal satisfaction because of the status they offer. Also worthy of note, is that merit itself implies haves and have nots. We cannot all be successful in the definition implied by the American Constitution, but we can all be successful within ourselves based on the learnings you can get from reading this book.

MONEY

Whoever said money can't buy you happiness: fuck you.
- Hector and the Search for Happiness (2014)

There is a saying that money can't buy you happiness, but that is okay because money can buy you wellbeing. Research has been conducted that has shown that money after a certain amount only makes you marginally happier. Someone going from earning US$20,000 to earning US$50,000 is going to be happier but then going anything above US$75,000, the amount of happiness felt becomes slight[87].

This has been the general consensus for many years now and is linked to the things we already know, hedonic adaptation, and the fact that we are never satisfied, we adjust to our new wealth and always need more to get that happy feeling. The funny thing is that as we have become richer and healthier overall, especially over the last 100 years or so, we aren't any happier than our grandparents were when all logic says we should be. Whereas beforehand we would treasure things handed down from generation to generation, and things were cherished and used to the very limits of their usefulness, now consumption is emphasised, not preservation, and buying has become 'throwaway' buying.'[88]

We pin our hopes on the latest thing to make us happy, whether that be a new car or a newer phone, each time getting that rush of joy at attaining the object but seeing that joy quickly evaporate and with increasing speed and intensity.

In many cases, the anticipation of getting the object is more than the joy we get from actually attaining it and so we wonder if we have made the right choice and then go out and buy another object because, hey, this has worked in the past, so it should work now, right?

Earning more money is usually coupled with more responsibility, which in turn leads to more stress, which can add to the lack of happiness. Add to this the commute to the job, as most are located in the city when you live in the sprawling suburbs, paying for a house that befits your elevated status. Include your equally elevated mortgage, and it starts to become easier to see why more money does not always equate with more happiness.

Your elevated status comes with social comparison, something we look at later, and who do you compare yourself with? It is not the rich and powerful but people just like you, your peers, family, and friends. As much as we may envy the lives of the super-rich with their mansions, yachts, cars, and seemingly continuous holidays, we don't compare ourselves to them. We are more likely to see our neighbours, old school friends, your sister's husband, or your workmate as a social comparison and aim to have a better job, car, phone or house than them. And therein is the thief of happiness. Where all logic says money should make us happy, it only does so when you have it and someone else doesn't. A large part of the reason we are not happier than our grandparents and great-grandparents etc., is the massive wealth we have now is used in keeping up with the Joneses, which of course doesn't make us happy, it makes us miserable.

So money doesn't buy you happiness, but it buys you wellbeing. How? Happiness is a part of wellbeing, and in many ways a big part but wellbeing is about you being a better version of yourself and leading a life you want to lead, full of happiness and wellbeing, not being better than the Joneses or having fancy cars and phones. Whereas we go through all of the ways you can find wellbeing within yourself, external factors will always come into play and a major external factor is money.

As much as people like to dress money up as the root of all evil, mainly because they don't ever have enough, it is and has become much more than that, especially as we bluster our way through the twenty-first century. Anyone who has been laid off, put on reduced hours, or dealt with inflation and increased mortgage rates, will tell you that money is not only necessary but also important and adds to their emotional wellbeing. The fact is that money, although it cannot buy you happiness, gives you security and safety, and most importantly, a sense of control over your life.

What is your opinion of money? Do you see it as an obligation or an opportunity? If you see it as an obligation, you see it in terms of fulfilling responsibilities; having to pay bills, pay expenses, pay for life. If you have this mindset in relation to money, you will likely never have enough. And that is the key word – enough. Knowing when enough is enough, whether it be of money or anything, is key to acceptance and happiness. The problem we have is that we see 'enough' as a sliding scale, relative to what we have here and now and relative to others. The goal posts keep moving. It is key if we are ever to find happiness, to stop them from doing so.

> *I looked about me and saw all the good things there were to bring happiness and contentment. And I realised that wealth increased the potency of all these. 'Wealth is a power. With wealth many things are possible.'*
>
> George S Clason, The Richest Man in Babylon

If you see money in terms of opportunity, the coin is flipped, and you see the value in what money offers you the opportunity to do. Money becomes an appreciation of what money does for you and the empowerment it gives you. If you can focus on providing value and less on earning, you will end up with more money, more happiness and more fulfilment.

How we each view money is unique, much like everything in our lives. Your life circumstances have coloured the way you see money. 'Your personal experiences with money make up maybe 0.00000001% of what's happened in the world,' says Morgan Housel in his book, *The Psychology of Money*, 'but maybe 80% of how you think the world works.' Your personal experiences when you were younger, especially in early adulthood, the economy you were bought up in, (was there high inflation? Low interest rates? A recession? Lots of unemployment?) your values, even your luck, all of these things will influence your view of money and how you manage it. So, how can we judge others for their decisions and have others judge us when we have all had a unique set of circumstances and experiences that dictate the financial decisions we make in life?

We can't, but of course we do and most especially with ourselves. How many of us curse ourselves that we didn't invest in this or that or take that job, start that business, or any other number of financial investments that have now paid off handsomely for someone else? To paraphrase Housel, our past experiences, conscious or not, have influenced us and all we can do is scramble together a narrative that works for us.

If you are looking at starting your own business, great! However, make sure that what you are doing is solving a problem, and it is scalable, otherwise you are simply a wage slave paid for by yourself. When we work for someone else, or in many cases for ourselves, we are essentially chasing money. Chasing money is like chasing the wind or happiness – futile, unfulfilling, and exhausting.

Instead of chasing money, chase solutions to problems people have. This is the key to making money. Rich people get rich because they think hard, not because they work hard. If you solve problems for people, they will pay you. If your solution is scalable, (it can be duplicated at little or no cost) then you have a solution that requires effort up front but is then replicable indefinitely. Think of franchises, books, apps, videos etc. Change your mindset about money. Making money is simple, not always easy, but simple. It is not a mystery held by the rich. Making money and getting rich is simple if you are willing to get over your limiting beliefs and try.

Money is important to wellbeing because it is not good or bad, it is a means to an end. It is a tool that enables you. With it, you can ensure your future, protect yourself and build a better life for yourself and those you care about. What you want to consider is money beyond that which you earn each week to pay bills and buy food and clothing. For most people, once those expenses have been met, it doesn't leave much left over to give you the freedom you deserve. In other words, having enough money stops you being dependent on a job just for money and having to tolerate a job you likely don't like because you live pay day to pay day.

What you need is multiple streams of income. Your job is one but if you lost your job, what money could you rely on? Sure, you may have some savings but that is not usually put aside to get you through hard times. Have a fund for that, but look at other income streams. It could be the share market, bonds, an investment, many things. This book is not about helping you find income streams or how to manage your money, however, there are hundreds if not thousands of books and other information channels that can help you with that. What is important is to have more than one income stream, enough that you are not dependent on being employed. When you are employed, you are paid at a value that someone else determines, not at a value that you determine. Multiple income streams will give you freedom, choice, and importantly, more control over your life. You don't have to live with anxiety and fear about paying your rent, mortgage, bills, or raising your family. Money gives you control and a sense of wellbeing over this aspect of your life. Money gives you the means to thrive, not just survive.

The thought of being a wage slave until retirement is a scary prospect, not just because you are living pay day to pay day but because once you retire, you are on an even lower fixed income and living week to week. If your idea of an income is solely having a job and you struggle to see beyond that option, you need to change your mindset towards money. Also, if you have a Lotto strategy to get rich, again you need to look at your mindset and instead of investing in lottery tickets, invest in options to increase your income streams.

A key to wellbeing is having interests and hobbies, a social network, and experiences. Of course, you don't necessarily need money to have these, but in many circumstances you do. Money pays for the nice meals out and events you attend with your social circle. It pays for the interests and hobbies, not to mention the travel you do, and many of the experiences you have.

> *Living like a millionaire requires doing interesting things and not just owning enviable things.*
> *– Tim Ferriss, The 4 Hour Work Week*

Instead of wanting and spending money on stuff, the real value you get is from spending money on experiences. Everybody thinks they want to be rich, but what they really want is to experience what they think only the rich can do. As already discussed, a lot of the happiness we experience is retrospective. Our memories can be embellished and selective. Even if, for example, you went on a trip to Europe, missed your flight connection, struggled with the language, got ripped off at the local markets, became fatigued by the endless number of cathedrals that all ended up looking the same, you can choose to remember the small moments of joy, the sunset over the beaches, the culture and the food, editing out the negatives from your narrative.

Remember also that an experience and the definition of this is subjective, unique to each individual. Buying a book is a thing, stuff, whereas reading it and getting lost in the story and becoming part of the adventure is an experience. The same goes for when you buy a tent, a skateboard, or a fishing rod. They are things but they can bring you extraordinary experiences that you can savour and repeatedly enjoy. Much like the Mastercard advertisements -

A fishing rod: $100.

Catching your first ever fish: Priceless.

Money and Time Affluence

Think about how much time you give to someone else in return for an hourly wage or weekly salary. If you include travel time to and from work and the time you spend thinking about work outside of your paid hours as well as the routine you have to put in around your paid hours, you are giving up a lot. We place so much value on money and the biggest price we pay for it is with our time. We are selling our time for money.

Now, there is no way that most of us can give up money for time. We need it to pay bills, rent, mortgages, to eat, pay for the kids' education, dance lessons, birthday parties etc. etc. etc. In a lot of cases, we need it to have fun! Less and less entertainment these days is free. We've already discussed money and how it is not a key to happiness but for better or for worse, it is needed and the need for it is the primary thief of our time. Even though money can't buy happiness, it can buy time and prioritising time over money does make you happy. Time affluence is having the time to do what you want when you want to.

How can you get more time if you still need to work for money? Instead of spending money on clothing and 'things', consider spending it on things that save you time, giving you more of that precious resource to do what you want to do. This century has seen a host of businesses start up that are designed to give you back your time.

- Instead of cooking a meal yourself, have one delivered (and I am not talking about fast food per se but more nutritious foods, although sometimes a fast food meal does hit the spot).
- Get a cleaner in to do your housework (and think how much happier you feel inside a clean house as opposed to one where your 'stuff' is strewn everywhere).
- Have someone do your taxes or mow your lawns.

Not everyone can afford to have these time saving services, but for most of us there is still time we can reclaim for ourselves. It is probable you work about an eight hour day with a half hour lunch on top of that. You probably work hard when you are at work and have a commute that adds at least another hour to your workday. You come home and spend time with your family, partner or housemates, have dinner, watch some television because you are too tired to do anything else and then perhaps read before going to sleep for about seven to eight hours before waking up and doing it all again. Life.

That is a typical day for many of us where you could say up to ten hours a day is spent doing work or actively involved in preparing for and getting to and from work.

Unfortunately, the facts show that people will choose money over time, a huge 69%,[89] yet those that prioritise time over money are happier people[90]. Many people feel that they are materially affluent and at the same time, time poor. Thinking about time and how you would spend it, such as on a holiday or a hobby, makes you feel happier and more social[91] than thinking about money. Thinking about money can make you feel stressed and worried, prompting you to think about work and removing any feelings of happiness or appreciation for time. Those that are time poor always feel stressed, rushed, overworked, overwhelmed, unappreciated and behind. Finding a balance is a delicate dance for although we need the security and freedom that money provides, we need it without losing our sense of happiness and wellbeing - our emotional stability!

The truth is, doing less makes you happier, so time is just as, if not more, valuable than money. Remember, money is a means to an end. Young people spend their time making money, whereas older people spend their money making time, wishing they had done so all their lives. Money spent on experiences brings us more happiness, just as money spent on things that give us more time, give us happiness. If we stop spending money on things that don't bring us either of these (the phones, cars, excessive clothing etc.) excluding those things that we need to live, we can lead happier, better, and more fulfilled lives as we will have more money.

Here are some ways you can grow richer with your time so as to allow you to become richer as a person:

- Get up earlier in the morning. Getting up before the birds and having the time to do what is valuable to you. It is difficult (especially if you are not a morning person) but it is true, getting up earlier, even if it is just thirty minutes earlier, gives you the opportunity to start each day on your terms. You are proactive, not reactive. You have time to prepare yourself mentally and physically for the day, maybe get in some exercise, eat a decent breakfast, meditate, or plan for the day ahead. Always remember to balance your need for sleep and rejuvenation with your need for time. Sometimes your needs will conflict with one another and you need to decide which you need more.

- Take time out. Remember to take some time out every few hours each day to reflect and focus on what you have done, not what you haven't. Spend time thinking about time, about your next holiday or the next social gathering you have, whatever makes you feel happier. Get away from the computer or wherever it is you usually work and either do some completely unrelated work or, better still, something unrelated to work at all. Go for a walk or a run, talk to other staff, swap stories, and completely remove yourself from thinking about work. If you are at home, do a little dance or get out into the garden. Whatever you do, do with intent and on a regular basis.

- Delegate. Not all of us have this luxury, but where you do, get someone else to do it, remembering too that they need time for themselves as well. If you cannot delegate, don't feel like you cannot ask for help. That can be the bravest thing you can do both for yourself and your work. Poor time management can lead to rushed work and mistakes costing both you and the business you work for, so getting help when needed is a sign of good management, not a sign of incompetence.

- On the seventh day. Sunday is traditionally the day of rest. In fact, whatever day you can, make it your Sunday. Treat it that way. Rest, relax, stay away from anything that can link you to work: your phone or email, in fact, all electronic devices. Do something that brings you joy and flow.[92] At the end of each day, leave time for yourself to reflect on what has been and what you did well. Don't worry about tomorrow, it will happen, and you can prepare for that when you get up. Focus on what you did well, then turn off both your mind to work and any electronics, read or write, and wind down for the day.

- Make time. Both in your life and in your mind. If you have regular errands each week, combine them so you are spending less time on them and have more time on other days of the week. When working on tasks, do those that you *want* to do first. They will usually be done faster and expand your sense of time and energy to do those tasks that *need* to be done.

Historically, money and success have been interchangeable. The more you have of the former, the more you have of the latter. Money isn't success and nor are the things that it can buy you. Success is an intrinsic thing unique to each of us and this book is littered with examples of how you can achieve real success and happiness in your life. If we continue to associate success with money, we will never find the things that really matter to us or have a true sense of wellbeing. Money is numbers and numbers are endless, there is always plus one, so if it takes money to make you happy, you will never have enough, you will always want more and you will never find happiness and wellbeing.

Jobs

The only way to be truly satisfied is to do what you believe is great work. And the only way to do great work is to love what you do. If you haven't found it yet, keep looking. Don't settle. As with all matters of

the heart, you'll know when you find it.
— *Steve Jobs*

When you are young, the world, as they say, is your oyster. Nothing is impossible; no dream is unattainable. Children know what they want to do when they are older. They don't allow the logistics of life to get in the way. They don't care about how much money it does or doesn't pay, just that they want to do it. Maybe they want to be a dancer or an actor. They aren't aware that most actors don't get regular work or get to be in movies and on television. They work in cafes and coffee shops to make money while they audition for roles and wait for the dream. For most, the dream never comes true and they get a 'real job' and settle down and be like the rest of us.

You have to admire them though, those few of us that actually go out to pursue their dream, taking a chance while they can in the hopes that with hard work and perseverance, they can live the life they want for themselves, doing something they love. Too many people do the exact opposite and live down to the expectations of others and sadly, in many cases, to the expectations of themselves.

A job should not define who you are. Working for a well-known brand, having a job that pays a huge salary, or owning your own business, all are things you should be proud of, but they should not define you. Because we are bought up to get an education and then get a job, it is easy to think that what you do for a living defines who you are as a person.

How many times do you meet someone new and one of the first things you ask them is what they do for a living? Does it really matter? Will you judge them by the answer they give you? Do you honestly really care what they do for a living, or are you fishing to see if you have what you perceive to be a better job than they do so you can feel better than them, probably because you have trouble defining who you are yourself beyond your job?

Nobody cares about you and what you do as much as you do. The opposite happens too when you have exchanged job titles and neither of you has any interest in pursuing the conversation, leaving an awkward silence. Perhaps the better question to ask is, 'What do you do in your spare time?' and find out what their interests are and see what you have in common and go from there. It is certainly a much more interesting discussion than what someone does for a job.

There is nothing wrong with having a job. People need to work and jobs need to be done. We need someone to clean the office, collect the trash, fix the plumbing, build the houses, and serve us at the supermarket. Reality bites and the need to earn money to live a life of means takes over the will to pursue the lofty dream jobs we had as children, but it doesn't have to stop there. We are talking of forty to fifty years of this gig. That is a long time!

> *Sometimes I can hear my bones straining under the weight of all the lives I'm not living.*
>
> *—Jonathan Safran Foer, Extremely Loud and Incredibly Close*

If you are working to earn an honest day's pay, be proud. Many people in the world would love to be in your position. If you are being motivated by the money your job offers, then you are being motivated by something that doesn't last. As discussed, you will never have enough money and you will always want more, never satisfied with what you have or the job you do.

The questions you ask yourself about a job need to change. Is the work meaningful? Are you being given the opportunity to develop and learn new things? Will you be given new responsibility and the opportunity for recognition and achievement? There is no reason for you to be in a job that doesn't give you these things. You need satisfaction, challenge, and reward. These things will truly motivate you.

This is not to say income is not important. Sometimes the need for money overrides the needs of yourself. Most of us, at some point, will need to support a family or partner. We all get old and as much as age discrimination isn't allowed, it is still something that is very real when going for new roles. Changing jobs isn't easy and changing careers is even harder, especially when you don't know if you are just moving from one unsatisfying job to another.

The thing is though, if your needs are not being met, your answer is 'no' to the three questions posed above, and you are in a position where you are no better off financially next week than you were last week, you need a new income stream. Whether that is another job or opportunity, all are supposed to be a means to an end, that end being a more fulfilled and meaningful life. If your job is solely to get you an income (and it is likely an income that isn't enough anyway) to support a lifestyle that doesn't give you any fulfilment but stress, fear and anxiety instead, you need to change.

Change is scary, especially when it can affect your main source of income and you have a family to support, or a mortgage or rent to pay, let alone the myriad of other expenses that pile up. Jobs change all the time and you need to be able to change as well. Forty years ago, the Internet didn't exist, personal computers were really expensive and not many people had one, apps weren't a thing and social media weren't two words you put together, yet now these things employ millions of people around the world. Looking at it another way, mining was a big thing as were factories where cars and machinery were assembled, but these are now gone, mined out, moved overseas, or taken over by robots. Change is inevitable in every facet of our lives, but especially within the working environment.

Maybe you think you are irreplaceable in your job and your work needs you? Don't believe it. You are replaceable and don't believe you are not. Don't believe you owe anything to your work other than what you are employed to do. If you were to die tomorrow, they would have someone else doing your job before you were buried. For that reason, you need to choose a job that gives meaning and value to your life, not one that only gives value to the business you work for.

To do this doesn't necessarily mean having to find a new job and for many of us, it isn't possible to just go and get another job – choices are limited by our skills, qualifications and experience. You can find meaning and joy in the work that you do. Of course, the work you do may not be the work you wish you did but you can introduce purpose in what you already do. Finding fulfilment is giving purpose to what you do, not what you wish you could do. You can use your signature strengths to increase your satisfaction and belief in what you do at work. We will go through how to discover your signature strengths in the chapter of the same name.

Attitude

There is always a choice about the way you do your work, even if it is not a choice about the work itself.[93]

The difference between a good day and a bad day at work is your attitude towards it. Whatever attitude you bring, your day will deliver, so if you come in with a bad attitude, you will have a bad day and if you come in with a good attitude, you will have a good day. Yes, it really is that simple. However, it is not always that easy to implement, especially if you feel you are a victim.

Barring extenuating circumstances, a victim is someone

who feels they have no control over their life, that external forces rule it, and a job is a prison they must endure because they have to. Maybe your self-confidence and self-esteem have been dented and you no longer 'feel it', you just go through the motions, the clock has stopped, and life is just one endless treadmill, a Groundhog Day on replay.

The thing to remember is you always have a choice. You choose the way you respond to situations and to life itself. The old adage of when life gives you lemons, make lemonade, rings true, but it takes practice and support, so involve others in your workplace if you feel they will help you and you can help them.

To change your attitude, change your perception of the work you (have to) do for a living. Doing so will give you a sense of personal responsibility, accountability, and proactivity. Observe those around you and see how they are at work. You will see a lot. Take note of those who are engaged in what they do and those who aren't. Who has a positive attitude? Who doesn't? Mimic those that do and feed off their enthusiasm. Take responsibility for your own happiness and seek challenges in what you do. Put some excitement and dynamism is your daily work routine.

Learning and growth is a natural human trait and one that you should embrace. If your workplace is worth its salt, it should be encouraging and motivating its staff to be the best they can be in order to enhance the success and growth of the organisation. Reach a level of flow, bringing your strengths and positivity into the workplace, connecting with your work colleagues, and having fun.

Have Fun

Work sucks when it is not fun. It can make an hour seem like a day. You spend at least eight hours a day in the company of the same people, doing the same thing day after day, week after week, for months and years at a time. The benefits of having fun and play at work include:

- Making it an enjoyable place to come to each day.
- People treat each other better when they are having fun, creating an enjoyable and creative environment.
- Creativity is the germ of growth, which is good for both the individual and the business.
- A fun environment is a healthy environment, seeding loyalty and commitment to a business.
- Being able to be serious about your work but not always serious about yourself.
- Social connection is important in having a job. For many, it is the most they have at all.

Stay Focused and Be Present

If you aren't in the moment, you are either looking forward to uncertainty, or back to pain and regret.

–Jim Carrey, actor and comedian

Our braincan only comprehend the here and now. The past and future aren't real, just figments of what was and what might be, infiltrated with delusions and misconceptions.

Being present in the here and now allows you to fully absorb what is happening. Stop and smell the roses. Remove autopilot and be in the current moment. When you are actively engaged in the now, you will be focused on your work, producing the best results you are able to. You will also be aware of your feelings and what works for you and what doesn't. You will be more engaged with your customers, whether they are internal, external or both, particularly when they need you most.

Don't wait to be successful at some future point. Have a successful relationship with the present moment and be fully present in whatever you are doing. That is success. — Eckhart Tolle

Make Their Day

Go ahead, make my day.
– Harry Callaghan, Sudden Impact (1983)

Your customers, whoever they are, are the reason you have a job. We are all beholden to someone, so if you think you don't have any customers, think again. Ultimately, it's your customers that make your job possible. Focusing on your customer keeps you present in the moment, focused on the task and on the positive effect you can have on them. Being kind is the selfish, selfless gift, not intentionally, but giving makes both the giver and recipient happy. Win-Win.

It is in our culture to go to school, maybe university, and then get a job and work for forty to fifty years before retiring. But why? As discussed, getting a job is an income stream. Unfortunately for most of us, it is our only income stream because that's the way it has always been done and one we are all led to believe we need. Look at the top 200 richest people in the world and you will find not one of them works for someone else. I am not advocating that we should all be aiming to be mega rich, as wealth is a relative term, subject to those we measure ourselves against. What it is saying is that we have this notion that we have to get a job to get money, when in fact, it is just one option, albeit the most obvious. What needs to happen is people need to change their attitude to jobs and stop seeing them as the only form of income they have. They need to look at other options available to them. For many, this requires a major change of outlook, the breaking down of walls, moving away from the tunnel vision of money only coming from having a job. This change in mindset will open up people's eyes to the opportunities out there.

How much is your time worth? We briefly looked at this when discussing the Time element of WEALTH. If I said I wanted to buy your life for the next forty to fifty years, you wouldn't sell. Yet you will sell by the hour and usually at a rate that is below what you are worth. Take a look at income streams as investment opportunities. First, let's look at your job. You have to invest nearly all of your money into your job, let's say it is worth $50,000 per year. If you are lucky, you might get a two to three per cent return on that investment (speaking solely financially, not in terms of job fulfilment, learning, and social interaction and so on) in the form of a pay rise, possibly more, probably less. On the downside, that investment can be lost in a day if you lose your job for whatever reason. When you work for someone else, your return on investment is always capped to whatever pay rise you can get and that is usually outside of your control just as the investment being taken from under your feet without much, if any, notice. Many who have lived through the COVID pandemic will attest to that, which is why multiple streams, whether it be multiple jobs or multiple channels of income, is very important.

> *My father could have been a great comedian but he didn't believe that was possible for him and so he made a conservative choice. Instead, he got a safe job as an accountant and when I was 12 years old, he was let go from that safe job and our family had to do whatever we could to survive. I learned many great lessons from my father, not the least of which*

was that you can fail at what you don't want so you might as well take a chance at doing what you love.

—Jim Carrey, actor and comedian

We live in an age where the ability to do something for yourself that can earn you money is greater than ever. Sure, you have your so-called social media influencers and bloggers, but that is a limited market. There are also channels unheard of in the past that can produce new income streams such as drop-shipping, selling products and services online, investing in stocks, shares, and crypto currency, and offering your services and skills to the local community.

Everyone has a skill that other people will pay for and it is simply a matter of getting off your arse and offering it to them. However, don't be fooled into thinking as you did as a child, that you can be anything you want. The only way that will happen is with hard work, an open mindset, a little talent and definitely some luck. Don't be one of those people who believes they are entitled to be whatever they want. It is merit, not entitlement, that matters. You can be a dreamer, but at some point, you need to act to make your dream a reality. Real life doesn't give out free passes to those who wait or feel offended for whatever reason suits them for not getting what they want in life.

Excuses are limitless.

I don't have time. *Yes, you do. Make time*

I don't have the skills. *Learn them.*

I don't have the confidence. *Do it anyway, confidence comes from action.*

I am too scared to fail. *Failure isn't failure. It is learning and experience.*

As the great basketball player, Michael Jordan said, 'I've

missed more than 9000 shots in my career. I've lost almost 300 games. 26 times, I've been trusted to take the game winning shot and missed. I've failed over and over and over again in my life. And that is why I succeed.'

Here's the upshot. You are the master of your own destiny – if you want to be. To lead your life, you don't need to give up your job to get the job or income stream you really want for yourself. In fact, don't give up your job. Minimise the risk of doing what you want to do and use the tools above to improve your work life. On the side, in the evenings and on the weekend, whenever you can make time, start building your dream. It will take willpower, self-determination, and motivation as well as good habits and you can learn these later in this book. If you want the opportunity for more freedom, more control, and more fulfilment, do what you want to increase your income.

Not everything will work, you will fail on occasion but success is yours to determine, you will chart your own pathway, make your own decisions (and mistakes) and above all, you will have experiences, becoming rich, not just financially but also in life as well. Alternatively, if you want less freedom, less control, and less fulfilment, stick with only working for someone else.

Now, you are probably thinking, starting your own business and becoming rich is not that easy, and I'm oversimplifying thing. You're right, it isn't easy, but nor is there any security in sticking with what you are doing for the next X number of years, living from pay day to pay day, knowing your potential and seeing it trickle away with each passing year along with your dreams and potential for a full life.

The worst thing is getting to the end of your working life and thinking 'what if'. That should scare you more than trying. The older you get, the more you realise how little time there actually is and how little anyone really cares about what you do, so say 'screw it' and do it anyway. You don't want to be at the age of 60 and wondering 'what if' and if you are at 60 or more, seriously, what have you got to lose? Remember, failure isn't failure. It is learning and experience, and that is never a regret. Take a chance on yourself. You are the key to your own wellbeing.

> *Don't attach yourself to a person, a place, a company, an organisation or a project. Attach yourself to a mission, a calling, a purpose ONLY. That's how you keep your power and your peace.*
>
> Erica Williams Simon, American Journalist

Stuff

Don't collect things, collect moments.

Do you ever go to open homes and look in awe at some of the houses and how immaculately presented they are, how amazing they look, what can be done with small spaces and how spacious they all seem to be? They are like billboard happiness – an illusion. Where's all the stuff? Real homes have stuff in them, walls being held up by stuff leaning against them for support, clutter in the corners of the room, ornaments on the furniture gathering dust, and every flat surface being used as a storage space. In a real home, a garage isn't where you put your car, it's where stuff goes to die or at least be stored because it may be useful someday and you paid far too much for it to be thrown away.

> *The things you own end up owning you.*
> — Chuck Palahniuk, Fight Club (1999)

The more stuff we have, the more space we need to put it in, and the more space we have, the more stuff we buy to fill it. It is a never-ending loop of consumption for the sake of consumption. Many people live in a McMansion, far too big for their needs but needed for the sake of appearance and to fit all the stuff they neither want nor need.

To hell with the cost and ongoing stress of keeping up with the Joneses. The same goes with having the bigger television, the SUV and sports car. The kids have to be labelled up with what they wear, not so much to show you are 'winning' at life but because all the other kids are wearing it and there is nothing as devastating to a teenager as not fitting in. The same can be said for the rest of society. We all fit into some group or tribe as they like to call it these days; people we identify with and want to be like.

Of course, to make things more interesting, our brains associate shopping with pleasure. We feel elation at the anticipation of buying something, which is then followed by the high of actually purchasing. This dissipates over the following days and weeks (sometimes hours) to liking the purchase and then feeling a neutral enjoyment of it until it becomes just another piece of stuff in your house or wherever it is kept. That initial feeling of elation and high of purchasing is gone, never to be felt again with this purchase, so what is the brain's solution to getting that feeling back? Do it again and again. It's why people choose to shop when they are feeling down. You feel great with the new pair of shoes or set of clothing you have purchased until you come home and it sits in the wardrobe unworn perhaps forever, until it is relegated to the garage – just in case.

When you shop, the act of doing so unleashes your primal hunter-gatherer urges. You are in a version of survival mode, similar to when there is the prospect of having sex on the table, both figuratively and literally! You are hot, ready for action.

Your judgement capabilities are low at this point and you think the purchase will bring you more satisfaction that it does and generally speaking, it doesn't. When it is all over and you are back to your normal chilled, rational self, you will look at your purchase and wonder what the hell you were thinking.

What you need to do is stop before you make the purchase and take a timeout. Do you really want this? Wander around different stores and again, ask, 'Do I really want this?' Do this especially if the stuff you want to buy is expensive. Go home, think about it. Take a few days or weeks. Monitor how many times you wish you had what you wanted. If it doesn't occur often, forget it and move on. Congratulate yourself on your self-discipline and think of all the money you have saved or the debt you have avoided. Moreover, remember this feeling the next time you have the urge to splurge.

Although it is becoming harder to do as more and more shops aren't accepting cash, if you are out shopping, take cash and don't use credit or debit cards. With your cash, make sure it is in large denominations. Why? Because of a thing called the Denomination Effect, which dictates that we are more likely to pay with small bills and save the big ones, which once broken are more easily spent, so we try not to break them in the first place.

> *It's a mistake to attach your sense of worth and wellbeing to something transient, like your looks, your job, money or fame, because these things may not last forever. Happiness isn't a passive entity which can be obtained. More exactly, long-lasting happiness can be achieved by changing how you spend your time and your outlook on life.*
>
> *- Oliver James, Affluenza*

Let's not mistake that we need stuff. We do. We have our basic human needs to fulfil, but the economic model that we in the West have adopted, feeds on the need for growth, increasing gross domestic product (GDP) based on consumerism and the consumption of stuff. It is a model that works, one that has increased the wealth of nations and those individuals (on the whole) within them, but at the same time promotes the idea of consumption for the sake of consumption. It doesn't matter what you buy (within reason) as long as it keeps the wheels of capitalism turning, and money being created and spent within the economy. Ultimately, this kind of consumption can lead to feelings of inadequacy, stress, anxiety and all manner of mental and physical health issues as the Joneses mentality is subtly promoted and adopted by the population.

To promote a healthy sense of wellbeing and sensible consumption, look at buying stuff that benefits you as an individual, stuff that helps you to grow to be your best self. Invest in yourself instead of another phone. Invest in your education. Spend money on a course or a subject that interests you or will develop your career or personal potential. Invest your time instead of your money, doing what makes you happy. The experiences you have in your life are worth more than the stuff you have in your life. Look at what you already have. Remove that which doesn't bring you joy or fulfil a need, as opposed to a want. For example, look at all the television options you have: hundreds of channels to watch on top of all the online content streaming into your living room and mobile devices constantly. There is so much, that at times, you become overwhelmed with the choices available and paralysed into inaction. When you have less to choose from, it is easier to make a decision. The expression, 'less is more', rings true, but only when you remove the fluff and superfluous clutter clogging up your life and closeting your happiness.

Stuff doesn't just include the things you can touch. Thinking stuff will make you happy is a mug's game, but so if the belief that you won't be happy until you have something. That could be marriage, children, or a degree. None of it will make you happy, any more than a new phone will. That said, the act of pursuing those things and achieving your goals will, whether the goal itself does or not.

The other thing about stuff is that it brings us anxiety and worry. We worry we will lose our stuff or have it taken from us. We spend a fortune each year on insurance to make sure what we have is protected or can at least be replaced. Is it a coincidence that those countries whose citizens don't have a lot of stuff have a higher rate of happiness and wellbeing than those countries that do, that seven out of the top ten happiest countries are socialist rather than capitalist? Worth a thought, at least.

Finally, remember, stuff is just that – stuff. It may mean something to you, but to anyone else, it is either rubbish or something they can sell. Think of when older people die. People are only interested in the money or assets they can inherit, not the stuff that has been accumulated over many years by the deceased. Sure, maybe there will be some mementos or family heirlooms that will be kept, but for the most part, it will be sold off or thrown out. Does that matter? If that stuff has aligned with your life purpose and values, then no, it has added to your life and experiences, making the life you had a better one for you.

Be thankful for what you have; you'll end up having more. If you concentrate on what you don't have, you will never, ever have enough.

– Oprah Winfrey

Key Points

- Happiness is not financial wealth and success.
- Money is an important part of wellbeing because

it brings you financial wellbeing, which supports your overall wellbeing.

- More money usually means more responsibility, expenses, and debt as we live to our means - and usually beyond them.
- Our perception of money can influence how we treat money. Do you see it as an obligation or an opportunity?
- Multiple income streams or sources means you are not reliant on just one, usually a job, and won't be beholden and tied to that job for better or worse.
- Choose time over money. You can never make more time, but you can always make more money.
- Choose a job that you love and if you cannot do that, then make the job into one that is meaningful.
- You won't find fulfilment in a job you are doing just for the money or status.
- Don't be defined by the job you do. You are more than that.
- To make the most of your job and feel fulfilled, have the right attitude, have fun, stay focused and be present, and make their day.
- Try to do what you love, even if it is just on the side. Having something you love doing will bring balance and enjoyment into your life.
- We buy stuff to make us happy, but this is short-lived and requires us to buy more and more to get that purchasing 'high'.
- Keeping up with the Joneses is an illusion. The Joneses are in debt up to their eyeballs and think you are the Joneses.

- If you are going to buy stuff, buy stuff that benefits you as an individual and gives you opportunities for growth and development.
- Spending money on experiences brings more happiness that is longer lasting than spending money on stuff.

PERSPECTIVE

A long time ago in a village far, far away, there was a place known as the House of 1,000 Mirrors. A happy little dog learned of this place and decided to visit. When he arrived, he walked happily up the stairs to the doorway of the house. He looked through the doorway with his tail wagging as fast as it could. To his great surprise, he found himself staring at 1,000 other happy little dogs with their tails wagging just as fast as his. He smiled and was answered with 1,000 smiles just as warm and friendly as his. Leaving the house, he thought to himself, This is a wonderful place. I will come back and visit it often. In this same village, another little dog, who was not quite as happy as the first one, decided to visit the house. He slowly climbed the stairs and hung his head low as he looked into the door. He saw the 1,000 unfriendly looking dogs staring back at him so he growled at them and was horrified to see 1,000 little dogs growling back at him. As he left, he thought to himself, That is a horrible place, and I will never go back there again.

– Author Unknown

What is the moral of the story? All the faces in the world are mirrors and life is a reflective portal – what you see is what you get.

Perspective is the way you look at something, your point of

view. Look up from where you are now, look out the window and see all that is around you. Do you see trees, birds, other people, cars, water? Now imagine being in an aeroplane thousands of feet above where you are now. The view is completely different, even though it is of the same thing. The same trees, birds, people, cars, and water, only from another perspective. The same, only different.

Perception and reality are not the same thing. Whereas perception is the way we regard, understand or interpret something, it is a mental thing, reality is the state of things, as they actually exist that is not subject to the way we perceive them to be. That said, our perception can alter the way in which we see reality.

We are influenced by our genetic predispositions, for example you may have a family history of depression or susceptibility to a specific disease. We are also influenced by our past experiences and knowledge, as well as emotions and other cognitive biases.

There is nothing wrong with having a high perception of yourself. For example, it can provide both psychological and practical benefits such as increased confidence, persistence and hope, but when that perception strays too far from reality, so-called delusions of grandeur, it can have the opposite effect and have people believing they can achieve unachievable things and consequently become unprepared for reality, leading to severe mental illness.

What is your perception of yourself? How do you see your future self? Is it the same person you are now or someone different? What about your past self? Is that the same person you are now? For most of us, we see our future and past selves as separate people, that we have distinct identities separated by time. The person you will be in twenty years' time is a different person. Why is this perception important to understand? Simply put, it explains why we act the way we do in the here and now with our present perception of ourselves. If we see our past and future selves as different people, we aren't beholden to them; they are strangers. The promise you made to go on that diet was made by a different person to the one you are now, so it doesn't matter.

Your present self doesn't identify with your retired future self, so you don't save enough money to support that person. You can see the issues that arise from not having a psychological and emotional connection to your past and future selves; it allows us to sabotage ourselves. There is no easy way to relate and connect your past, present and future perceptions of yourself, however, there are now tools available that can help.

Using face-ageing software, researchers at New York University's School of Business found that when asked how they would spend $1,000, students who looked at an older version of their face using the software answered dramatically differently to those who simply looked a reflection of themselves in the mirror, choosing to place a large portion of the money into a retirement fund as opposed to an immediate indulgence selected by students looking into a mirror. The thought of saving for their retirement didn't even enter their minds. The thought is, that if you look at your aged self, using the software, further and further into the future and on a regular basis, you start to associate yourself with who you will become and be more likely to take care of yourself now, both in health and financially, so you are better prepared for when you are your older self. Set the foundations now so you have a better future then.

> *I'm like everyone else - I see the world in terms of what I would like to see happen, not what actually does.*
>
> - Paulo Coelho, The Alchemist

How do you choose to see the world? What is your attitude like? Do you have a positive attitude or a negative one? Do you see the glass as half full or half empty? Our perception moulds, shapes and influences our view of people, events, and everything around us, even our emotions, and more than that, our perceptions influence our experience of life itself.

Those who perceive things in a positive light experience higher levels of happiness and wellbeing. Our perception of ourselves is closely related to our story of who we think we are. The influence of our past experiences, feelings, memories, and the biases we have been brought up with are massively influential, but they do not define us. The reality of our past is not unchangeable and we shouldn't fall into the trap of believing that it is.

Our perception can change and we can choose what we want to remember and how we want to remember it. Too many people allow the past to define them or use it as a crutch to stop them from moving on and achieving what they really want in life. Our past doesn't prevent us from achieving what we want to do, but we can allow it to facilitate that. Some of us have had pretty traumatic things happen in the past and it is hard to just forget about them and move on, but that is not what you need to do.

You need to come to a point where you are able to look at past events and be able to accept them for what they were, placing them in the story of your life's journey and growth. Maybe the thing that is holding you back is the thing that can drive you forward with a different perspective. Perhaps, instead of focusing on the angst and hurt you are getting from your problems, you need to change your perception so you can start thinking of solutions. Don't believe negative thoughts, they are just thoughts. Question them. Look at them for what they are and move on.

Chances are you don't know how you are perceived by other people. Take a step back and try to see yourself as others see you. Have you considered how much of the perception you have of yourself is constructed by the expectations of others and society, the opinions of others such as parents and loved ones, or even by your culture itself? Determine for yourself if the things you do are the things the person you want to be, would do. If not, then it is time to change them. Identifying your behaviour is the first step.

Our brains are predictors; they like to make life easy so base a lot of what we do on expected outcomes based on certain cues or triggers. Once we do it automatically, we stop paying attention to it. If you are doing something without thinking about it, you have adopted a habit. Using another perspective and seeing what you do from an outside point of view, becoming aware, can help in determining your habits, good and bad, and from that, making changes when desired.

You can't go on blaming others for your circumstances. The government, your work, family, people you don't know. Blaming any and everyone else is easy, but you need to sort your own life out before going after others. It is true that people may be to blame for your unhappiness, but you are responsible for your unhappiness. At some point, you need to take responsibility for yourself. You have the freedom to change how you perceive the world and your circumstances. It is all your choice.

Life isn't fair. Our society is competitive. It is in our genes, survival of the fittest and all that. The winner gets the accolades; the loser gets forgotten. It's the way we operate. You don't have to be subjected to this pressure. You are not always, if ever, going to be the best at anything, but you can be the best you can be. If that still makes you worse than everyone else, so what? Change your perspective. You have bettered yourself and at the end of the day, the most competitive person you will face in this life is yourself. It is all about you. No matter what you may have been led to believe, every one of us has our own issues and demons to fight.

> *'As in Chess-play, so long as the game is being played, all the men stand in their order, and are respected according to their place; first, the King; then, the Queen; then, the Bishops; after them, the Knights; and last of all, the common Soldiers and pawns: but when the game has ended, and the table taken away, then all are randomly tumbled into a bag, and happily the King is lowest, and the pawn upmost.'*[94]

At the end of the game, we are all the same.

In life, you can choose to be one of two things: the victim or the victor. It's just a matter of perspective. Every life has its problems. You can choose to accept them as the victim or the hero. It's your story, so choose how you want to tell yours.

In his book, *The Alchemist*, author Paulo Coelho says, 'He realised that he had to choose between thinking of himself as the poor victim of a thief and as an adventurer in quest of his treasure.' A lot of this can relate to what is called the locus of control. Those with an external locus of control will have a victim mentality because they focus on what they cannot control. If you find yourself in this situation, ask yourself how much time and stress you are giving to something that you cannot control compared to something that you can. We will discuss the locus of control in more depth shortly.

You can be bitter at the world because you don't have what you want and you feel that everyone else is getting ahead, but the truth is (no matter how bitter it is to accept), you are blaming others because you refuse to blame yourself for the fact that the real reason you are not where you want to be is because you haven't done anything about it.

It is easier to blame someone else for what is or isn't happening in your life. This was especially predominate during the COVID-19 lockdowns imposed across the world. People lost the control they were used to having, or felt they had, in their lives and blamed everyone else for their lack of security. Let's blame the Government, the incoming travellers, Bill Gates(?!), the secret world government, anyone but ourselves. We are the victim! The problem isn't mine, it is someone else's.

The thing with problems is that people see them as something preventing them from moving forward. They become roadblocks to advancement and achievement and, in too many cases, excuses to stop. With this mindset, people start to create problems and disasters in their lives, bearing in mind it is all perception, because they are afraid of living their lives. It is a way of procrastinating and avoiding moving forward with your life, and staying within your comfort zone. The irony is that problems are not roadblocks, they are moments to pause, look at the problem and think about how to overcome them.

> *The impediment to action advances action.*
> *What stands in the way becomes the way.*
>
> *- Marcus Aurelius*

The action you take will cause you to think and behave differently, becoming the spur or motivation you need to live the life you want for yourself, even if it takes you in a different direction and on a different journey.

When you think about what you want to do with your life and what you have or haven't achieved, don't see it as a negative but a different journey adding to your story. We can only change some things, and the past isn't one of them, only our perception of it. Some may have thought they would travel the world and instead end up married with kids, and that isn't necessarily a bad thing. Some may have thought they would be rich bankers but end up working as administrators in some back office. In the end, you have to make the most of what you have.

Do you think Russian Roulette is a safe game to play? Most would say no, for obvious reasons but from another perspective, if you had to play, you'd have a five in six chance of being completely safe. That is pretty good odds (83.33%), something most would take a gamble on, if it wasn't with their life!

What about luck? Do you believe you are lucky? Maybe you haven't won the lottery so you think you aren't lucky but the fact you are alive, have the ability to read, drink fresh water, make your own decisions, choose how you want to lead your life, does that make you lucky? People aren't lucky. Luck is believing you are lucky and in many cases, making luck happen for yourself through action.

People see luck as getting the job they wanted, winning the lotto, or the bus stopping for you when you are running late. However, if you ask people who have won the lottery if they are happier, most will say no (and for the same reasons as mentioned earlier about happiness levels and habituation) and who is to say that things would not be better for you if you had not won the lottery, missed the bus or were turned down for the job. You never know what is just around the corner. As the Dali Lama once said, 'Sometimes not getting what you want is a marvellous stroke of luck.' It is like in the movie *Sliding Doors*, where two scenarios take place: one where the main actor catches the train and one where she misses the train and the consequential actions from each. Such too is life. It is only theoretically that we live in multiple universes.

> *As in a game of cards, so in the game of life, we must play what is dealt to us, and the glory consists, not so much in winning, as in playing a poor hand well.*
> *- Josh Billings on Ice, and Other Things'*
> *by Henry Wheeler Shaw who used the*

pseudonym Josh Billings.

Happiness should be seen as a verb, an action that needs to take place. Where does that action come from? Thought. Everything starts with a thought. It is thought that has created our reality. It is this union of thought into action that has allowed us to evolve as we have. Every advancement we have made as a species has first started as a thought.

Consider Einstein's theories that started as thoughts and ended with nuclear power, satellite navigation and radar guns, among many others. Michelangelo's masterpieces started as thoughts and ended up as some of the most admired pieces of art in world history. If you are going to change the world, even if it is just your own little world, you need to change your thoughts, to change your mind. This means changing your perspective and perception of things, seeing barriers not as problems but as doorways to new thoughts and actions that will better your life and those around you. To change your perceptions requires you to change your beliefs.

This isn't easy. You can't just say, 'I will change the way I think.' That won't work. Try telling someone to stop believing what they have always believed. They are not going to do it, no matter how many times they tell themselves otherwise. No, to change your way of thinking you need to pursue experiences that will change your thoughts and make them real to you and consequently your beliefs and your life.

The mind is everything.
What you think you become.
- The Buddha

Saying you will change your perception is a lot easier than actually doing it, which is why pursuing the experience is so important. Once you have experienced something, it makes changing your perception so much easier. Having had a bad experience or feeling is one thing and does not equate to a bad day or bad life, just a bad experience. To overcome the negative feelings and self-talk in your head, that little voice that says, 'This is stupid. I can't change' and other negative phrases, consider doing the following enough to allow action to take place:[95]

1. Listen to the voice and see if you can identify where it is coming from and who is saying it to you. Is it you, your parents, your partner, your boss?
2. Validate what you are being told. Is what you are saying valid? If so, why? If not, ignore it and take action.
3. Change negative self-talk into positive self-talk through the use of neuro linguistic programming techniques (NLP).[96]

The key to changing your perception is to see and know that everything is an opportunity to experience. This is quintessential to wellbeing. Most people would say they get to have sex as opposed to they have to have sex; they get to go on a holiday as opposed to they have to go on a holiday. So why do most people say they have to go to work as opposed to they get to go to work, or they have to go to the dentist as opposed to they get to go to the dentist? Okay, maybe the dentists is a bit of a stretch, but we are lucky that we have good oral health care available and healthy teeth and gums, especially in this world where hygiene and good teeth are seen as important.

The point is to see everything as an opportunity, not an obligation, because then we can start taking advantage of them rather than trying to avoid them. Too many spend far too much time avoiding everything and wondering when life will be good to them. Wake up! The only thing holding you back from living the life you want is you, your perceptions, and your inability to act. Changing your perception takes time and practice, as well as persistence, but like everything, it will happen with concerted effort. Sure, there are things that block you and that you can't control, but there are many more that you can including the way you choose to react.

This is not to say you will get or achieve everything you want but it is so much better to be doing something towards it than lamenting why you haven't.

CONTROL

*God, grant me the serenity to accept
the things I cannot change,*

Courage to change the things I can,

And wisdom to know the difference.

– Reinhold Niebuhr, The Serenity Prayer

During the COVID pandemic, we had multiple waves, variants and lockdowns, meaning we thought we had COVID under control only to realise that we didn't. Restrictions on our movement were imposed and then lifted before being re-imposed by the Government meaning we were unable to leave the house unless we were getting food or supplies, exercise, going to work (if we could not work at home) or getting medical care. If you were one of the unlucky ones, you may have also lost your job or been stood down from working because your place of work had to close because of restrictions. There were restrictions on visiting friends or going to a movie, getting a drink at the bar or meal at a restaurant. You were possibly stuck at home with limited income because you were unable to work, your kids couldn't go to school and had to be home schooled, and you couldn't visit your family or elderly parents who may have been quarantined in an aged care home. With these restrictions came a lot of anxiety and loss of control, and that was scary.

The government had taken control of your ability to do what you wanted, when you wanted, and with whom you wanted. Your sense of autonomy and freedom had been stiffled.

This feeling that you have lost control and have a lack of choices is common and not always in such an extreme example as the one given. Wanting control may sound like a bad thing as you come across as controlling, but it is anything but. It is important to our mental, physical, and emotional wellbeing that we feel in control. It is part of our survival instinct to feel in control and that is key, to *feel* in control, not necessarily to *be* in control. Feeling in control gives us a sense of security and peace of mind, a feeling that we are dictating the direction of our lives, that we are in the driver's seat.

In life, we all have different experiences that can be positive or negative. We can have success or failure in what we do. There are things we can control and others that we cannot. The difference between people is how they react to these experiences and the causes of them. Generally, we can attribute the results of our experiences internally or externally, that is, based on what we have done or on events outside our control. Simply put, when something goes wrong in your life, do you blame yourself or someone else? As mentioned earlier, these are known as the locus of control.

Locus of Control

Internal locus of control is a belief that your actions have a direct effect on the outcome, whereas an external locus of control is the belief that it is mainly external factors that account for what is happening in your life. Of course, we can be in both camps at different times with different experiences but in order to lead a life where you feel happier, healthier and more successful, we need to build a way of thinking that puts us in the internal locus of control camp. Here is why.

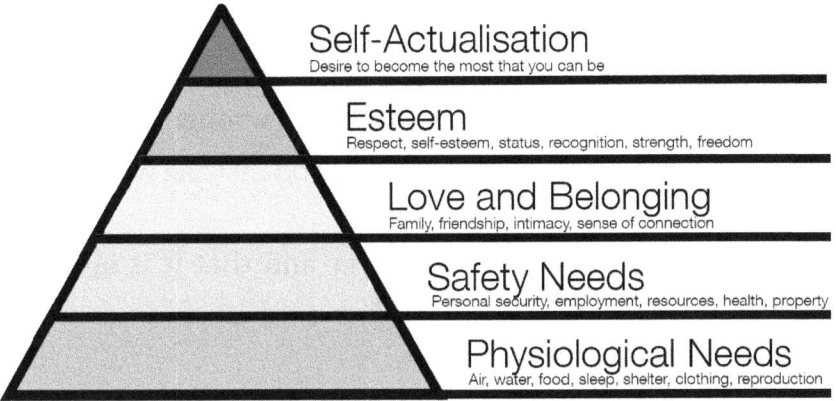

Maslow's Hierarchy of Needs

We have a hierarchy of needs. This was laid out by the psychologist, Abraham Maslow[97] as a five stage model where the lower stage needs (physiological and safety) have to be met before someone can progress up the pyramid to achieve the more complex needs such as growing and developing as a person in order to achieve their potential. The hierarchy of needs has been studied and improved upon many times over the decades[98] however the core principles remain the same. If we are not able to meet the needs we have for food, water, shelter and sleep, the things necessary to survive, then we cannot progress as individuals to achieve our full potential. You need more control at the bottom of the pyramid: these needs take precedence over all other needs. When we lose control, especially of these physiological and safety needs, the locus of control kicks in. There is a problem in the form of greed. The fifth level of the pyramid is all about growth and self-actualisation, reaching our fullest potential. However, greed tries to ground us in the lower levels of the pyramid where our anxiety is based on our psychological and safety needs. Moving up, the anxiety shifts to existential anxiety, something greed tries to protect us from, but which at the same time prevents us from ever reaching the pinnacle of our growth.

People who have an external locus of control are inclined to do the following:

- Blame others when things go wrong.
- Believe in good luck and good fortune when things go well for them.
- Feel they have no power and that it is all in the hands of someone else.
- Feel helpless.
- Believe nothing they do will make a difference.
- Are influenced by other people.
- Are passive and accepting.
- Have a fatalistic attitude.
- Will generalise more.
- Become depressed or anxious.
- More likely to believe conspiracy theories.

Those who suffer from depression and anxiety are more likely to have an external locus of control. They may use social media as a channel to extol the hardship that is their life. They will put up 'Woe is me' posts, the epitome of a fatalistic attitude, passive and accepting of their position but are not willing to do anything to improve their position. Many will see this as their way of calling out for help, but help that is offered is never taken.

Some people find comfort in being a victim. Others tend to blame anything not going right in their life on others, usually people in power, such as politicians and governments. When they really do have a loss of control, such as with the coronavirus pandemic, their anxiety really comes to the fore and this person leans heavily on such things as conspiracy theories as to why they have lost their feeling of control. It is always easier to blame others for what is not going right in your life, the uncertainty and unfairness of it all, even if the blame is on unsubstantiated beliefs.

Our society has instilled in us that negative feelings such as fear, pain and anxiety are bad and that happiness, love and joy are good. The things is though, that when you want to do something that you love, such as dating, getting married, starting a business and so on, you put yourself into a vulnerable position. You are going to feel fear and anxiety, the very things we are conditioned to avoid. Is this going to stop you doing what you want, what you really love? No! On the contrary, these feelings are not barriers or roadblocks but indicators that you are doing something new and exciting, something scary but worthwhile, something you want to do because it interests you. If you didn't have these feelings, it means you are indifferent and not really invested in it, anyway.

> *And obsessing on the things we can't control is useless. It takes us out of the game. We have to choose to be in the game.*
>
> *– James Altucher, Choose Yourself*

An external locus of control can make you feel like you are on a runaway train. You feel overwhelmed and helpless. The pace of life today can seem exhausting and you barely have time to breathe, being pushed and pulled from all directions with no sense of control or belief that you have any good in your life. To feel in control, you need to have an understanding of why things are as they are. That way, we can know the reason why something happened and whether we can repeat the action that caused it to happen or avoid it altogether. We need consistency and to feel competent as achievement is a great way to feel a sense of control. When you are not achieving, you feel swamped, pressured, harassed and anxious, completely out of control, triggering all sorts of negative emotions.

We need to feel safe and that we have enough to survive, with good health, somewhere safe to sleep and food on the table. Those with an external locus of control are more likely to be indecisive, prone to poor health, and quick to quit. On the other hand, they cope better with failure, at least in the short-term, are quicker to accept failure when something goes wrong and more likely to give praise to others when working in a team as they appreciate the influence of others and not so much of themselves.

People who have an internal locus of control are inclined to do the following:

- Take responsibility for their actions.
- Believe they are responsible for their own successes or failures.
- Believe they are in control of their own future.
- Believe that with hard work, they can succeed in life.
- Believe in their own abilities.
- Are not influenced by other people's opinions.
- Feel they can face challenges with confidence.
- Will generalise less.
- Are proactive and challenging.

The Locus of Control is a spectrum as opposed to two distinct options, and we all sit somewhere along the spectrum. An internal locus of control is considered the better of the two loci because, from a wellbeing perspective, those who are more internal than external feel happier and more successful in their lives. They believe that what they do can make a difference through their actions. They are less prone to anxiety and depression and are driven to perform better and achieve because they believe their results are a direct result of their own actions.

Now, many people are on the external part of the locus of control spectrum and changing your way of thinking is a massive undertaking, especially when events have resulted in external forces taking away your control. By allowing yourself to become a victim, you are also allowing yourself to become a villain, a villain to yourself – your own worst enemy – because in doing so, you are taking away your own power, handing it over to whatever may be instead of what you want to do. Look at the example given at the beginning with the coronavirus pandemic. With external factors such as that influencing your thinking, it is easy to see why it was frustrating. However frustrating it may have been, there are things that can be done to change your attitude or way of thinking.

Focus on what you can control and leave alone what you can't.

Trying to control things you cannot is a recipe for frustration and mental and emotional fatigue, depression, and anxiety. Look at the coronavirus pandemic. There was nothing you could do about it or the way it affected your ability to work, earn an income and see your friends and family. It was difficult not to become frustrated at these things, but there really was nothing you could do. Ultimately the best thing you could do was to find things that you could control and influence.

As with anything beyond your control, you can control the way you react to the situation, especially in front of your family and children. In our example, you could have used the time you had stuck at home to improve yourself through learning, spending more time with the family, starting a new hobby, or completing that task you have always put off. For everything that you cannot control, take a step away from yourself and look at what you can control. You always have a choice; you just have to make it. Even when things are beyond understanding and reason, you ultimately determine how you will react to it and the actions you take going forward.

Step back

Practice some metacognition and think about what you are thinking about when feeling you have lost your sense of control. Ask, why am I reacting this way? Are conscious of the way you are behaving? You can equally change the way you are behaving, just focus on changing your mindset. Critique what has gone wrong instead of criticising yourself or others. Be objective in doing so. Don't berate yourself over mistakes made or things not done. Simply take responsibility for your actions and learn from them. Take an honest look at your strengths and weaknesses and cultivate your strengths while at the same time avoiding situations where you feel vulnerable or at a loss. Of course, this will not always possible, but being aware puts you in a strong position. Remember, even though experiences and situations can make us feel vulnerable and without control, they are all part of our unique story, building neural pathways and adding wisdom and understanding in our life story. They will ultimately make you feel stronger.

Think of being on a roller coaster ride. You sit in the seat, the harness clicks into place and the rollercoaster starts moving forward. You are helpless at this point, with absolutely no control at all. You are reliant on the rollercoaster working as expected and that you won't come flying out of your seat as it goes through one of the loops or bends at breakneck speeds. The anxiety and fear as you move forward is intense because you have no control, but like many things that make us happy, it is not until afterwards, upon reflection, that we think it was a great and satisfying experience. Such is the same with many of the things we fret and feel anxious about.

> *Fear of suffering is worse*
> *than the suffering itself.*
> - Paulo Coelho

Live, right here, right now

By focusing on the present moment, you can ignore what is happening elsewhere. As previously mentioned, start by making your bed each and every day. Do things, even small things, with vigour and effort. Small accomplishments add up to making you feel able and competent so you can end your day feeling in control of aspects of your life that matter to you. Seek support from friends and family. Do what matters to you. That means taking action, not just thinking about it. Find your mojo, your passion, your values and take action to living a life where you are doing something that you care about.

Befriend the beast

Anxiety is not something you should consider an impediment in your life. Anxiety is one of the main reasons you and I are here. The fight-or-flight mode, of which anxiety is a part, has kept human beings around for millennia. The chances are that if you have a disabling amount of anxiety in your life, it is likely because you aren't addressing 'the beast' or at least the major issue in your life that is causing it and then taking action on it. To aid you, there are acceptance and defusion techniques that come from Acceptance and Commitment Therapy (ACT), a therapeutic approach to dealing with anxiety and unhelpful forms of worry, which are supported by over 330 clinical trials[99]. They include:

- Accept what you can't control

- Step back from your thoughts
- Focus on the present moment
- Remove limiting self-definitions
- Live by your core values
- Take action towards what matters

Did you know that poet, Emily Dickinson; English naturalist, geologist and biologist, Charles Darwin; and activist, Martin Luther King Jr, all struggled with anxiety? We can't ask them how they dealt with it, but we can take some more suggestions from Sarah Wilson's book, *First We Make The Beast Beautiful*[100].

1. Develop a gratitude ritual. Why? Because you cannot be grateful and anxious at the same time.
2. Eat to curb anxiety. Of course, this means eating real foods as opposed to those that will only make you feel worse.
3. Study others. Look at other people who have anxiety or fret and worry. See how they behave to see how you behave and modify from that.
4. Forget FOMO. Instead of worrying and getting anxious that you are missing out on something (FOMO – fear of missing out), say, 'fuck it' and grab a beer, wine, soft drink, whatever, order some takeaway, and plant yourself on the couch for the night. With friends, even better.

You can't control everything in your life and when things seem bad, remember this: When things seem especially rough, just ask yourself 'Did I shit my pants today?' and if the answer is no, you're doing alright.

YOU CANNOT CONTROL

The length of your life, but you can control its width and depth.

The contour of your countenance, but you can control its expression.

The other fellow's opportunities, but you can grasp your own.

. . .

Why worry about things you can't control? Get busy controlling the things that you can.

- Exchange.[101]

Framing

Just as they say the pen is mightier than the sword, so too are your words. The way we talk to others and more importantly, to ourselves, determines a lot about the outcomes we will see. As Mary Kay Ash, businesswoman and founder of Mary Kay Cosmetics Inc., famously said, 'If you think you can, you can. If you think you can't, you're right.' This is especially true of the verbs we use. Scientists have shown that when we use positive sentence structures, they result in positive actions.[102] Our brains are negatively geared and resistant to change, so framing how you think and speak becomes a very conscious effort. We all have that inner voice that seems to do everything it can to cast doubt and talk us into doing nothing in order to keep the status quo. To overcome this, we need to be conscious and observe how we talk both to ourselves and to others.

Think of these two common expressions used on memorial days – *Lest we forget,* and *We will remember.* The sentences tell us what to do but we pick up only the keywords: *forget* and *remember.* Saying these words makes them real. The subconscious mind does not process negatives. Consider the following: *Don't think of a clown.* What do you do? You think of a clown, even though you were told not to. Look at it another way. Someone says to you, 'don't be upset.' Your brain ignores the negative *don't* and what are you left with? *Be upset!* Alternately, when we use a phrase like, 'You'll be okay,' the brain processes that as it is, a positive message.

The same goes for self-talk when you use limiting words like *try* or *can't*. When you say things such as *I can't*, by saying so, you have already closed your mindset and have proved yourself right. Instead of saying *I can't*, reframe it and say something like *How can I?* Robert Kiyosaki, in his book, *Rich Dad Poor Dad* demonstrated the power of reframing in the story of his two 'dads,' one rich and one poor. His poor dad always said, 'I can't afford it.' His rich dad always asked, 'How can I afford it?' By posing a question, it gets your brain thinking, looking for a solution and ultimately changing, *I can't* to *I can*. Positive words reinforce positive actions and memories.

> *Your beliefs become your thoughts*
> *Your thoughts become your words*
> *Your words become your actions*
> *Your actions become your habits*
> *Your habits become your values*
> *Your values become your destiny*
> *- Mahatma Gandhi*

'Buts' cancel anything said before them especially in self-talk. Consider the following: 'I made some good progress today but I could have done better.' You ignore that you made good progress and focus on the part after the *but*. This can be especially important in a work or social situations with friends and colleagues. A simple way to reframe the wording to keep it positive, is to simply switch the word *but* for *and*. Let's look at the comment now – I made some good progress today and I can do even better. There is no negative or conflict causing connotations at all, and any advice or criticism is seen for what it should be: constructive and positive feedback.

The 'but' stops here!

> *It isn't what you have or who you are or where you are or what you are doing that makes you happy or unhappy. It is what you think about it.*
>
> — *Dale Carnegie, How to Win Friends and Influence People*

Once, long ago, there was a wise king who ruled a large kingdom. Each night he would sit with his son before he went to sleep. He would pray that his son would grow up and have the wisdom to rule his vast kingdom for the betterment of his subjects. With that thought, he summoned the wisest men in the kingdom and asked them to gather all the acquired wisdom in the world and put it into a book that he could give to his son so that he might be a wise ruler.

The wise men realised the mammoth task they had ahead of them but agreed, and one year later returned with all the wisdom they had acquired. It was a huge book and amounted to twenty-five volumes. The King looked at it and said it was too big. They had to make it shorter. Undeterred, the wise men left with the book of wisdom and after one year returned, this time with just one volume. Again, the King looked at it and said it was too much. Make it shorter. Dismayed, the wise men left and one year later returned again, this time with just one piece of paper with one sentence written on it. The King asked one of the wise men to read out what it said and he read, 'This too shall pass.'

Much of our life, attitude, and perception towards it is led by our philosophy towards life. Some live by the philosophy of *Que Sera Sera*, whatever will be, will be (are you singing the song in your head, too?), whereas others by *Carpe Diem*, Seize the Day. Others go by the philosophy of *Shit Happens*. *This too shall pass* is another that covers both the good and bad things that will happen in your life. Nothing is permanent, so appreciate and savour the good things that happen in your life because they won't last and realise the same of the bad things, they won't last forever either. In fact, as discussed, they may be the doorway you need to rethink and start on a new direction to a better life for yourself.

As the great stoic, Marcus Aurelius said, 'The universe is change; our life is what our thoughts make it.' Our perception is our reality, but we need to make sure that our perception is as close to reality as it can be.[103]

- Your perception is not reality – just your reality
- Accept that others have perceptions that are different to yours but just as valid so respect their perceptions as they may end up being right and yours wrong.
- Your perceptions may be wrong, so don't cling onto them too firmly as it will take courage to admit you were wrong.
- You will have biases that will distort your perceptions. Identifying your biases will help keep your perceptions close to reality.
- Use experiences and metacognitions to challenge your perceptions to see if they marry up with reality.
- Use experts and credible sources to validate your perceptions. Friends and families do not fall into this bracket, as they will likely have the same perceptions as you do.
- Be prepared to admit you are wrong when the majority of proof demands it. It is better to admit you

are wrong as opposed to sticking to what is blatantly wrong.

At the end of it all, remember to 'always look on the bright side of life' - Eric Idle.

Key points

- Our perception of things can change the way in which we see reality.
- Our perception of ourselves greatly influences the story of who we think we are.
- Our past does not define us but many use it as a crutch to prevent them from moving forward and achieving what we are capable of.
- Consider how other people perceive you. Consider how much of your self-perception is shaped by the expectations of others and society.
- Consider what you can and cannot control. Focus on what you can.
- Don't blame others for what you cannot control. Choose to be a victor, not a victim.
- Don't see problems in your life as roadblocks but as moments to pause, look at the problem, and think how to overcome it. Challenge yourself.
- If you are going to change the world, even just your little piece of it, you first need to change your mind.
- Consider how you frame things. Asking yourself if you can do something gets the brain looking for a solution; telling yourself doesn't.

ROCK

Waves crash against me and try to
knock me from my feet
But I am a rock and I shall not be moved.
Time will eventually count against me
and the waves will wear me down
But for now I am a mountain and
I rise high into the sky.

Birds flock to my steadfast sanctuary
Aware that they can lean on me for support.
Other mountains crumble and fall around me
But I am a rock and I shall not be moved.

I bear the weight of the world upon
my heavy shoulders
But I stand tall and the sky lifts me to new heights.
I feel drained by the constant pressure upon me
But I am filled with the vigour of life that abounds.

The sun warms my heart and lights my way
As I steer myself through this maze.
Others get lost in the darkness and stumble

But I shall not be moved.

This long and arduous journey has left me wanting
  But wanting for something already within me.
  I take solace in the fact that I have a reason
  But a meaning to it all forever escapes me.

HAVING A VISION AND MEANING IN YOUR LIFE

Don't underestimate the power of vision and direction. These are irresistible forces, able to transform what might appear to be unconquerable obstacles into traversable pathways and expanding opportunities.

- Jordan B. Peterson

If you are looking for a meaning to your life, then it is likely you are not living it.

There is no universal meaning to life. It is unique to each individual just as they too are unique. But why do we need meaning? How does having meaning make our lives better? Surely, the only universal constant with life is that it evolves. Research done in the field of positive psychology suggests that having meaning in your life accomplishes two functions in our lives. 'Firstly, it provides the necessary bedrock foundation which enables us to be more resilient and to bounce back from adversity. Secondly, it gives us a sense of direction, enabling us to set goals and targets to aim for.'[104]

What road do I take?

Well, where are you going?

> *I don't know.*
>
> *Then it doesn't matter. If you don't know where you are going, any road will get you there.*
>
> *– Lewis Carroll, Alice in Wonderland*

Finding what meaning you have in your life is not as easy as you might expect. It would be easy to choose a life in the pursuit of pleasure. Epicurus, the Greek philosopher born in 341 BC, believed pleasure was the goal of a happy life. You could choose to follow your impulses, live for the moment, consume, cheat, steal, lie. These are easy options, but options that ultimately leave you feeling empty inside.

Our brain likes to have direction. If we move through life with no sense of direction or purpose in what we do, nothing good can come from it, only disillusionment, despair, and no reason to go on. In his book, *Man's Search for Meaning*, Victor Frankl, a renowned neurologist and psychiatrist as well as a survivor of the Holocaust, stated that individuals have the power to create meaning in life, rather than it being prescribed. By this, he meant every individual has their own unique, context-specific meaning to life. There isn't one universal meaning to it. We give meaning to our lives by what we do, what we create, what we experience, and how we choose to respond to situations. What we do determines what meaning we give to life.

You could argue life has no purpose and consequently nor do we as human beings, or that God created us and therefore has a purpose for us – the meaning of life – but we don't know what that is or whether it is meaningful at all, at least to us. Therefore, it is better for us to determine our own purpose in life and be the authors of our journey rather than to adhere to a pre-determined purpose we do not know, or alternatively have no purpose at all.

> *When a person can't find a deep sense of meaning,*
> *They distract themselves with pleasure.*
> *– Victor Frankl*

Referring back to Marlow's 'hierarchy of needs', the need to fulfil our physiological needs such as food, water and shelter, then safety and security, social, and esteem needs, like climbing a ladder, before we even contemplate personal fulfilment and actual meaning in our lives can seem too simplistic and doesn't take into account the reality of human psychology. You could quite easily argue that you need meaning, and the opportunity for growth and self-actualisation, and reaching your fullest potential, in order to want the other needs, for what is life without hope? At the very least, the hierarchy should be seen more as a circle of needs where you can take pieces of each 'level' at any point in time and they can work alongside one another.

Look at your own life. You have a job, and it may be one that gives you meaning. In fact, a job that gives you meaning makes you more productive and less prone to peer pressure. You may have friendships with people who share your ideals. We all need to believe that we have opportunities for growth and self-improvement, whether we are barely able to put food on the table or able to fulfil all the needs identified by Marlow. We all, as part of our human nature, have a desire to be a better version of ourselves.

Nevertheless, you may still consider meaning in your life to be pointless, after all we are all guaranteed to die at some point and meaning adds nothing to the experience of life but meaning does in fact have a strong impact on a long and happy life. People decline quickly when meaning is taken from them. Research has shown a 21-fold increase in the risk of heart-attack within the first 24 hours of losing someone close to you[105], and a 40% increase in the probability of depression when retiring[106]. In other words, if you have a clear meaning and purpose, you are less likely to become lonely and bored, leading to the possible complications above.

> *A wise man was asked, 'What is the meaning of life?'*
> *He replied, 'Life itself has no meaning. Life*
> *is an opportunity to create meaning.'*
>
> *– Unknown*

It could be argued that a midlife crisis is a crisis of meaning. You get to the halfway point and realise you're halfway to dead. The kids are growing up and don't need you as much anymore. Younger, better people are occupying your workplace. Your job is just that – a job. The things that gave you meaning no longer do. The certainties of life are no longer there. You need something, but what? The extrinsic motivators and meaning are going or gone. A Harley-Davidson motorcycle or affair won't cut it. It is time to look inside yourself. What was meaningful is changing. It is time to examine yourself, get to the essence of who you are, find your soul and get to know who you really are and what life really means to you. What gives your life meaning?

In order to find meaning, it is best to establish something to focus on, a direction in life, as soon as possible and seek help where we can to make sure what we are doing is purposeful and worthwhile. Purpose is not something you just come across as you amble your way through life. It is something you need to build into your life, built from the ingredients 'of your own past, of your own affections and loyalties, out of the experience of humankind as it is passed onto you, out of your own talent and understanding, out of the things you believe in, out of the things and people you love, out of the values for which you are willing to sacrifice something.' [107]

Like you, these are unique, and only you can put them together into a cohesive design that will be your life. It is your choice to make a life, taking the good and the bad, the successes and the failures, building a life that has meaning to you.

Author Emily Esfahani Smith[108] argues that it is more important to have meaning in your life than to be chasing happiness, which comes and goes. Having meaning gives you something to hold on to, something that can help you build a better self. There are four pillars of meaning, according to the author.

The first is belonging. It is the relationships we have where we are valued for who we are, not what we believe or whom we like or hate, but who we are simply as individuals. The same goes for the way we feel about the people we have a relationship with, we value them simply for who they are, nothing else.

The second pillar is purpose. Purpose is about what you give as opposed to what you want. It is about using your strengths to help others. Most of us do this through work; it's how we feel valued and needed, but we need to have a purpose beyond what we do at work as it gives us something to live for and pushes us forward. When we go ahead into new ventures without purpose or direction, very little positive comes from it. We feel exhausted, disillusioned and a failure as we give up. Before starting, it is best to focus on what we are doing, seek help from others when needed, and ensure what we are doing is purposeful and meaningful.

There is some general advice that states that men and dogs are very much alike. When a dog is shepherding animals or bonding with and helping a family, it has a purpose, but when it doesn't have a purpose it becomes agitated, depressed and anxious. When this happens, they start digging holes in the backyard because this gives them a sense of purpose. It is very much the same with men. When they don't have a sense of purpose or direction, they start digging holes in their lives, maybe through drinking, drugs, overeating, or depression, and this hole becomes deeper and deeper highlighting the importance of having purpose and direction in your life.

The third pillar, Esfahani Smith says, is transcendence. What she means by this is removing your sense of self and rising above the bustle of life and feeling connected to a higher reality. It is getting into the zone, a sense of flow, where you lose all sense of time and place.

Finally, the fourth pillar is storytelling. This is the narrative or story you tell yourself about yourself. It is how we determine why we are the way we are and how we got here. Seth Godin said in his book, *This is Marketing*, that we each have our own narrative, that little noise inside our head, 'the world view that is unique to us, the history, beliefs and perceptions that shape who we are and what we choose.' The key to storytelling is that is all subjective. We are the authors of our own story. We determine the emotions and background story. It is our perspective that makes our story what it is. We can change it to be whatever we want. We can turn negative experiences into excuses to explain why we are where we are or we can turn those negative experiences into positive experiences, events that teach us things about ourselves and allow us to grow into fuller, better people. That is, after all, what wellbeing is about.

> *For the mystery of human existence lies not in just staying alive, but in finding something to live for. Without a concrete idea of what he is living for, man would refuse to live, would rather exterminate himself than remain on this earth, even if bread were scattered all around him.*
>
> – Fyodor Dostoevsky, The Brothers Karamazov[109]

Vision

When you have meaning in your life, you can create a vision that compliments the meaning you have given your life. This gives you the ability to think about or plan for the future using your imagination and acquired wisdom. A vision should naturally lead to well-defined and more focused goals. This will also aid in keeping you motivated to achieve what you want. The great thing is that when you can see a future that is better, you are more likely to make changes needed for you to reach what you want.

When creating a vision for yourself, there are several things to remember. Your vision should include what you want to be. To do that, you need to know who you are now. This includes understanding and being honest with yourself. What are your habits, your attitudes and biases? If you don't know who you are now, how can you be clear about who you want to become?

What is your vision? What do you want? Where do you see yourself when it is fulfilled? Think or dream as big as you want. Maybe you want to be rich, healthy, slim, or successful? There are no limits with visions, but make them fit within your meaning of life. Detail how you see your life and give it some substance. Visualise what it will look like. When it feels real, it is easier to feel passionate about it and motivated to achieve it. Start setting goals and plans in place to get there. A hope and a prayer are not enough. You need to act to make it happen. Once you start moving towards your vision, aspects of it will start coming true, which will motivate and inspire you even more. A vision is important for moving towards a life you want for yourself. It gives you the ability to see beyond your current reality and circumstances, and create an image of what could be, what you want for your life. The great thing about visions is that they can cover all aspects of your life, whether that be physical or emotional, and give you an insight into what your future could be.

The ability to practice metacognition, as we mentioned, is a double-edged sword. It allows us to envisage a future and build a pathway towards it but in asking us to create a vision where we live 'the dream', some of us can become obsessive, to the detriment of ourselves, as our thoughts focus on the 'what if' scenarios. In these cases, it is important to remember to focus on the things that give your life meaning and purpose, not otherwise.

Once done, you can focus on your passion, one that has been built with meaning and a vison.

Passion

Your work is to discover your world and then with all your heart give yourself to it.

– The Buddha

Do you ever find people just amble through life, filling time, but with no life, no spark, they just seem to wander aimlessly from one highlight or calamity to the next? They are waiting for something, unwilling to commit to life until they have a reason to, waiting for a purpose and a passion. They don't know what to do with their lives and think it will all come right when they find their passion. The problem is they don't know what it is and worse still, they don't know how to find it. Worse again is the supposition that a passion is something to be found.

Passions are not something you magically discover. Passions, by definition, are a powerful or compelling emotion or feeling. They can be positive or negative, such as 'I love you with a passion' or 'I hate you with a passion.' Of course, when we talk of passion, we are talking about the doing of something that you really enjoy. This has typically been corrupted by people, leading the population to believe that your passion can be your job. Do what you love, and you'll never work a day in your life. How many times have you heard that, and how many times have you thought, I don't even know what I like, let alone love, and I wouldn't even know how to make a living from it? And so, you get people looking for their passion, only to discount it because there's no way they could make money doing it, whatever 'it' is.

To be honest, if you are having to ask what your passion is, you likely don't have one or equally so, won't acknowledge your passion. The notion many have that your passion should be your job is ridiculous. Steve Jobs, in his 2005 Stanford Commencement speech,[110] is inspiring, but unrealistic for most of us. Although he never mentions the word passion, he says essentially the same thing: do what you love.

Do what you love, but you don't have to make a living out of it. It can just be something you do in your spare time. Do it because it sparks your passion. These days many people think they can be the next Steve Jobs because he said to do what you love. How many people think they are entrepreneurs and how many more feel pressure to be doing what they love even though they don't have any passions or know how it would be possible to make money from their passion? Kudos if you do, but even those who are able to make a living out of their passion have to admit that it is not all flowers and chocolates.

Mark Manson, author of *The Subtle Art of Not Giving A F**K*, himself says that every job sucks sometimes and he still hates what he does about 30% of the time[111]. We all do things we don't want to do. That make us unhappy, and all it does is make us resentful. We do a bad job, our energy gets zapped and we lose motivation to do what we really want to do, realising we have wasted yet more of our valuable time and life. Passion comes from inside you. It is a fire that burns, simmering, waiting for you to let it rage. Nothing external will nurture your fire and every time you say yes to something you don't want, your fire starts to go out. You burn out. Your passion keeps you alive inside.

> *If you're struggling to find your passion, think about what gives you energy. What do you do that you seem to do effortlessly? What makes time fly? What do you look forward to doing more of as soon as you finish doing it? What makes you smile? What do you raise your hand to volunteer for? What gives you goosebumps?*
>
> – Bradley Charbonneau, Every Single Day

So, how do you know what your passion is? You can start by looking at your natural talents and abilities. It is true that what you are good at may not be something you are necessarily interested in, let alone passionate about, and the truth can be said of people who know what their passion is – you may be passionate about something but that doesn't mean you're any good at it.

Referring back to Mark Manson again, 'you're awake 16 hours a day, what the fuck do you do with your time?'[112] We all have something that interests us, something we like to talk or think about, some topic that takes up a good portion of our free time. That could be your passion. Have you ever explored the option? Having a passion presupposes that it is singular and fixed, but in reality, like most things, passions change and evolve as we get older, learn more, and have more experiences[113]. The things you were passionate about when you were younger are not always the same things you are passionate about now, they have been replaced with new things.

The supposition that we have to find our passion implies that once we find an interest, that pursing it will be easy but with most things, challenges and roadblocks will occur and with the 'it will be easy' mindset[114], once you hit these obstacles, you are likely to quit, sending you back to the couch wondering again, what your *real* passion is and where to find it. The truth is, it probably wasn't a passion in the first place.

The problem with this kind of mindset is that it is not open to exploring new things, which ultimately limits those with this mindset 'finding' their passion.

Instead of finding a passion, this needs to be replaced with developing a passion. This makes so much more sense too. Like riding a bike, you don't do it initially because you love bikes, you do it because your parents want you to or because your friends all ride bikes. You will fall off and hurt yourself, but over time you will learn and develop the skill of riding a bike, riding with no hands, doing wheelies, skids, and bunny hops – you will become a proficient rider. And like learning to ride a bike, you can learn to develop your passion. It isn't always fun and maybe it isn't going to make you a lot of or any money, but it makes you happy.

Passions can be something you do on the side. Look at Einstein. He worked in a patent office and in his spare time worked on what he was passionate about, giving us the Special Theory of Relativity. You don't have to change the world like Einstein did, but you can change your own world by developing your interests through taking the time to work on them. Sometimes, having a simple interest in something can lead to a passion, maybe developing a set of specific skills that you can build an expertise in, becoming a dilettante, that is someone who is interested in a subject but not with any special knowledge or commitment. As Gregory Walton says in his paper on finding passions, 'If you look at something and think, 'that seems interesting, that could be an area I could make a contribution in,' you invest yourself in it. You take some time to do it, you encounter challenges, over time you build commitment.'[115]

Still don't feel like you have a passion? Don't worry about it. Ask others what they think your passion is. You may be surprised what they say and then you may have one of those lightbulb moments. Maybe even take the view that having a passion isn't needed to have a fuller life. Do as suggested and choose an area of interest, build on it and develop a passion for it, even if you have to make yourself do so – better still, do it for something where you can make money or make a positive difference. Look at the possibility that your passion doesn't even exist yet. How many people have a passion for flying? 120 years ago, that wasn't an option. Maybe it is online gaming? thirty years ago, that didn't exist. Alternately, remember that everyone is an individual and what works for one doesn't work for all.

Passions are very personal and self-centred. They are all about you and what you can take from life. Looking at another commencement speech, this time by Ben Horowitz, American businessman, investor, blogger, and author, he says that passions take a very 'me'-centred view of the world. 'When you go through life, what you'll find is what you take out of the world over time – be it money, cars, stuff, accolades – is much less important is than what you've put into the world. So, my recommendation would be to follow your contribution. Find things that you are great at, put that into the world, contribute to others, help the world be better and that is the thing to follow.'[116] So, instead of finding what excites you and gets your emotions and feelings going, maybe your fulfilment will come from giving back and contributing to all the good that is and can be done in the world.

> *I heard this story about a fish. He swims up to an*
> *older fish and says, 'I'm trying to find this thing they*
> *call 'the ocean.'*
> *'The ocean? the older fish says, 'That's what you're*
> *in right now.'*
> *'This?' says the young fish. 'This is water.*
> *What I want is the ocean!'*

The above quote comes from the Disney Pixar movie, *Soul*.

It is a parable about finding meaning and purpose in our lives. We can spend our whole lives looking for it when all along what we have been searching for is right in front of us. We think reaching a goal will make us happy, doing this or doing that, and are disappointed when it doesn't, but we can find happiness right in front of us, where are right now. We just need to live more in the moment and savour life's simple joys.

Key Points

- Having meaning in your life gives you direction and enables you to set goals and targets to aim for.
- Having meaning gives you something to hold onto and can help you build a better life.
- According to author Emily Esfahani Smith, there are four pillars of meaning: Belonging, Purpose, Transcendence, and Storytelling.
- Having a vision will compliment your meaning, giving you the ability to think and plan for the future, leading to well-defined and more focused goals, keeping you motivated to achieve what you want.
- To make your vision a reality, you need to act on it.
- Finding your passion is not as easy as it would seem.
- Passion comes from finding your natural talents, asking yourself what you do with your spare time? What do you like to talk about?
- Passions change just as you do, and you can develop a passion by taking an interest in it and over time building expertise.
- If you don't have a passion to follow, follow your contribution and build what you give back to the world.

SAVOURING LIFE'S JOYS AND LIVING IN THE MOMENT

Life moves pretty fast. If you don't stop and look around once in a while, you could miss it.

– Ferris, Ferris Bueller's Day Off (1986)

Who didn't like the movie, *Ferris Bueller's Day Off*? It was a great movie because he did what we would all love to do. He was living in the moment and making the most of each experience. We all know a Cameron Frye, Ferris' best friend, who is too scared to do anything or an Ed Rooney, the school principal, who sought to bring down Ferris and made sure everyone played by the rules because that is what we must do every day. We get up, work, pay bills, do homework, make meals, clean the house. We do what needs to be done without causing too much disturbance, avoiding upsetting the status quo.

From that state, our lives fall into a routine and become, essentially, boring. Boredom is a way of telling you that you are not making use of your time and that you should be doing something more enjoyable, useful, or fulfilling. To fight boredom, we look for distractions, sinking ourselves into entertainment such as television, video gaming, and bingeing on a plethora of entertainment options, all at our fingertips. To emphasise how much time we spend combating boredom, the global entertainment and media industry is expected to reach US$3.5 trillion in 2029.

All the entertainment options, instead of making things better, end up making them worse as we don't feel satisfied but desensitised, needing more and more stimulation to increase our dopamine levels. It is a classic case of hedonic adaptation. Those that suffer chronic boredom are also at a risk of developing psychological problems, including depression and addiction. Boredom removes us from the present and needs to be seen as a signal and catalyst for change, a change where we are present in the here and now.

When we are living in the moment, you are happy at a non-conscious level. Our brain doesn't understand the future, it can only comprehend now. That is why saying you will be happy when you do this or that or after this or that has happened is redundant. You can only be happy now – if you choose to be. This isn't some ideal reserved for the enlightened Zen-like people, it is the only way to live a life that isn't subverted by illusions of the future and of what might be. Think of children and how they spend their time. They are happy in the here and now, not thinking of or planning for the future when they might be happy. They live for now.

> *Because I don't live in either my past or my future. I'm interested only in the present. If you can concentrate always on the present, you'll be a happy man... Life will be a party for you, a grand festival, because life is the moment we are living in right now.*
> *- Paulo Coelho, The Alchemist*

To make the most of now, you need to stop deferring the present in favour of the future. The future holds your success, or so you believe, so you keep looking at now or any given moment in context of your whole life to see if you have had success and can be happy yet. The problem with this is that now is now, not representative of your life as a whole. You need to see now, the present, as it is independent of your past or desires for the future and be in the moment.

Don't live in the future. Live in the moment.

Don't collect things. Collect moments.

Remember what was said in Part One of this book? Each and every day, something positive is likely to happen to you. We all experience happiness but not many of these moments are remembered in the normal memory process. This is because they don't stick or become long-term memories as we haven't experienced them for long enough, more than a few seconds, or they haven't been million dollar moments, and the memory simply gets pushed out by the influx of new experiences or just information flooding the brain.

So, how can we make these positive experiences stick? Stop and experience the present moment. Feel the sun shining on your face. Pay attention to the positive things that happen to you and stop to let it sink in. The neurons in your brain will fuse together to create positive memories.

> *Never let the future disturb you. You will meet it,*
> *if you have to, with the same weapons of reason,*
> *which today arm you against the present.*
>
> *– Marcus Aurelius*

We have all, at one time or another, lived in the moment, experienced what those in the know, call a sense of flow, being so absorbed in what we are doing that we lose all sense of time and self. Flow is when you set a goal, immerse yourself in an activity and pay attention to what is happening, enjoying the immediate experience. It is total involvement with life. Flow can happen at any time, in any place. With flow you get a sense of deep enjoyment, creativity, and participation in life. It can have a massively positive impact on work satisfaction, academic success, and overall quality of life.

Flow happens when your skill levels are stretched; it is a challenge, but not by too much; it is one you are still able to meet.

It is the sweet spot between anxiety and boredom.

In it, you feel completely absorbed with what you are doing and don't have the excess capacity to evaluate or judge what you are doing.

Time becomes lost and passes more quickly or slowly than you expect. You are focused only on the present moment and not the end goal, just what you have to do next. For example, in tennis or squash, you are focused on the next shot.

In flow, you feel in control and are unconcerned about failing.

You don't feel self-conscious, but feel that what you are doing is intrinsically rewarding.

When in flow, you are relaxed and constantly learning in new ways, maybe unexpected ways. Particularly when you are in high flow, really absorbed and skilful, you can exhibit charisma and people will find your talent and skill attractive. People like others who are in flow because it allows them to be a part of it, to share in the experience. Think of a professional game of football or tennis with the best players in the world. You become part of the action as the players compete with one another, completely immersed. Alongside them you get into a state of flow, as if you are in the match yourself and your flow doesn't affect or come at any cost to them. It is able to be shared.

Flow itself is neutral; it is neither good nor bad. You can achieve flow doing both 'good' things such as sport and 'bad' things such as gambling. What then comes as no surprise is the fact that activities that get you into flow can become addictive. A lot of the time we don't even know we are in a state of flow until after the fact, much like happiness.

Flow is why it is important to get a job that plays to your signature strengths. When you do something you enjoy, you can experience flow and the positive impact it has on your wellbeing. If you don't have or can't get a paying job that gives you flow, then do something in your own time that you love and believe in. Dale Carnegie, author of the bestselling, *How to Win Friends and Influence People*, said it best:

> *Are you bored with life? Then throw yourself into some work you believe in with all your heart, live for it, die for it, and you will find happiness that you had thought could never be yours.*

If you want to be in flow and make a difference, find out what you are good at, what the world needs, and what you enjoy doing. These, says Sir Ken Robinson in his book, *The Element*, put you in your element; in a state he calls Ultimate Flow. To truly enjoy flow and identify when you are in it, set goals, become immersed in the activity to achieve the goal, pay attention to what is happening in the moment, and learn to enjoy the immediate experience. That is flow and living in the moment.

Your life won't last forever, and no-one is going to make it happen except you, so take a different route, change your routine, do something different, just do something and have the experience. The fact is you are better off spending your money on experiences. Experiential purchases are better than materialistic purchases as they allow you to acquire a life experience, have social value, and are less susceptible to negative social comparison. It is about doing things rather than having things. You can laugh about it, as we tend to remember the good things and forget the bad, as experiences improve with time. Experiences make you happier than material purchases.

Ichi-go ichi-e (pronounced 'ee-chee go, ee-chee eh')

Loosely translated, this means 'Once in a lifetime.' Every moment, every circumstance, and every person is unique. It is about taking pleasure in and embracing every moment, even if it was unexpected. It is about being present in the here and now and learning from others; putting your phone away and focusing on those you are with and what is around you. It sends a message that you are with those with you now and not distracted, that they are important and mean something to you. You are focused and experiencing the moment.

Spend time with other people, your parents, friends, and children. Absorb yourself in the experience of being with them. Savour the moment. Be with them because you want to be. Play with your kids, take a vacation, go on a holiday, see that music concert, but be there to experience it. Don't record it from behind a camera or on your phone, and instead, engross yourself in the moment and be there. Bono, lead singer of the band, U2, said performing had changed and he didn't enjoy it as much as he used to. No longer was he performing to an audience who was engaged with him and the band as they performed, now he was performing to a sea of phones recording him, people trying to immortalise the event instead of living in and savouring the moment.

> *We should concern ourselves not so much with the pursuit of happiness but the happiness of pursuit.*
> *– Professor Corman. Hector and the*

Search for Happiness (2014)

There is nothing like the experience of failure to make you appreciate that of success. In many ways, success is the end and usually comes as an anticlimax, the journey along the way being the fun and exciting part (especially in retrospect), not knowing whether the gamble is going to pay-off or not. At least with failure, the game is still on, you can go back and start again, but once you have succeeded, that is it.

Prosperity comes from the experience of doing what makes you better, makes you that bit more fulfilled. There doesn't have to be money involved, nothing financial at all and that is what prosperity should really be about, not the attainment of a goal or money but the feeling of doing something that makes you feel happy and fulfilled. The prosperity is in the experience, not the result.

If you hear someone say, 'I used to go fishing,' or 'I used to dance,' or 'I used to do that,' whatever that might be, ask them why they don't still do it? If it brought them pleasure and they are still physically able, it is a concern because the moment someone starts saying 'I used to' is the moment they have stopped investing in their emotional and physical wellbeing. If this sounds like you, stop, look at your life, and see where your personal needs are in relation to everyone else's. Where are you putting your needs on the priority list? It is time to make your needs and wellbeing a priority and you can do this by replacing 'I used to' with 'I will.'

If living in the moment occurs at the time, savouring is recognising that moment and noting what is happening, what is making you happy and why this is a special moment.

How will savouring the joys of life make me happy? Let's look at what savouring can do for you. Savouring can boost your mood in several ways.

    1. It can ward off hedonic adaptation.

You remember that. The thing where we want the quick fix but get used to our new circumstances, so want something new again. Savouring helps us remember the good things in life without having to buy something to feel happy.

2. It can stop your mind wandering.
Savouring keeps us on point. On average, we spend over 46% of our day mind wandering and unfocused. Savouring is a form of meditation in that it focuses our mind by keeping us in the moment.

3. Savouring can increase gratitude.
Savouring can make us thankful for the experiences we're having as we're having them.

How do we make the most of savouring?

To start with, you need to take part in a positive experience, and then you have to savour during that experience. To do this, stop and recognise why it is making you happy. Now, as much as I just said to be in the moment and not to record it, take a photo, if you need to, and use it to help you remember the moment later. Later, when you are alone, think back on the day and what you enjoyed and appreciated the most. Take as long as twenty minutes to replay the positive experience/s. Reminisce and write down what you remember. Use the photo/s you took to recall the event and jig any memories. Doing this will make you relive the experience and bring back the feelings of happiness you felt at the time. Tracking what you savoured in a twenty minute replay, can turn your savouring of a moment into a habit and bring on a general sense of wellbeing as you will learn to live in the moment more often and savour each moment for longer.

Savouring is a process, not an outcome.

Here are some activities that will enhance savouring as well as some activities that will hurt savouring an event.[117]

ACTIVITIES THAT ENHANCE SAVOURING	ACTIVITIES THAT HURT SAVOURING
• Tell other people how good it felt.	• Focusing on the future as soon as it is over.
• Share it with other people.	• Reminding yourself it will be over soon.
• Think about how lucky you are.	• Telling yourself it was not as good as you hoped.
• Think about sharing it later with others.	• Thinking it will never be this good again.
• Laugh.	• Thinking of ways it could be better.
• Be proud.	
• Think only of the present and become absorbed	• Feeling like you don't deserve this good feeling.

Living in the moment and savouring the joys of life is an essential part of wellbeing. They allow you to be completely present in the here and now. We are, however, subject to mind wandering and drifting, thinking of things done or to be done, the past and the future. We can counter this with the practice of meditation, the subject of the next chapter.

> *And me? I still believe in paradise. But now at least I know it's not some place you can look for. Because it's not where you go. It's how you feel for a moment in your life when you're a part of something. And if you find that moment... It lasts forever.*

– Richard, The Beach (2000)

Key Points

- Boredom is a way of telling you that you are wasting time and should be doing something more enjoyable, useful, or fulfilling.
- When we are living in the moment, you are happy at a non-conscious level.
- Your brain only knows now, so stop deferring the present in favour of the future.
- Saying you will be happy when or happy if means you are not living now but in the future. Choose to live in the moment, not in the future.
- Be aware of the here and now. Pay attention to the good things that happen in your life, even if they are small. Stop and experience the moment, allowing the brain to process them and add them as positive memories.
- Flow is when you set a goal, immerse yourself in an activity and pay attention to what is happening, enjoying the immediate experience.
- When in flow, you are relaxed and constantly learning in new ways, maybe unexpected ways.
- Experiential purchases are better than materialistic purchases as they allow you to acquire a life experience, have social value, are less susceptible to negative social comparison.
- It is time to make your needs and wellbeing a priority and you can do this by replacing 'I used to' with 'I will.'
- Savouring can boost your mood by warding off hedonic adaptation, limit mind wandering, and increase gratitude.

- Savouring is a process not an outcome, so recognise what makes you happy, noting what is happening in the moment and why it is a special moment.

MEDITATION

If it weren't for my mind, my meditation would be excellent.

- Pema Chodron

Once upon a time, there was a fox and a turtle. They met in the forest and the fox thought, *Yes, I am going to have a good meal today.*

The turtle thought, *Bugger, I am in trouble here. Do I run? No, I am not fast enough,* so he retreated into his shell. The fox paced round and round the turtle but eventually grew tired of waiting and left.[118]

What does this story have to do with meditation?

When you see a problem in your life, whether it is stress, tension, depression, anxiety, sadness, worry, or whatever, be like the turtle. Don't run away from your problems, but stop and observe your reaction to them. Engage with your problems and appreciate that these things are passing products of your own mind and you control your relationship with them. Instead of surrendering to problems, learn to accept and befriend them.

What is meditation?

The goal of meditation isn't to control your thoughts, it's to stop them from controlling you. It is a practice of turning your attention away from distracting thoughts towards a single point of reference, such as breathing, bodily sensations, compassion, or a specific thought.

It sounds so simple, but it is not an easy thing to do. Trying to quiet your mind and focus on a single thing for a period of time is incredibly difficult, especially in our lives full of activity and things to do. Meditation takes time, as your mind likes to wander, to think about the past; the future; what you need to do; what you should have done; what you could be doing instead; and of course, just thinking about thinking.

Mind wandering takes up nearly half[119] of what we do on a daily basis[ii]. This means that half the time we are on autopilot in what we are doing on a daily basis! Think of the times you have been driving and before you know it, you are at your destination. You didn't even think about driving, you just did it on autopilot, thinking about what you had to do when you got to your destination, the argument you had with your partner and what you should have said, or why you have never seen a baby pigeon. Do they even exist? Maybe they are born fully-grown? Mind wandering can lead you down many rabbit holes.

Mind wandering does, however, serve a useful purpose. Our brains are wired to wander, with mind wandering being associated with brain activity in the cortical region when the brain is at rest. It allows us to digest data as we wander, of which we do a lot when we are sleeping. There are strong links between mind wandering and creativity, but overindulgence in mind wandering can be debilitating. This is called obsessive rumination. Those who do it tend to dwell on negative thoughts and emotions, and unsurprisingly there is a strong correlation between rumination and depression. It can be like 'being stuck in a self-defeating movie of our own making, starring us.'[120]

In a study[121] by psychologist, Daniel Gilbert and Matthew Killingsworth, of 2,250 people, it was found that mind wandering did not make them happy. Let's focus on that for a moment. Something we do nearly half of the time doesn't make us happy. Using that information, you can see why living in the moment is so important to having a sense of wellbeing. Mind wandering, it turns out, is as good, if not a better predictor of happiness as the events that people do. You can see from this why different things make some people happy and others not so much.

If you are immersed and focused on a task, such as completing a jigsaw puzzle or reading a book, it can be quite pleasant. But let's say you're doing your taxes – if you get frustrated and annoyed with the process, it can feel like quite the opposite. In fact, people in the study reported that their mind wandered no less than 30% of the time, no matter what they were doing with the exception of sex. For most guys, that's probably just a few minutes of being in the moment.

> *If you think you are too small to make a difference, try sleeping with a mosquito.*
>
> *– The Dalai Lama*

Meditation stops mind wandering and because it puts you in the moment; it makes you feel happier and calmer. The problem is still meditating at all. Many people don't like it. It is actually very hard to stop and quieten you mind when so much is going on both inside and outside of it. Mind wandering is like the mosquito buzzing around you when you are trying to sleep, always there, trying to get in. The stray thoughts buzzing around, trying to take away your focus are forever present. It takes time, practice, and perseverance to make meditation work, and the temptation to give up and walk away is very strong. Like a muscle, you need to exercise your mind to focus.

And, just like the mosquito, even though it may seem like a small thing, doing even just ten or fifteen minutes of meditation per day can make a big difference to your wellbeing.

Benefits of Meditation

There would be no point in doing meditation if there were no benefits, so what are they? On top of stopping mind wandering, the benefits of meditation include:

- Meditation increases your grey matter.

Research[122] shows that meditating can increase the grey matter around your frontal cortex, that is the part of the brain linked to decision-making and memory. Cortexes generally shrink as people get older but research has found that those who averaged twenty-seven minutes of meditation per day, with other studies showing results with as little as fifteen minutes a day, the amount of grey matter stayed the same as those half their age. To put that into context, 50-year-old meditators had the same amount of grey matter as 25-year-olds.

- Meditation improves focus and focus improves memory.

In a 2013 study at the University of California, Santa Barbara, it was shown to improve memory, focus, and overall cognitive function.[123] Emotional experiences are remembered more than those that are not, which is why you remember the emotions on people's faces. For example, you remember a face showing anger or smiling more than a face with no emotion.

- Meditation reduces stress.

There have been many studies[124] that show the benefits of meditation in reducing stress. Stress reduction comes with better physical, emotional and social rewards.

- Meditation can reduce feelings of depression and

anxiety.

Meditation has been shown to help with depression and anxiety, studies showing that it disrupts the entire stress cycle in the brain. 'As a result, we are more insightful and regain the power to ignore the negative feelings, and can successfully overcome depression and emotional liability.'[125] In a study done by Richard Davidson at the University of Wisconsin, it was found that meditation can change the shape of the amygdala, the part of the brain that regulates serotonin. Where antidepressant medications are serotonin inhibitors, they stop the process, meditation can help the amygdala process serotonin and therefore alleviate symptoms of depression. This was supported by a study[126] that found mindfulness meditation has the same effect as antidepressants in managing depression and anxiety. 'It isn't a magic bullet for depression,' says Study researcher, Madhav Goyal, 'but it's one of the tools that may help manage symptoms.' Additionally, a study has shown that meditation doesn't help anxiety disorders as clinically diagnosed but can help improve anxiety symptoms.[127]

- Meditation can help control pain.

Believe it or not, meditating can reduce mental and physical pain better than morphine! Other research done on 'mindfulness meditation has been shown in clinical trials to reduce chronic pain by 57 per cent. Accomplished meditators can reduce it by over 90 per cent.'[128] Meditation can also be of benefit in the treatment of chronic pain.[129]

- Meditation can boost your immunity.

Several types of meditation, including mindfulness and yoga, have been shown to both strengthen your immune system[130] [131] and make you resistant to viruses and infections.[132]

On top of these benefits, it has been shown that certain types of meditation can make you feel happier and more socially connected, kinder, able to fight addictions, improve sleep, decrease blood pressure[133], improve self-awareness and self-esteem, become more creative, and improve cardiovascular health[134]. There are ample reasons to give it a try!

Here is an interesting side note on the study done by Richard Davidson on meditation and depression. The type of meditation done in this study was 'tonglen', a mediation created by Tibetan Buddhist monks in which a person pictures or imagines healing someone or something of an illness. The interesting part is that the act of meditating or imagining healing someone or something outside of yourself actually heals you. In other words, the act of helping someone is an act to help ourselves. The study, which has been running for over ten years, has shown through MRI tests that this is true. It throws a new perspective on the power of prayer, not for others, but for ourselves.

> *You should sit in meditation for 20 minutes a day, unless you're too busy, then you should sit for an hour.*
>
> *– Zen Proverb*

Types of Meditation

There are many types of meditation out there, hundreds of meditation techniques, in fact. There is no universally accepted 'best one' and it is up to you, the individual, to determine which is best for you.

There is both guided and unguided mediation. In guided mediation, you are guided through the meditation process either in person or through a recording, such as online or via audio. If you are a beginner, then having someone guide you through the steps is a good starting point as they can help you get the most out of the experience. In unguided meditation, you do the meditation alone. This may simply mean sitting in a quiet place and paying attention to your thoughts, your breathing, or your body for a period of time.

Nine of the most popular types of mediation include:

1. Mindfulness Meditation:

Mindfulness meditation involves paying attention to thoughts as they pass through our mind, but not to judge them or become involved in them. It is like standing on the street and watching cars go past. You observe and take note of patterns. It is helpful to focus on an object or something, such as your breath or sensations in your body, thoughts, or feelings. This form of meditation can be guided or done alone and can reduce fixation on negative emotions, impulsive and emotional reactions, as well as improve relationship satisfaction, focus, and memory.

2. Breath Awareness Meditation:

This form of meditation encourages mindful breathing. In it, you breathe slowly and deeply, either counting or focusing on the breaths. The goal is to focus on the breathing and ignore all other thoughts that enter your mind. It is very important to understand how you breathe and to focus on it. It is after all the first thing you do in life and the last, so a focus on this elixir of life can vastly improve many parts of your being and more specifically Breath Awareness Meditation is known to reduce anxiety and give improved concentration and greater emotional flexibility.

3. Spiritual Meditation

Similar to prayer, spiritual meditation has you reflect on the silence around you and seek a deeper connection with the universe or God. The use of essential oils is commonly used to heighten the experience and it is beneficial to those who thrive in silence and want spiritual growth.

4. Focused Meditation

This form of meditation involves focusing on any of the five senses, such as your breathing or listening to everything around you. It is designed to bring focus into your life but can be difficult to master as most of us find it hard to focus on anything for more than a few minutes so it will take practice - as will they all!

5. Movement Meditation

As the name suggests, this form of meditation requires movement, whereas most other forms of meditation have you sitting. In movement meditation, you can do a gentle form of movement such as walking through a forest, gardening, or qigong. It is a good option if you find peace in action and prefer to let your mind wander.

6. Guided Meditation

Sometimes called guided imagery or visualisation, this form of meditation has you form mental pictures or situations that you find relaxing. This form is usually led by a teacher or guide, hence the name, and brings calmness.

7. Mantra Meditation

This meditation is most famously stereotyped by the 'Ohm' sound people make as they sit, legs crossed and eyes closed. It uses a repetitive sound to clear the mind, hence the 'ohm', but it doesn't matter what the sound is or if it is said out loud or in your head. This form of meditation is supposed to bring you deeper levels of awareness.

8. Transcendental Meditation

This is a spiritual form of mediation where you remain seated and breathe slowly, focusing on a mantra or repeated word or series of words in order to rise above, or transcend, your current state of being. This form of meditation gives both spiritual experiences and heightened mindfulness.

9. Loving Kindness Meditation

The goal of this meditation is to cultivate an attitude of love and kindness towards everything, including people and things you hate. The key is to repeat a message of love and kindness until you feel an attitude of loving kindness. This form of meditation is supposed to increase positive emotions and has been linked to reduced anxiety, stress, and depression.

> *It is very rare to find a human being today. They are always going somewhere, hardly ever being here. That is why I call them 'human goings.'*
>
> *– Ajahn Brahm*

How to Meditate

Different types of meditation have different requirements, however, no matter which type of meditation you want to do there are the four 'P's to consider. These are Priority, Place, Purpose, and Plan.

1. Priority:

Make mediation a priority. Don't let other things come between you and your time for meditating. Prioritise it over anything else. Build it into your routine and regular schedule, and do it at a specific time each day. Commit to regular practice.

2. Place:

Find a suitable place to do your meditation. Select or design an environment that makes meditating as easy as possible.

3. Purpose:

Determine the purpose for your meditating and what you want to achieve.

4. Plan:

Look at the methods you will use for your mediation. Have a goal. Maybe it is just to meditate for two minutes a day, maybe longer. Make sure you know when and where you will do it each day. Make yourself accountable in order to help build the habit of meditating and reward yourself for good behaviour to reinforce the good habit you want to form.

When doing meditation such as focused or breath awareness meditation, try the following:

- Find a suitable place; somewhere quiet, where you are unlikely to be distracted or disturbed.
- Find a comfortable sitting position, usually cross-legged on the ground. Have a cushion to sit on and a relaxed posture, but try to keep your back as straight as possible so that you can concentrate on inhaling and exhaling. Have a relaxed disposition and wear comfortable clothing.
- Choose a time that works for you, when you are comfortable and feel able to relax.
- Check what your emotional state is before starting and pay attention to the small things.
- You may want to have a timer on hand so you aren't looking at your watch or phone all the time.
- Don't worry about where to put your hands, maybe just leave them in a relaxed position on your knees.

- Close your mouth and relax your jaw.
- Breathe in and out of your nose, focusing on the breathing but only observing it, not analysing it. You are trying to be present in the moment and letting it happen.
- If you find your mind wandering, bring it back to listening to your breath.
- As mentioned, meditation is difficult to get into. Your mind is a mosquito and forever buzzing. Turning the volume down takes time, practice and perseverance, but the rewards can be invaluable.
- There many videos on YouTube and free (and paid) apps available that can help with guided meditation. Many local gyms and businesses now offer mediation sessions, so take a look around. If you want to try unguided meditation, search for more in-depth how-to guides online.

Alternatives to Meditation

Getting in a meditative state can be a difficult ask. As simple as it sounds, it takes a lot of practice to let thoughts enter your head and tune them out and to be in the moment, focused on just your breathing or whatever you choose. There are alternatives that are gaining traction, including Hygge (pronounced hoo-gah), a Nordic practice, which basically means embracing positivity and enjoyment in everyday experiences – living in the moment. In countries like Denmark, it is a common word, used as a noun, adjective and a verb, and is not so much a lifestyle, as opposed to a way of living and doing things. It is a focus on togetherness and prioritising people in your life and removing anything annoying or emotionally overwhelming (this includes people! We can assume that all of us have some people in their lives that fall into the annoying and emotionally overwhelming category).

Another alternative closer to meditation in definition is the Northern European practice of Niksen. The word means 'nothing' or at least 'doing nothing' or doing something ,but with no use. In other words, the Dutch practice is about doing nothing or something without achieving anything or being productive. You might think that is just like watching TV. Well, not really. Niksen is about letting your mind wander, pretty much the opposite of meditation. Whereas meditation wants you to be present in the moment, niksen is about letting your mind wander, rather than focusing on what you are doing, for example, breathing.

Of course, as was discussed, mind wandering can have its disadvantages and lead to ruminating and overthinking, so it needs to be something that is practiced. The benefits of the practice include reduced anxiety, strengthening the body's ability to fight viruses, curbing the ageing process, and increasing your creativity and problem-solving ability. Like meditation, niksen – the art of doing nothing – isn't as easy as it sounds. This is because when practicing niksen, you do nothing. For people who are used to doing something, even watching TV, sitting down and staring out the window can be quite disconcerting and uncomfortable. You can try active passive things such as walking or even knitting and the advice is to push through the discomfort, try it for short stretches at a time and slowly build up to longer stretches, making time to do so. Like meditation, you have a time and place for yourself. Niksen is something to be practiced, fitting in with your lifestyle. Too much of doing nothing can be detrimental but mixed with a balance of active and productive activities, when you *niks* regularly, you can find a stronger self of self-efficacy and inner peace.

Key Points

- The goal of meditation isn't to control your thoughts, it's stopping them controlling you.
- Meditation takes time as your mind likes to wander.
- Mind wandering takes up nearly half of what we do on a daily basis.
- Mind wandering doesn't make us happy.
- Meditation stops mind wandering and because it puts you in the moment, it makes you feel happier and calmer.
- Like a muscle, you need to exercise your mind to focus.
- Meditation can increase your grey matter, help with memory, control pain, boost immunity, and reduce stress and feelings of anxiety and depression.
- There are many types of meditation available and all consider the four 'P's: Priority, Place, Purpose, and Plan.

SIGNATURE STRENGTHS

The challenge needs to be equal to our skills.

The Japanese have a word, *Ikigai*, which, when translated into English, means 'thing that you live for' or 'the reason for which you wake up in the morning.' It is used to specify what is of value in your life or makes your life worthwhile. Thought to have originated on the island of Okinawa, it is considered the Japanese secret to a long and happy life. So, what specifically is it and how can it help in making you happier?

Ikigai is the sweet spot of four primary elements:

- What you Love (your passion)
- What the World Needs (your mission)
- What you are Good at (your vocation)
- What you can get Paid for (your profession)

Ikigai is unique to everyone, none of us being exactly the same and so too our reasons to get up each morning differ as well. So, whereas you may think you get up each morning because you have to go to work to earn a living to pay for your lifestyle or because you have kids and they need to be cared for, *Ikigai* is more than that. It incorporates your mental and physical state as well as economic.

It is easy to know what your profession is (if you have one) and maybe even what you are good at, but then again, maybe not. Knowing what your passion is for some of us ever elusive and we can spend our entire lives trying to work out what fires us inside and as for our mission, what is our purpose? Many times, that is lost in the daily grind and we amble aimlessly through life with no clear purpose other than to get to the end of the day, sleep and do it all again the next day.

So, how, if we don't know where to start, can we find what these elements mean to us?

You can start by making four lists, one for each element

and writing down whatever words, ideas or phrases come into your head. Take your time and walk away when you can't think of anything or feel yourself becoming frustrated. The thoughts will come and when they do, write them down. See where there are areas or ideas that overlap or relate to one another and slowly, you will come to a point where your ikigai will start to show itself.

Of course, books have been written on Ikigai, one of which is called, *Ikigai. The Japanese Secret to a Long and Happy Life*, by Hector Garcia and Francesc Miralles. In it, they break down the ten rules that can help you find your own ikigai, some of which will sound very familiar if you continue this book:

1. Stay active and don't retire.
2. Leave urgency behind and adopt a slower pace of life.
3. Only eat until you are 80% full.
4. Surround yourself with good friends.
5. Get in shape through daily, gentle exercise.
6. Smile and acknowledge people around you.
7. Reconnect with nature.
8. Be thankful for anything that brightens your day and makes you feel alive.
9. Live in the moment.
10. Follow your ikigai.

So, what is the reason you get up and out of bed in the morning? What do you choose to do when you have nothing else to do? If you still don't know or sort of do, but still aren't there yet, you can use some tools to help you find your signature strengths. These are the character strengths that are most essential to identifying who you are. Afterall, it is Signature Strengths that is the title of this ingredient for wellbeing.

Character Strengths are the positive parts of your personality that impact how you think, feel, and behave and are the keys to you being your best self. Character strengths reflect the 'real' you — who you are at your core.[135]

Twenty-four strengths have been identified and we all have them to varying degrees. They vary from your creativity, honesty and perseverance to your kindness, fairness, and humility. You can take a free 15-minute survey to find out what your key character strengths are. It is worth doing just out of interest but even more so because it focuses on pulling out your strengths. It can help guide you towards identifying where your passion, mission, and vocation lie and perhaps even where you should be looking for a profession to find true purpose, meaning and wellbeing.

Do the test here: **http://www.viacharacter.org/www/Character-Strengths-Survey** – then come back and read on.

How did you find it? Some of it probably even surprised you. Knowing your character strengths is great and opens up a whole new world of possibilities for you to reach your true potential. However, until you use them and apply them in your everyday life, they are just knowledge and will soon be forgotten. In order to stop this from happening and enable you to get a sense of wellbeing and purpose in your life, based on the survey results, it is recommended that you to select your top five character strengths. These are your signature strengths. It is these strengths that you need to focus on applying in your everyday life on a regular basis. Chances are, you already do, but because many of us suffer from personal strengths blindness, we tend to underuse our strengths.

To get things started, here is a challenge: For one week, use your top signature strengths in a new and different way. Here is an example. If curiosity is one of your strengths, enrol in an online course, get a non-fiction book on a subject that interests you from the library or shop. If social intelligence is one of your strengths, help someone who isn't as socially adept as you to fit in when in a social situation. The thing to remember is to do something different every day for a week using each of your top four or five strengths. Also, remember that, although you will be excited to start using your strengths more strongly, not to overplay them, especially in the workplace. Know your audience and when to tone it down if they start creating difficulties or you start colliding with others. Find a happy medium and that may mean, with your new knowledge on what your strengths are, that you are working in the wrong place and your strengths lie elsewhere. What you should find, and studies have shown this, is just one week of using your signature strengths in a new and different way each day will have an enduring impact on your happiness. Not only that, when at work, you will be more productive and satisfied with your job when you use your signature strengths. In fact, you will enjoy work more and see it more as a calling when you use about four signature strengths.

That brings us full circle back to your ikigai. Do you feel like you have a better understanding as to what it is now? If not, rinse and repeat this chapter and, as said, take your time. Practice your signature strengths and by continually applying them on a daily basis, you will come to a point where your ikigai, your reason to get up in the morning, becomes clear and you will start to lead a purpose-driven life.

Focus on your strengths instead of trying to fix or improve your weaknesses.

> *Focus on a better use of your best weapons*
> *instead of constant repair.*
> *– Tim Ferriss, The 4 Hour Work Week*

Key Points

- What gets you out of bed each morning helps to determine what you live for.
- It is summed up in the word, Ikigai, which means 'thing that you live for.' It is the sweet spot of your passion, your mission, your vocation, and your profession.
- Character Strengths are the positive parts of your personality that impact how you feel, think, and behave, and are key to being your best self.
- Focusing on and applying your top character strengths in a different way helps you to build upon them and use them in your everyday life.

LEARNING

I'm still learning.

- Michelangelo

Learning is one of the pillars of happiness and wellbeing. Without it, we would just have WEATH and that isn't even a word! The reason this is also an ingredient is because learning in and of itself can bring wellbeing into your life. The learning in WEALTH is about learning from your experiences and actions whereas this learning is done with purpose for the attainment of knowledge and because you want to better yourself.

We all know that learning doesn't end when our formal school education does, but too few of us actively engage in the skill of lifelong learning. A formal education gives us the building blocks we need to be a productive member of society. We are taught in a structured and regimented style, one that has not changed much in hundreds of years. It is based on a mix of learning in order to remember rules and processes as opposed to learning to understand. In many schools, it is still the one size fits all approach to education and learning, and for many children, that just doesn't work.

We all learn differently and although the majority of us will get through the schooling system, how many are put off wanting to pursue any kind of learning afterwards? Education is a function, whereas learning is an experience and mindset. Formal education also misses on teaching fundamental subjects that are relevant to real life. Whereas we push mathematics and english as part of the curriculum from the first year right through to the last, little, if any, education is given on mental health and money management, although both crucial if someone is to lead a healthy and productive life.

Throughout our life we learn new skills, maybe without even realising it, from learning to ride a bike, making a bed, doing a job, using a smartphone, or driving a car. The benefit of lifelong learning is that you choose to do it. It is voluntary, self-initiated and motivated, and usually informal with the purpose of achieving self-fulfilment.

As human beings, we are driven to explore, learn and grow. Learning can help improve your sense of self-worth, confidence, and quality of life. Your sense of accomplishment and satisfaction can come from a continued effort to learn. Learning doesn't have to be formal, such as going to night school or doing an online course. Lifelong learning is just that – lifelong. You may choose to improve your career and job prospects by learning for your professional development, but lifelong learning comes from learning about what interests and benefits you.

Anyone who stops learning is old, whether at twenty or eighty.

– Henry Ford, automobile entrepreneur

What are the benefits of lifelong learning?

Today we live in a learning and knowledge economy. There are very few jobs left that don't require you to continually upskill if you want to get ahead. Those jobs that don't require this are probably pretty close to being automated and completed through machines, robots, and AI. From an economic point of view, learning for professional development is imperative to staying ahead of and even just in the game.

The nature of work is changing exponentially and many jobs that we are doing now didn't exist ten or twenty years ago. With that being the case, how many jobs don't even exist yet? In five years' time, there will be jobs we'd never think of today. If you want to be an asset and earning better money, you need to be learning so you can get those jobs. It will make you a more efficient and capable person as well as lead to better job satisfaction and opportunities for advancement.

Learning conveys intellectual benefits, increasing knowledge and the ability to use that knowledge in different and significant ways. You can practice new skills, challenging cognitive bias and conflicts, and getting pleasure out of achieving new things. Lifelong learning opens your mind to the exchange of ideas and different points of view. It allows you to escape your biases and increases your wisdom. It helps put your life into perspective, allowing you to understand and learn from the why's, what's, and how's, of past failures and successes, ultimately understanding yourself better, living your life both consciously and deliberately.

Learning is good for your brain. It improves your cognitive skills including attention, memory, problem-solving, and decision-making. A healthy brain equals a sharp and focused mind. Lifelong learning, especially as we get older, can help prevent cognitive decline, sustaining the strength of the mind and leading to a longer life, all other things being equal. Combined with better sleep and physical health, your mental health improves immensely though the conscious act of lifelong learning.

The social benefits of lifelong learning are huge. Ongoing learning opportunities increase your social connectedness, contacts, and opportunities for further growth. When we engage in learning, it is usually with others, whether in person or online. We tend to be with people who we learn with or want to learn from. The benefits of social connection make you happier and engaged.

Learning benefits you in a multitude of ways. Your self-confidence increases as you get satisfaction from your sense of accomplishment. It rises through your increased knowledge and being able to apply what you have learned. Whereas formal education teaches us skills to be productive in and benefit our society, lifelong learning enables you to learn practical skills that benefit you. You learn for personal development, building skills in such areas as creativity, problem-solving, leadership, critical thinking, interpersonal, adaptability, and more. These skills increase your motivation, giving you the drive to learn more. It can drag you out of a rut where you have been just going through the motions doing what you have to do, putting you back in the driver's seat and in control of your life and destiny. Learning can enrich your life, reducing your boredom and the mundane activities you spend your time on, giving it meaning, especially if what you are doing is meaningful. It enables you to develop your natural abilities, abilities you may not have known you had if you hadn't taken a chance and tried something new. By doing so, you push through your instinct to stick with what you know and learn to experience life, adapting to change and seeing that it isn't so bad, in fact, it is quite invigorating and life-affirming. Most of all, learning becomes fun because you are doing it because you want to do it.

An unexamined life is not worth living.

– Plato

As the saying goes, you learn something new every day, but how many of us are consciously taking in the lessons as opposed to be guided by our instincts, emotions, and desires, whether they are ours or others? Time needs to be devoted to learning, self-reflection and reviewing to see what we have learned and how we can use that learning to do things better. Doing so will help improve our work, relationships, and lives in general. Learning for the sake of learning is fun, but if you want to make the most of what you have learned, it is not enough. You need to put into practice and take action with the knowledge you have gained and make use of it, otherwise it is just motion, not action.

To become a lifelong learner, you have to take it personally. Lifelong learning is about you and what you want, not what others want or expect of you. You need to recognise what your personal interests and goals are; what it is that motivates you.

Examples are:

- learning new skills, such as public speaking, sewing, or cooking.
- self-taught study, such as learning a new language.
- learning a new sport or activity, such as football, golf, or surfing.
- learning to use technology, such as programming, web development, or new software.
- acquiring new knowledge, such as carpentry, the history of ancient Egypt, or positive psychology.

Using the above as a starting place, make a list of the things you would like to learn and then do some research on how you can learn more about the subject. It is now easier than ever to learn from home. You could use a search engine to find more information. There may be books, magazines, blogs, podcasts, websites, videos, courses or talks you can listen to or attend.

The thing then is to determine what your goal is. Saying you want to learn more is very broad and easy to ignore or abandon. Maybe you want to get a certificate or degree in a subject or understand how something works so you can build one, for example, a car engine or a bookcase. These are finite goals. Once determined, make a commitment to learning, purposely fitting it into your day, no matter how busy it is. It doesn't even have to be long but you need to commit some time. If you are passionate about learning then you will be motivated to achieve your goal no matter what but if not, there are methods to encourage you to build habits that can work for you. Lifelong learning shouldn't be a chore. You should be doing what you want to do, not what you are required to do. There may be times when your motivation is lacking and 'life' has other things that require your attention. Maybe you simply can't focus, you don't have the cognitive ability to settle and get down to the business of learning.

In these circumstances, here is something to try: write your first name on a piece of paper. Now, with your non-dominate hand, write your name again. No doubt, the second time didn't feel comfortable but if you wrote your name using your non-dominate hand another thirty times and then compared it to what you wrote with your dominate hand, the chances are it will look pretty similar. This process sets up neural pathways in the brain. It feels uncomfortable to start with and the temptation to quit and do something familiar and comfortable is huge, but with any new skill, feeling that discomfort when learning a new skill or job, is vital.

Creating neural pathways is key to learning anything new including things we want to learn. Feeling the discomfort means your brain is working and that you are learning. You just need to embrace the feeling, stick with it, as it will pass, and you will come out the other end with the benefits of learning, and the satisfaction and sense of accomplishment of what you have achieved.

In life, many of us are prone to dwelling on bad decisions and what we could have done to avoid bad outcomes. In these situations, we tend to focus more on the negative emotions as opposed to the learning benefits that can be gained from them. This is a hard habit to change as this adaptive trait is important to the brain and its need to learn from errors made.

It is however, something that is difficult to regulate internally, knowing how much to learn from it without obsessing over it, and something even more difficult for those with depressive disorders who get caught up in obsessive counterfactual thinking (thinking about things that have not happened or aren't factual).

To overcome this kind of thinking and absorb the learning, practicing metacognition allows us to examine the elements of the decision and outcome without being consumed by the emotions of it. With a focus on the actual (non-counterfactual) realities, inner discussion, where you are not self-destructive or self-demeaning about yourself, can help in examining different ways of thinking though an issue and finding learnings from it as opposed to the negative emotions.

Learning is a skill, one we can all acquire. So far, we have discussed the skill of learning through being taught, whether that is a teacher, book, online or other source, but the learnings we can have from the experiences of everyday life are immeasurable. A skill of learning is being able to listen. In fact, you should listen far more than you talk. Treat every experience as an opportunity to learn and don't go into situations thinking you know more than everyone else. That attitude shuts off your willingness and ability to learn and turns on your ability to be shown up and taken down a peg or two. Learning is a key tenet and pillar of happiness and wellbeing because it is a part of all the ingredients. Your experience of life and wanting to better yourself is pivotal on your ability and willingness to learn.

Key Points

- Learning is a lifelong activity.
- Lifelong learning is usually a choice, self-initiated and motivated, informal, and with the purpose of achieving self-fulfilment.

- Learning is good for your cognitive skills including memory, attention, problem-solving and decision-making.
- Learning opens your mind, challenges cognitive biases and conflicts and gives you pleasure through the achievement of new things.
- Learning increases confidence, motivation, natural abilities as well as those you didn't know you had.
- All experiences should be seen as an opportunity to learn. Believing you know something already closes your mind to learning more.

GROWTH MINDSET

Growth itself contains the germ of happiness.

- Pearl S Buck, American writer and novelist

A man worked for over forty years, most of those to support a family. He worked as a clerk and then manager at a retail store for most of that time. It was not a job he would have grown up wanting to have, but he was taught; you go to school, you get an education, and you get a job. End of story. He didn't hate his job, but he didn't love it either. Well, that is not true.

By the end, he hated it, but he did it, working five days a week for decades so he could support his family and save some money in the bank. The man had several hobbies that he did in his spare time: fixing bikes, building things, and cycling, all of which he was talented at and he enjoyed. By their mid fifties, both the man and his wife had paid off their house and were able to save a little more money, finally able to buy a new car and get some nicer things for themselves and the family. When they retired, they had some money in the bank and an income from their pension and superannuation, but both were limited and less than what they had been living on. They still had to pay bills and their bank savings were earning less in interest than inflation was rising, so effectively they were losing money by having it in the bank. They had spent their entire lives working to get by, but never got ahead.

How many people can identify with this story?

How many people can identify their parents with this story?

There was a book published in 1997 called *Rich Dad, Poor Dad*[136] by Robert T. Kiyosaki in which he compared the approaches taken by his two father figures towards earning and saving money. The gist of it was that the mindset of the two fathers was different. The poor dad earned and then saved his money, whereas the rich dad used his money as a tool, putting it to work to actively grow his money. Whereas Kiyosaki applied this to the financial mindset of people, the same applies to the life mindset of people as well. There are those with fixed mindsets and those with growth mindsets.

A fixed mindset is one where a person believes their abilities are fixed. They are therefore less likely to prosper than those who have a growth mindset. The difference? A person with a growth mindset believes that their abilities can be developed and grow, rather like the rich dad's money. Similar to the Little Engine that Could's, *I think I can, I think I can*, the growth mindset focuses on goals and achievement. It believes it has the ability to improve and will, as it has the motivation and belief to bounce back from failure and therefore increase its likelihood of success.

As Thomas Edison said when asked why he didn't give up on inventing the lightbulb after he had failed 10,000 times, 'I didn't fail 10,000 times, I found 10,000 ways not to do it.' A growth mindset believes that abilities can be developed through dedication, effort, and hard work. A fixed mindset sees 'effort' and 'hard work' and says, 'Yeah, nah, that's not for me. I can't do it.' They want good grades to come naturally, not with hard work. The fixed mindset thinks if they have to work hard then they aren't smart, so why bother, instead of thinking that if they work hard, they will get better. If they fail at something, they see themselves as a failure. They focus on the outcome as opposed to the learning, which will in due course provide a good outcome. With all that said, and the glowing impression of someone with a growth mindset, they, those with a growth mindset, require lots of sustained motivation and active coping mechanisms for when things don't go as planned.

> *You don't get in life what you want.*
> *You get in life who you are.*
> – Les Brown, motivational speaker

A fixed mindset is not something you can just change at the flick of a finger. A fixed mindset is like an external locus of control, except it is a locus of belief. What you are being asked to do is abandon your entire belief system, what you have been brought up to believe and how to behave since you were a child, and all at an unconscious level. And being asked to change your belief system is like being asked to change your identity. This is very difficult to do.

Do you remember when you found out that Santa Claus wasn't real? Do you have kids who still believe or maybe are starting to cotton on that maybe Santa isn't real? How do you tell them? They have spent their entire life believing that someone who lives at the North Pole comes to their house every Christmas and leaves them presents. They will know that you have lied to them, you have betrayed them, and they will never have the same trust in you that they did until then. Their whole belief system has been upended and thrown out the window. It is a hard pill to swallow, and the same goes with our fixed mindsets.

We are all born with no preconceptions about life. We are not born to think we suck at anything or have limiting beliefs about ourselves. As we grow, we start to have negative self-talk. In fact, that voice in our head can flood us with its internal monologue constantly. It is that little voice in our head that says you can't do it, you suck. That inner critic, our own little saboteur, may convince us that we don't deserve something or can't do something and essentially stop us from achieving our potential. It is not others that stop us being the best version of ourselves, in most instances, it is ourselves doing it!

We are programmed to believe we cannot change, that we are what we have been brought up to be and because this is subconsciously implanted into our psyche, we will sabotage our own attempts to break the mould.

Your teachers, friends, and other people you hold in authority have put limiting beliefs inside your head, but most of all, it is your parents.

Life is a struggle.

Things are hard.

You can't make it.

Who do you think you are?

You're not smart enough.

We'll never be rich.

Get a job.

It is not you. Once you realise it is not you, but someone else who has put these limiting thoughts inside your head, you can start the process of letting go of those beliefs and moving forward, actually caring for and loving yourself. Don't resort to an external locus of control and blame your parents. They are like you; they were brought up to believe what they taught you to believe. It is about breaking the cycle of limiting beliefs.

Start by naming your limiting belief. What is giving you a fixed mindset? Your mindset is largely created by whatever you focus on the most. It is not always easy to know what your limiting beliefs are, as they are beliefs you have had all of your life, of which you are not always consciously aware of. Listen to the voice in your head, the inner critic, and when it criticises you or tries to stop you doing something, ask why?

Actively listen to people, especially your parents, and the way they speak. What negative talk and beliefs are they feeding you without even knowing it? Think of something you want to do, but which the inner voice inside your head keeps quashing, such as investing in a start-up business, maybe even starting your own business, and mention it to others and see how they react. What are they saying? Most of us have fixed mindsets and don't even know it, but once you realise that your fixed mindset is the result of other's limiting beliefs, you can start to cast them away, creating new beliefs, beliefs that give you confidence and make the beliefs you once had, look ridiculous.

> *Some people see things as they are and say, 'Why'?*
> *I dream of things that never were*
> *and say, 'Why not?'*
> *- George Bernard Shaw*

How do we go from a fixed mindset to a growth mindset and stay there? After all, we all start projects with the intention of completing them, but the start, as well intended as it might have been, soon stutters and then comes to a complete stop and there lies another unfinished symphony.

We are negatively geared as human beings and to develop a growth mindset, we need to force ourselves to both look at and believe the positives. Fortunately, you have discovered your signature strengths. You know where your talents lie and where you are more likely to succeed. This self-awareness is one step you can use in developing a growth mindset. Coupled with knowing your strengths, you can see from the character strengths where you are not so strong, where your challenges lie. You don't need to work on these, but you do need to identify them and accept them as areas in which you do not excel. Once you have accepted this and sometimes it is hard, especially if you thought that maybe it was a strength, you open up your mind again to growth. To paraphrase the Serenity Prayer,

'Lord, grant me the serenity to accept the things I do not excel in, the courage to excel in the things I do, and the wisdom to know the difference.'

Others will not always be there to support you. They still have a fixed mindset and cannot or will not understand why you want to change. We discuss this later in the book. People with a fixed mindset generally have a 'now' mentality. They look at what works for them now instead of looking ahead into the future and what will be good for them then. They acknowledge opportunities that will benefit them now and don't want to partake in anything that will not see dividends straight away. The limiting talk will come up and the temptation to stay as you are and listen to the voices will sway you. But they are just voices.

'Stay away from negative people,' warned Einstein. 'They have a problem for every solution.' It can be a lonely and uncertain journey to walk your own path, but with time and perseverance, you will find your solution.

Acknowledge the effort you are making to achieve something and not just the results. Studies have shown that kids who are praised for the effort they make and not just the results they achieve are more likely to develop a growth mindset because they become focused on the process (the learning) rather than the result. You will too. Positive feedback aids intrinsic motivation (engaging in a behaviour where you enjoy the activity itself as opposed to extrinsic motivation where you are engaging in a behaviour in order to earn external rewards, for example money or to avoid punishment.).

Your Jedi mind tricks won't work on me.
- Jabba the Hutt, Return of the Jedi (1983)

It is not easy to convince yourself out of something you have believed all of your life, no matter how many times you tell yourself otherwise. Your mind is full of LIEs and BS. These are acronyms for Limited Ideas Entertained (LIEs) and Belief Systems (BS). You allow limited ideas to permeate your belief system that aren't necessarily true, but you give your time and energy to them. Change the way you look at things. Switch your way of thinking 180 degrees. Instead of thinking you have failed, think you are still learning, you have just not mastered it yet. 'Yet' implies it is ongoing, still to be learned, so when you haven't learned something, you have not failed, you just haven't master it yet.

Value the process as opposed to the end result and enjoy the learning, not getting it over and done with. Instead of asking questions, 'Why am I in a dead-end job?', ask positive questions like 'How can I get out of this job?' As we have discussed, you will start thinking of solutions and the questions will direct your focus. Just don't allow your fixed mindset to squash your ideas before they have even taken form.

Stop and reflect on what you have learned each day and not just on what you have achieved. This is especially important in the workplace. It is not always easy to appreciate learnings when you have deadlines, but by doing so, you are increasing both your growth mindset and your value because by reflecting you are putting in place longer term memories and therefore increasing your knowledge and skills.

Remember, the brain is a muscle and to be effective, like a muscle, it needs to be flexed and worked out. Learning is the brain's way of having a workout. Also remember that you can't learn everything straight away. Some things are harder and take more time than others, so allow yourself time and extra effort to get to your desired result. Things change as well. How and what you learned may no longer be the same.

As an example, look at the way children do mathematics compared to the way their parents learned. The way they do multiplication and fractions is completely different to the way their parents were taught and when the children ask for help, the parents are like an old dog, too old to learn new tricks, and resort to the way they were taught, confusing the children even more, even if the old way is the better and easier way – at least, in their opinion. The children's way just seems too difficult and as hard as it is for older people to relearn (they likely have neither the desire nor inclination), they have to for them. Changing your mindset is in the doing. Like cultivating a garden, it takes time, patience, persistence, and effort.

The subject of mindset is enormous. There are hundreds of books on the subject and we will cover it more in the final part of the book on how to build habits as, in order to make sure what you learn in this book lasts beyond the turning of the final page, you need to know how to develop habits and a growth mindset in your life on an ongoing basis.

Changing your mindset from fixed to growth is an ongoing effort. The more you do it, the easier it becomes and still, it takes a conscious effort for a long time. Like letting go of Santa Claus, letting go of lifelong held beliefs means rewriting a painful past. Think of the things you have identified from your past that have been limiting your beliefs. Think also of the things you may have done that have caused you to limit your beliefs. Maybe things where you have embarrassed yourself and the shame has stayed with you ever since. Maybe you had to do school athletics and came last, maybe kids called you fat, or you fell over and people laughed at you. The options are limitless, just as the remedies for them are. Don't bury them in the past, subconsciously allowing them to stop you being a better you. Own them. We all did dumb, embarrassing things when we were younger but instead of allowing them to limit your future, share them as anecdotes of how you were but are not any longer. Rewrite your past. Stories like that can be cathartic as well as good laugh for everyone as you no longer make it personal.

Another way to look at your fixed mindset is to associate it with pain. Look at your limiting beliefs and what they are doing to you in the here and now. Look at what you are missing out on and change the neuro-association you have to feel pain and discomfort. For example, your fixed mindset may be preventing you from interacting socially with others and instead you stay home alone on a Saturday night, missing out on spending time with friends, having fun, and potentially meeting your future partner. They are having a good time while you are watching an Agatha Christie movie marathon on TV.[137] Screw that. Feel the envy. Hate your mindset. Hate it so much you want to change. Then make that change.

As you develop your growth mindset, associate your identity with it. When you learn new things, take pride in it and share what you have learned with others. When you overcome a limiting belief, take pleasure in what you have achieved. Start associating enjoyment with opportunities that give you growth. Opportunities are often not transparent. Whereas you might have stayed inside watching the Agatha Christie movie marathon, going to a social event or work party might end up changing your life. Sometimes it is the events we would usually pass up that end up sending our lives in positive new directions.

Get excited about learning more and expanding your horizons. Learning is a major factor in moving from a fixed to a growth mindset. Reframe your negative thoughts, coming up with reasons to push on instead of reasons to fail. Be excited about breaking new bounds and learning new things. See failure as a chance to learn, not a chance to quit. Persevere with growing, changing a little every day. Building new neural pathways takes time and repetition.

In his book, *Jonathan Livingstone, Seagull*, author Richard Bach shows the power and attributes of ambition, hard work, and curiosity. The story celebrates the power of self-belief and voyaging into the unknown and trusting yourself to obtain your desires while at the same time acting as a guide for others to follow so they too can achieve growth. That is what you can be to others when you move from a fixed mindset to a growth mindset. Push the boundaries that you have imposed upon yourself. Expect more of yourself. Challenge the negative thoughts and beliefs you have, replacing them with positive thoughts and embrace your curiosity and ambition and then allow others to follow in your wake.

A growth mindset will give you increased self-esteem. It is a continuous sense of respect for and belief in yourself. It isn't so much about how much self-confidence you have or even how you are perceived by others, but how much confidence you have in yourself to manage your life. With increased self-esteem you are in control of yourself and you no longer feel the need to compare yourself to others or feel superior to them in order to feel good about yourself, only who you were. After all, you are only working to be better than you were yesterday. Self-esteem gives you the confidence and sense that knowing everything will be alright even in the face of challenge and adversity. It is not so much a sense of 'She'll be right' but a belief that you can manage your destiny and if the proverbial shit hits the fan and everything starts to fall apart, you can find a way to put it all back together again. You are alright because you are capable of making things all right.

The things you think about determine the quality of your mind. Your soul takes on the colour of your thoughts.

- Marcus Aurelius

Key Points

- There are two mindsets: Fixed Mindset and Growth Mindset.

- A fixed mindset is one where a person believes their abilities are fixed.
- A person with a growth mindset believes that their abilities can be developed and grow.
- Limiting beliefs come from those around you, such as your parents and teachers.
- By naming your limiting beliefs, you can start to overcome them.
- Understand what you can and cannot control and focus on the things you can control.
- Focus on the effort you make and not the results. This will help to build a growth mindset.
- Stop and reflect on what you have learned each day and not just on what you have achieved.
- Changing your mindset from fixed to growth is an ongoing effort. The more you do it, the easier it becomes and still, it takes a conscious effort for a long time.
- As you develop your growth mindset, associate your identity with it. When you learn new things, take pride in it and share what you have learned with others.

KINDNESS

A Lion lay asleep in the forest, his great head resting on his paws. A timid little Mouse came upon him unexpectedly, and in her fright and haste to get away, ran across the Lion's nose. Roused from his nap, the Lion laid his huge paw angrily on the tiny creature to kill her.

"Spare me!" begged the poor Mouse. "Please let me go and some day I will surely repay you."

The Lion was much amused to think that a Mouse could ever help him. But he was generous and finally let the Mouse go.

Some days later, while stalking his prey in the forest, the Lion was caught in the toils of a hunter's net. Unable to free himself, he filled the forest with his angry roaring. The Mouse knew the voice and quickly found the Lion struggling in the net. Running to one of the great ropes that bound him, she gnawed it until it parted, and soon the Lion was free.

"You laughed when I said I would repay you," said the Mouse. "Now you see that even a Mouse can help a Lion."

No act of kindness, no matter how small, is ever wasted.

– Aesop

The act of giving is like a mirror. You make someone feel good because of your act of kindness and it reflects back on you. The act gives you a sense of wellbeing and happiness as well. Think of Christmas time when you are giving presents to others. Many times, the feeling you get from giving is better than the one you get from receiving a gift. It is better to give than to receive[iii]If you have money, there are ways to spend it that will make you feel happy beyond the time it takes to eat your favourite food or appreciate the expensive coat you purchased. Buying for others can and does make you feel good. Just remember to make sure to give within your means. It is all well and good to get a buzz from seeing the look on someone's face when you buy them a gift, but it isn't worth you paying for it for the next few months or even years. Give but give within your means.

Aside from the feeling you get from being kind to someone else, their gratitude also makes you feel good. Being kind improves your heart rate and circulation, enabling you to process more blood efficiently as well as reducing hypertension. Your heart expands and relieves pressure when you are kind.

In a study [iv]done by David Cregg and Jennifer Cheavens at the Ohio State University, it was found that the act of helping someone else can cure or alleviate symptoms of depression in the person doing the helping. Suffice to say, the act of helping someone else is also an act that helps yourself.

Everybody likes a compliment.

– Abraham Lincoln, American President

Research[138] also shows that doing small acts of kindness throughout the day can provide a significant boost against the impacts of stress. The more you can be of service and help others, the better your mental health will be. Those who participated in the research reported higher levels of resilience to daily stressors, as evidenced by higher levels of positive emotion and self-evaluations on their mental health. The gestures don't need to be big. Simply opening a door for someone or saying hello, is enough to improve your mood as well as providing a layer of emotional protection.

Random acts of kindness can make the biggest difference. Of course, you can plan acts of kindness, but it is those that are not planned, those that pop up when the opportunity presents itself that make for the most happiness. Be wary though, not to fall into the habit of doing the same act of kindness. Much like anything else, your brain gets used to it and the feel-good hit you get dissipates and then disappears. Vary it up and try new things. It doesn't have to be a grand gesture. In fact, at any one time in our society, one in five people are feeling lonely, that's twenty per cent! The simple act of saying hello may be the sole act of kindness and social interaction that person gets all day, and it costs you nothing. You really don't know the positive effect you may have on someone's life just by being kind to them.

> *While others search for what they can take, a true king searches for what he can give.*
> *- Mufasa, The Lion King (1994)*

Helping others can make you feel happy, but only to a certain level. Helping someone cross the street or holding the door open for them is fine, but you cannot always make others feel happy and it's not your responsibility to do so, no matter who they are, for example, child, parent, or partner. Doing so will only serve the purpose of making you feel unhappy. If that someone is unhappy or depressed or an addict, do what you can, but don't take all the responsibility as you need to look after yourself too. Accept their unhappiness and don't blame yourself for it.

Give them different options to be happy, but don't make yourself the only option they have for happiness as you need your own happiness too. Be happy you did what you could do and don't feel guilty you couldn't do more. There is only so much that you can do. People need to take responsibility for their own happiness and it shouldn't be at the cost of yours.

Our society is known for being very individualistic and isolationist as opposed to group and community based. Everyone strives to be better and have more, competing for jobs, attention, 'likes' and recognition. Everybody feels they have to be in control, be protective of themselves, and their perception of themselves and the world, whereas we know that there is only so much that we can control and we need to accept that.

Still, showing kindness can be seen as a sign of weakness, that you are a pushover, even naive, instead of what it is – simple kindness. This all stems from our negative bias, albeit unconscious, where it is easier to be mean and stoic and not being seen as emotional and soft. There are two great examples of this: Superman and Batman. Superman, in his blue and red outfit, is kind, friendly, and truthful, a symbol of hope and justice for all, whereas Batman, in his black outfit, is dark, harsh, unfriendly, fearsome, and violent. Already, we see Superman as the kind superhero, even his alter ego, Clark Kent, is this way, soft and nice. Batman is hard, unyielding, and abrasive. Regardless of which you prefer, the comparisons are stark.

Because of our negative bias and the lack of trust endemic in our society, acts of kindness are often viewed with suspicion. Why are you being kind? Why aren't you looking out for yourself first? What do you really want?

As Marcus Aurelius said, 'Some people, when they do someone a favour, are always looking for a chance to call it in. And some aren't, but they're still aware of it – still regard it as a debt. But others don't even do that. They're like a vine that produces grapes without looking for anything in return.'[139]

The irony is that although kindness is seen as a weakness by many, it is really a strength. It demonstrates a level of emotional and psychological strength and resilience. The benefits of kindness far outweigh the costs and, as much as the perceived weaknesses of kindness have been emphasised, it is not something we encounter in most situations. Most see kindness for what it is and are grateful when the act of kindness is given.

> *An argument arose between the wind and the sun about who was the stronger of the two. They decided to settle the issue by seeing who could be the first to get a passing traveller to take off his cloak. The wind blew with all his might, but the harder the wind blew, the tighter the traveller grasped his cloak and wrapped it around himself. The sun then shone its soft, kind rays and as the traveller felt its friendly warmth, he removed his cloak. The sun won the argument.*
>
> *- Aesop*

Kindness is a great persuader. People respond more favourably to kindness and persuasion than they do, brute force, whether that be physical or verbal. If you want something from someone, you are better off being calm, humble, and kind, as people will respond to kind words over angry yelling. Kindness, as the saying goes, is the language that the deaf can hear and the blind can see. Be to others, as you would have them be to you.

As much as we should be kind to others, we also need to be kind to ourselves. Once we start to look after and be kind to ourselves, we will more naturally treat others the same. So many times, you will find yourself being kind and of service to others, usually family or close friends, without reciprocation. You can become lost in the service of others and do little to help or be kind to yourself.

Being kind to ourselves is not as easy as it sounds. How many times do we sabotage ourselves with negative thinking? You need to get over it and forgive yourself; we all make mistakes. You need to accept yourself for who you are. To do this you need to look at yourself and show some self-compassion. This is self-care. It is turning away from the bad habits of becoming self-critical (fighting with yourself), abandoning and not confronting issues (running away), as well as getting stuck in the 'why me?' loop of thinking (freezing), which can lead to all kinds of mental health problems.

Using self-compassion, you can use comforting words with yourself, take a nap, or do some breathing meditation, acknowledging when you are having trouble, and talking to someone you trust. It is not what you do, but why you do it. Acknowledging your concerns and addressing them, even to yourself, asking questions, gets your subconscious thinking of solutions. When you are at peace with yourself, you will open up the doors for joy in your life, and consequently be able to bring joy and kindness into the lives of others.

> *You know, the ancient Egyptians had a beautiful belief about death. When their souls got to the entrance to heaven, the guards asked two questions. Their answers determined whether they were able to enter or not.*
>
> *'Have you found joy in your life?'*
>
> *'Has your life brought joy to others?'*
>
> *-The Bucket List (2007)*

Key Points

- The act of giving is like a mirror. You make someone feel good because of your act of kindness and it reflects back on you.
- Acts of kindness help boost against the impacts of stress, and improves heart rate and circulation.
- Spontaneous acts of kindness bring the most happiness.
- It is not your responsibility to make others happy. Doing so will only serve the purpose of making you feel unhappy. At some point, they need to take responsibility for their own happiness.
- Kindness can be seen as a weakness, as it stems from our negative bias, albeit unconscious, where it is easier to be mean, stoic, and untrusting, believing there is an ulterior motive.
- Kindness really is a strength. It demonstrates a level of emotional and psychological strength and resilience.
- As much as it is important to be kind to others, we also need to be kind to ourselves.

GRATITUDE

*Gratitude is not only the greatest of virtues,
but the parent of all the others.*

- Marcus Tullius Cicero

This is, of course, a quote from a man who had his head cut off, so gratitude was probably missing at that time in his life. Cicero was a Roman philosopher who lived at the same time as Julius Caesar, Augustus Caesar, and Brutus, and it was his association with the latter that caused him to lose his head. Gratitude is a grateful attitude and a feeling of thankfulness or appreciation for something. The problem is a lot of us do not even recognise when we should express gratitude, so caught up with the me, me, me attitude and chip on our shoulder that we can only see what we don't have and not what we do have.

It is odd that gratitude, for all the benefits it offers, is so uncommon. It seems to be opposed to our human traits and need for control. How can we show gratitude to someone when it makes us look weak, that we are not in control, and need help and support? We like to credit ourselves for success and blame others for failure. It is almost as if showing gratitude is an attack on our ego when it is, in fact, a sign of our emotional maturity. Charles Dickens said, 'Reflect upon your present blessings, of which every man has many, not your past misfortunes, of which all men have some.' And that is it. If you love someone, tell them; if you are thankful to someone for something, tell them.

In the case of marriage, you may have been with your partner for twenty years. Over time, you get used to one another and don't express or perhaps even realise how grateful you are to them and what they do for you and bring into your life. Gratitude is best when it is unexpected and writer G.K. Chesterton summed it up nicely when he said, '... I hope it is not pompous to call [this] the chief idea of my life; I will not say the doctrine I have always taught, but the doctrine I should always have liked to teach. That is the idea of taking things with gratitude, and not taking things for granted.'[140]

Things are taken for granted because you do it all the time, having become lazy and going through the motions and meeting expectation, such as giving the children's teacher a bottle of wine at the end of the school year, or your mum a bouquet of flowers on her birthday. It is not gratitude, it is simply appreciation. Still, not a bad thing, but gratitude comes with surprise or genuine emotion and feeling to the benefactor.

People struggle with gratitude as they struggle with the idea of knowing what they are grateful for. The truth is that everyone could come up with a dozen things they are grateful for. How? Instead of focusing on what we don't have, it is recognising the things that we do.

> *It is said our lives on this Earth are brief and filled with insufferable anguish. But there's a way to avoid all the trials and tribulations of mortal existence. Those who know this secret are always merry and forever blessed with good fortune. They are well-loved and welcomed.*
>
> *A very wise old man once told me if you carry a pocketful of this magic ingredient with you, you'll never go hungry and you'll never want for laughter, music and good company.*
>
> *The secret that unlocks all these wonders is a simple one.*

Gratitude.

- Caiseal Mor, King of the Blind

Like kindness, expressing gratitude doesn't just make the recipient feel good, it makes you feel good too. The feeling of gratitude focuses you on the positive things in your life. The fact is, the experience of gratitude can lower your stress levels and increase your mood. Consequently, it can have physical health effects, including the strengthening of your immune system and the lowering of your blood pressure.

Gratitude can make you feel a stronger connection with people, which itself has many positive benefits. Gratitude doesn't always have to be about being grateful to other people, it is also about a wider appreciation of your life. When we are healthy, it is hard to be truly grateful for our good health as we take it for granted. It is only when we get sick or have an accident that we appreciate how good we had it. Gratitude is counting your blessings for, as the expression goes, 'There is always someone worse off than you.' At times, that can be hard to believe, but just saying to yourself the things you are grateful for, no matter how small or seemingly insignificant, can improve your wellbeing as described above. Believing is receiving.

How do we make the most of this ingredient?

Start each day by thinking of things you are grateful for. It may be as simple as your health and your family and their good health, and the opportunities you will have today to make a difference and be the person you want to be.

You can also start by writing things down that you're grateful for. Aim for three things you are grateful for per day. The simple act of writing things down for which you are grateful, let's call it a Gratitude Journal, will make you look for things to be grateful for and before long, you will actively become more grateful. In your household, as an example, at dinnertime, you could ask those you dine with what they were grateful for during the day. At first, they may struggle to come up with anything, and remember, expressing gratitude doesn't have to be some grandiose gesture, it can be a simple 'Thank you', which might mean nothing to you but might make someone else's day. In time, if you keep asking the question, you will start getting great examples of gratitude as people will start actively being grateful and of course, in turn, you will start seeing what you too are grateful for and hopefully you will all strive to express gratitude in your lives.

With practice, this can become a great way to feel happiness and wellbeing in your life. Just remember to be honest in your gratitude, mean what you say and do to express gratitude to others. Authenticity is key in your pursuit of happiness.

How to practice gratitude.

1. What was the best thing that happened to you today?
2. Who am I most grateful for today and why?
3. What am I most looking forward to most about tomorrow?

According to the Resilience Project,[141] in 21 days, you will rewire your brain to start scanning the world for positive, becoming three times more likely to notice positives.

In 42 days:

- Less likely to get sick.
- Have higher levels of energy.
- Feel happier.
- Be more enthusiastic.

- More focused.
- More determined.
- More optimistic.
- Have a better quality of sleep.
- Have lower levels of depression and anxiety.

Gratitude and kindness go hand in hand, kindness preceding each act of gratitude. An act of genuine kindness should result in an equal act of gratitude if we allow ourselves to lower our guard and accept it. Real gratitude is a rare attribute, succinctly summed up in the Aesop fable of an escaped slave who pulled a thorn from the paw of a lion when he had sought shelter in a cave.

Time passed and the slave was recaptured. He was to be fed to the lions at the Colosseum. In front of a crowd of thousands, the lions were released. Bounding out of cages, the lions roared and ran towards the slave. However, upon recognising the slave who showed him kindness, the lion fawns all over the slave, rubbing up against him, licking his face and protecting him. 'Gratitude' concluded Aesop, 'is the sign of noble souls.'

*My wish for you is that you are happy
with what you've got.*

- Jack, Three Wishes (1995)

Key Points

- Gratitude is appreciating what you have and not what you don't.
- Showing gratitude demonstrates emotional maturity.
- Gratitude comes with surprise or genuine emotion and feeling to the benefactor.

- The feeling of gratitude focuses you on the positive things in your life.
- To increase your gratitude, start writing down things you are grateful for in a journal. Over time, you will start looking for things to be grateful for.

SOCIAL CONNECTION

Happiness is only real when shared.
- Into the Wild (2007)

They have sent another rocket into space to release a probe to explore the universe. The cost is hundreds of millions of dollars, perhaps even billions, as this isn't the first one. They are looking for other life in the universe. It doesn't matter if it is an alien being like ET or just microbes. They just want to find life. With all that we have accomplished as a race, all the conquests, the advances in our understanding of life and ourselves, the dominance we have attained over all other living things, we will go to almost any expense to show that we are not alone, that we belong to something bigger.

Everybody wants to belong, to be a part of something. A sense of belonging is a sense of one's own identity. Whether it is within yourself, another person, a group or a place, everybody wants to belong, to know that they are not alone in how they feel, what they believe, or who they are. Belonging bridges the gap between you as the insecure, emotionally inept loner and you as the assured, happier, driven person. Whether you belong because of a shared interest, belief, or mindset, you are, as part of that sense of belonging, a stronger, healthier, and more humane human being.

Our search for belonging begins within each of us. We identify with our family, our roots, and customs – our heritage. We feel at home with who we are, where we have come from, and where we are going. A sense of belonging on this level brings a sense of accomplishment and confidence. We are a part of something that is bigger than we are, but is who we are at the same time.

Belonging then becomes more layered as we leave the bounds of ourselves and weave through the tapestry of connections outside our front door. The social and cultural communities we are a part of lead us to who we are and aspire to be as individuals. We are a part of something bigger. As we extend ourselves, we increase our sense of belonging to others and can respect what gives them a sense of belonging, feeling a sense of belonging ourselves in many cases. We can take responsibility, honouring the values, concerns, and interests of others, as they are, at the end of the day, our own. The search for belonging is lifelong and if all goes well throughout our lives, we will weave an ever-larger tapestry of belonging of which we are a part so that in the end we can feel that sense of belonging and feel at home no matter where we are.

The problem many of us have with social connection is the society we have been brought up in. We are social creatures by design, but our society conflicts with this because it praises the virtues of individuality and freedom, pushing us to better ourselves as individuals, not as part of the whole. Most of us don't know what we want or who we are and or what we are supposed to do with our lives but we plough on, becoming lonely and having no-one to turn to, distrusting of others, with a crisis of meaning in our lives.

Loneliness is isolation and feeling that you are alone and having to figure all this stuff out for yourself. Loneliness and conflict become partners in crime. Research has found a neural connection between the experience of loneliness and being attracted to human conflict.[142] The adage, 'Misery loves company' rings true as those who feel socially isolated seek out conflict.

Think of a typical office or cantankerous elderly neighbour.

They always seem to find something or someone to hate and argue with or about. Feeling isolated means we feel we have no-one to turn to in order to feel connected but ironically the chances are that others are feeling the same way as you are. David Brooks in his book, *The Second Mountain*,[143] believes that there are two figurative mountains in life separated by the Valley of Despair. The first is the mountain of individuality and the second is the mountain of commitment. They represent the two paths you can take in life. Most of us take the first one, but he believes we should be pursuing the second, which offers a committed purpose-driven life of togetherness and meaning; that putting the needs of the community ahead of yourself is what matters and gives your life meaning and purpose and a better future for everyone.

A study started in 1938 at Harvard University, called the Harvard Study of Adult Development[144], initially tracked 724 US men made up of a mix of Harvard students and low-income workers in Boston. The aim of the study was to determine what makes a good life, and instead of stopping after a period of time, the study has continued to this day, tracking the same people and their families, now up to three generations. After thousands of questions and hundreds of measurements, including bloods and brain scans, it has come to down one thing, just one, that has more effect on both mental and physical health, as well as longevity than anything else – good relationships. Quality, strong social connections are what strengthen us against the trials and tribulations of life. It doesn't matter if you are rich, poor, single, or married, if you have good relationships with others, you are happier and healthier.

Innately, we know social connection is important to our wellbeing, yet many of us still resist it, lamenting the change we would have to endure, opening ourselves up to others and possibly to ourselves and the way we truly feel. But even if you are stuck on a deserted island with only a ball called 'Wilson' for company, you need social connection.

Our children innately understand this. If you ask them what the most important thing is to them, they will say their family and friends. This is not to say you need many social connections, in fact, it is the quality of the connection that matters, not the quantity of connections. Social media is a key social tool, although it could be argued that it isn't really a social tool at all and could, in fact, be the exact opposite. Nevertheless, for all its cons, social media does act as an important tool for social connection. For many youths, it is the primary form of contact they have with their friends and has proved invaluable, especially during times of crisis, for keeping in contact with friends and family.

It provides a gateway for those who would otherwise be unable or unwilling to be part of a social group, even if that social group is otherwise unaware of each other. This could be through the sharing of posts with friends, real or otherwise, the sharing of photos, videos, and memes, among many others.

The most concerning part of social media is its ability to allow people to be bullied on a global scale and especially among youth, who live vicariously through their social media accounts. This can have devastating consequences as well as give unrealistic expectations on those who think life is what they see on social media and that they could be the next social media influencer, or star. Social media is very much a juxtaposition of the words 'social connection'. The way the algorithms are set up on social media channels makes the likelihood that your friends and followers will see your posts increasingly remote. Only a tiny fraction, about 2% of people that follow you on Facebook, as an example, will see your post and even less will engage with it.

I never liked you, and I always will.
- Samuel Goldwyn, Film Producer

Some of you may be saying, 'But I'm not a social person. I hate socialising.' It is a common feeling. Having to make small talk, God, you would rather someone just shoot you now. You don't follow a football team, don't care about whatever reality TV show people are talking about, and let's not even get started on the weather.

The problem with being socially isolated, made worse when it is a choice (which for many it isn't), is that it is a major risk factor for mortality. (Holt-Lunstad, 2015)[145] The fact is that you don't have to be the extroverted socialite, going to parties and every social event under the sun, you just need to find something that interests you – your Signature Strengths – and find like-minded people. We live in the digital age, so there are tonnes of easy ways to find people with the same interests as you. Go online and search for social groups. A good one is **meetup.com**, which has groups related to almost every subject you can think of and if you can't find one you like, or there are none local to where you live, you can start one yourself.

> *Really, you don't need someone to complete you.*
> *You only need someone to completely accept you.*
>
> *– Rapunzel, Tangled (2010)*

We all need a friend. As the 1980s movie classic starring Bud Hill and Terrence Spencer tells us, *Who Finds a Friend, Finds a Treasure*. It is true. Having someone you can share your experiences with is much better than doing it alone. A true friend is worth more than money. Experiences bring much more happiness than material things. Sharing those experiences that you can then reflect on later makes them even more special and happier.

A lot of us work and that is the major social connection

we have each day away from our families. Think about it. You probably spend more of your day with your work colleagues than you do with your family. But how many people that you work with do you really know? Now, many people go to work for that purpose only – to work. They aren't interested in sharing their 'real life' with work colleagues. That is fine.

That said, we are human beings and by default we are social creatures. You don't need to know your work colleagues' life stories and they don't need to know yours; just being in the company of other people is good, being socially connected. Saying 'hello' and smiling at someone each morning can make a world of difference and you wouldn't even know it. Challenge yourself to talk to a stranger. It could be as simple as a 'hello' in the street or striking up a conversation at the bus stop, train station or water cooler, you name it.

That may sound like a scary prospect and fill you with apprehension. After all, they might think you are some kind of creep or that you are trying to hit on them. The fact is, however, research, and there has been plenty of it done by many specialists in the field of positive psychology, shows that 'talking to strangers makes us happy. Even if you are reluctant to talk to a stranger, you and the stranger get a happiness boost after talking to each other. Sharing experiences with another person makes them better.'[146] So, what to do? Start small. Smile. Simple. When walking past someone, just smile at them as you pass. Not some suggestive, 'hey, how you doing?' smile, or over the top, toothy smile, just a simple smile. Work up to a 'hi' as well and then, with people you are familiar with or see often but don't really know, such as at the supermarket checkout or someone you work with, start with inoffensive conversation. The weather is an easy one even though it is completely banal, but generally won't offend anyone, which seems so easy to do these days.

Then, once you get your confidence up and see how easy it

is to do and that it does make you feel happier, you can start working up to talking with complete strangers. Contrary to what we are led to believe, most people welcome having someone greet them or ask how they are doing (unless they are in a shop and it is a sales assistant asking every thirty seconds!).

One of our ingredients for happiness is kindness. You could mix social connection with kindness and volunteer - give back to the community. A supportive social network in the form of community groups and participation in their social activities gives you social connection. Examples of community groups include the church, service clubs, and professional or political associations. Maybe you are a stay-at-home parent, retired, unemployed, or want to get away from the television at night after working all day. Community groups are always looking for people to help them out and are a great avenue to meeting new people with similar interests to yourself.

Remember, you need to take care of yourself, and being socially connected is a critical part of that. People matter more than things. We all know that, but sometimes we seem to forget which is more important. Talk to people. Just be in their company. It is very therapeutic for all. At the end of your day or, in fact, whenever during the day, tell people what you have been up to, listen to what they have been up to, give, share, and support others.

> *Happiness quite unshared can scarcely be called happiness; it has no taste.*
> *- Charlotte Brontë*

There is a joke that people chose marriage and children over wealth and freedom, but the truth is that we are drawn to find a partner so that we have someone to share life with, the good times and the bad times and everything else in-between.

A relationship with someone, however, does not fill a void in your life. You need to be happy with yourself before you can be happy with someone else. Therefore, a relationship is not about receiving and expecting from your partner or friend, but giving.

Nurture your talents, which your ideal partner will appreciate, give them the best of you and be free to be yourself. Appreciation of your partner's talents and personality should complement you and build a stronger relationship. Research done by the University of Chicago's National Opinion Research Center (NORC)[147] between the 1970s and 1990s found that 40% of married couples said they were 'very happy' compared to about 25% of those who had never married. People who are in committed, happy and stable relationships tend to be happier but this comes with the caveat that you need to choose a partner wisely because if you get it wrong, divorce makes everyone miserable and even worse are those that stay in an unhappy relationship.

He chose... poorly.

- Knight guardian, Indiana Jones and the Last Crusade (1989)

Our choice of friends is important. Some will be there for the long run and some just passing through. Some people are part of your journey and not your destination. Make friends with those who want the best for you, remembering that friendship is a reciprocal arrangement and you have the want the best for them as well. It is not selfish to choose people who make you better, nor is it selfish to move away from people who no longer fit your life goals and direction. The same works from their point of view as well. For example, if you are trying to quit drinking and your friends keep wanting to go to the pub or come over for a drink, where is the support and friendship? If they are not supporting your goals, they are not the best company to be around. They will only hinder your progress and development.

> *A dad was dying on his bed. He called for his son and gave him a watch. He told him the watch used to belong to his father before him and his grandfather before that and was 200 years old. He told him to take the watch to a jeweller and see what it was worth. The son did so and came back, telling his dad that the jeweller valued the watch at $150 because it was old. The dad then told him to take it to a pawnshop and see what it was worth to them. He did so, came back and told his dad that they had valued the watch at $10 because it was worn and old. The dad then told the son to take it to a museum and see what they thought it was worth. He did so and came back, saying they had valued the watch at $500,000. The dad then said to his son, 'This shows you that you have to know your value and worth and not accept those that don't value you.'*
>
> *- Unattributed modern fable*

After reading this book, you may choose to better your life, which will require change. By doing so, you make it known to others that there are things missing from your current life that you want to change so you can have a better future. Friends may not like this. They will want you to stay with the status quo, to stick within your comfort zone, and be with them in theirs. You are highlighting not only the inadequacy of your current circumstances, but also theirs. They may no longer value you or support your need to develop and grow as a person. You are ready to move on, whereas they are not.

Leaving can and will be difficult. You will be alone and your brain will resist the change, as will your friends, but remember that growth requires you to leave your comfort zone and enter the unknown because it is there that experience and your destiny lie. A true friend is someone you can tell a bad thing to and they will listen and empathise. They won't judge you and say why that bad thing happened to you, that it was your fault. You can also determine a true friend when you tell them good news and they will help you celebrate. They won't say, 'Wow, that's great' and then proceed to tell you about something good that happened to them or someone else they know. They will give you your moment and genuinely celebrate it with you.

Social connection is important for our emotional wellbeing, which is why the scourge of loneliness is sad to see. Reports of a loneliness epidemic make this all the more alarming with polls saying three quarters of older people in the UK are lonely[148], many saying they can go an entire day without speaking to anyone. This is tragic, and we will all experience loneliness at some point in our lives. It can and does affect everyone.[149] Many of us do like solitude, which is the joy of being alone, which is empowering. We all require alone time to process and go through problems and issues. It is why we sleep, our body giving us timeout, removing the distractions, influences and restrictions put on us by others. Solitude allows us to develop and consider ideas, practice metacognition, reconnect with what is meaningful to us and with ourselves. While solitude is empowering, loneliness is damaging, which is why we need to put ourselves out there and develop social networks. Not all of us are able to do this, with some of us physically unable to do so and others mentally. Most of us probably know someone who is lonely and simply calling in for a cuppa or just giving them a call can make all the difference in their lives – and yours too.

> *Surround yourself with human beings, my dear James. They are easier to fight for than principles.*

- Ian Fleming, Casino Royale

Making friends is not as simple as saying 'go out and meet people.' The social networks we have are not based on our choice alone. We are all limited by the opportunities we have to meet other people, whether they are geographic, current social environment, or otherwise, which is why taking the opportunities to experience different things can lead to new friendships, opportunities, and networks. Our pool of friendship choices is generally limited to work, existing friends, family, and social clubs such as your golf club or local pub. Much of the time, we like to keep these networks separate but, in many cases, supported by research, they do tend to overlap. The Framingham Heart Study[150], one of the largest studies on emotional contagions, found that happiness is highly contagious and its effects long-lasting. It found:

1. Happiness spreads over three degrees of separation (a friend of a friend's friend, or your brother's friend's sister, and so on).
2. If you are with happy people in the near term, there is a greater likelihood that you will have future happiness.
3. Happiness is a powerful force for gluing people together, sticking together, irrespective of whether those people were similar to begin with.

So, with all of that said, how do we connect? How do we make friends, especially as adults, and gain social connections that will give us the glue of lasting happiness?

Firstly, understand that friendships don't just happen. If you believe that if it is meant to be then it will happen, then you will likely be sitting alone in five years' time, still waiting. Friendships don't happen through luck. Like all good things in life, making friends takes effort.

You need to be where the people are. It could initially be through a social network or dating site but even then, you can't be passive, like at a high school dance, waiting on someone else to make the first move. No-one likes to feel they are not in control and no-one likes rejection, but you need to take hold of the idea that you are in control more than you think and be purposeful about meeting others. It is all about perception. If you go to an event and you mingle with people, talking and listening, you are going to come away from that event thinking it was good, and the people were friendly, whereas if you go to an event and keep to yourself, you are likely going to perceive the event as bad and unfriendly, much like the house of a thousand mirrors.

Research has shown that simply 'being there,' where the people are makes you more likeable even if you don't interact with them at all.[151] People notice you and if you are there as much as they are, you become familiar and people tend to like that more than someone who turns up less often. This seems like a long way to make friends but bares out the idea that you are more likeable than you probably think. More research has found that people underestimate how much people like them.[152] So, as you stutter your way through a conversation with a stranger, feeling awkward and like an idiot, remember that the person you are talking to probably doesn't see it like you do and probably likes you.

Some people have a knack for making friends at the click of a finger. They seem to have some aura or magnetic attraction that people are drawn to. We seem to have the most friends when we are in our early twenties and they slowly decline as we age. This loss can lead to feeling down and lost, an identity crisis, as we try to work out who we are now and how we fit into the broader scheme of things with friends marrying, divorcing, dying, and moving on with their lives. If you feel or have felt like this, it is important to know that this is normal and healthy and that making new friends at different times in your life is a good thing. Friends generally are friends when you have something in common. When this thread disappears, the friendship usually isn't far behind.

In many circumstances, friendships haven't ended as much as drifted apart, for various reasons already mentioned. A key to making friendships is to rekindle old, existing friendships. It is easier than ever to find old friends through the Internet and social networks. Reminiscing about the past is a great joy, but be aware that we tend to romanticise the past and block out the bad parts. If you want to rekindle an old friendship, do so with the intention of building it into a new friendship, not one based on the past where you are unable to move forward because that will only fail and ruin your memories of when things were good together. You have changed and so have they, so consequently your friendship has to change as well.

Another key to making your interaction with people purposeful and meaningful is to act as if this may be the last time you will ever see them, much like not knowing how many more times you will see your parents again. This will change the way you interact with people. No longer falling back on the weather or other neutral subjects, you will actually get to know them and understand them, to appreciate them and let them know what they mean to you. Imagine doing that each time you caught up, what a valuable connection you would end up having with them. Your interactions would be valued and authentic, meaningful, and lasting.

Maybe you don't like socialising, perhaps it makes you feel unhappier? Believe it or not, this could be because you are really smart! In a 2016 study published in the British Journal of Psychology, it looked at the effect of friendship on people's life satisfaction and happiness levels. It found that, in general, people are happier when they spend time with their friends. However, for people who were extremely intelligent, this situation was reversed. It found that they feel unhappier and dissatisfied with their lives when spending time with other people. Now, why this is, is not clear but one theory is that smart people like to spend time alone working on their personal pursuits, while another theory posturises that from an evolutionary point of view, intelligent people don't need as much help with adaptation and adjusting to their environment so they can go it alone more easily.

Whatever the case, making new connections and new friendships is not easy, but that doesn't mean you should give up at the first hurdle or roadblock. It gets especially harder as you get older. Midlife means being settled and knowing who you are and where you fit, not having to explore and trying new things. Right? Well, no. This book is about dispelling that. Life is about experience and taking action to lead a full and meaningful life.

It is true that as you get older, you know what you do and don't like, and that makes it more difficult for you to make new friends because you are pickier and basically stubborn. You expect people to conform to your view of the world but like the person who waits for the other to make the first move, if you think that way, you too will be no better off or further forward in five years' time. You need to move, both literally and in terms of moving your expectations and barriers. Move in small steps, using your interests as a stepping-stone to meet people by joining a club, taking up a hobby with others, and if you are not outgoing, using existing friends, family and acquaintances to meet new people. When it comes to making friends, there is no-one size fits all formula or overnight friendship magic potion. Like a fine wine, developing deep and meaningful friendships takes time, and sometimes over a fine wine, deep and meaningful friendships are made.

Key Points

- Social connection comes in many forms.

- We have been bought up in a society that values independence and individuality, values that contradict social connection.
- Many people feel lonely and isolated but resist social connection.
- Connecting with people who share your values and interests works because you accept each other and what you have in common.
- Being connected with others is a critical part of self-care and emotional wellbeing.

EXERCISE

Nothing happens until something moves.

– Albert Einstein

Do you, or someone you know, relate to the following?

You wake up each morning, get out of bed, sit down and have some breakfast, if any at all. You get in the car or on a train or bus and go to work where you sit in front of a computer for about eight hours, maybe stopping for a short break to have lunch in the staff room or café or possibly at your desk. Afterwards, you get back in your car or on the bus or train and head home. You spend some time with your family, sitting down to have dinner before putting the children to bed and then sitting down in front of the television or online until it is time to go to bed where you lie down to sleep until waking up again the next morning and doing it all again.

This is a simple example of a typical week for many people, with the weekends a little less structured but still relatively idle.

Did you notice how much sitting or lying down was in a typical day? From lying in bed for eight hours to sitting down for breakfast, sitting in the car, sitting behind a desk, and then sitting again in the car before sitting down for dinner and then sitting down in front of the television before doing the same thing over all over again. Life is very sedentary. And it is so easy to be so these days. We don't even have to leave the couch to change the channel, no longer have to get out of the car to open the garage or leave the house to get groceries or dinner. Everything comes to us. We don't have to move.

This information is very concerning. A study[153] done in the United Kingdom in 2017 by the non-profit organisation, *UK Active*, found that adults spend an average of three hours and nine minutes on the toilet each week, compared to one hour and 30 minutes of physical activity during the same time period. In other words, people spend more time taking a shit than giving a shit about their physical health. Now, that is shit!

Modern humans spend far too much time sitting and not enough time moving. We are bipedal and have two legs for a reason: to move. Moving is important, if for nothing more than to keep our heart pumping effectively. Believe it or not, even though your heart is a pump, it needs help from other parts of the body to keep it supplied with sufficient quantities of blood. For example, the muscles in your legs act as a pump when they contract, so when you sit for too long, you aren't doing much good for your blood circulation. When you get up from sitting, move around so your legs muscles can contract and pump blood around. Take into consideration gravity and helping get blood back up to the heart. Moving around helps your heart, which helps your health. Any way you look at it, sitting for too long, as many of us now do, is bad for our health.

Fortunately, there is a very simple fix, something so quick and easy that it will greatly improve your health. In fact, the benefits are astounding, to say the least. Exercise is a quick and easy way to both physical and mental good health.

There is a tonne of evidence from a huge number of studies on the benefits of exercise. The general medical consensus is that exercise:

- Increases life expectancy.
- Reduces the risk of a stroke.

- Lowers the risk of heart disease.
- Lowers the risk or slows down the onset of dementia.
- Reduces the risk of breast and colon cancers.
- Lowers the risk of osteoarthritis and osteoporosis.
- Increases self-esteem.
- Boosts energy levels.
- Manages weight.
- Lowers stress levels.
- Elevates mood.
- Lowers the risk of type 2 diabetes.
- Enhances quality of sleep.
- Boosts good cholesterol.
- Improves body tone.
- Strengthens joints, muscles, and bones.
- Prevents constipation.
- Reduces the risk of suffering from depression.
- Prevents impotence.
- Reduces levels of aggression.

In a nutshell, exercise is good for you and it works. Moreover, it doesn't have to be that difficult. You don't need to be at the gym every day, pumping iron or working up a sweat, spending your hard earned money on a membership. Exercise is something you can do anytime, anywhere, and the biggest commitment you have to make is time. In fact, it doesn't even have to be that strenuous. Results can be achieved from the simple task of walking for only thirty minutes a day, around three hours per week.

As much as walking is a good exercise for your physical

health, it is also good exercise for your brain, stimulating the production of neurotrophic factors, molecules that cultivate the creation of new neurons and synapses, which as we know are critical to wellbeing. Associated with this is the benefit of simply getting outside and being in the daylight. Research has shown that getting outside each day, especially in the morning, even just for a few minutes, stimulates dopamine production in your brain, which as we know is the feel-good chemical.

What it also does it set a clock for about sixteen hours later to help you get to sleep. Quite the opposite happens when you stay up late, meaning between 11pm and 4am, with lights on, whether they be screens, TV, computer, phone, or house lights. This light limits the production of dopamine for up to two days, so if you do this regularly, you are setting yourself up to feel anxious and depressed, not to mention your energy levels will be very low. Set a goal to walk every day for at least thirty minutes. This simple exercise has huge benefits, not least of which is the mood benefits of just twenty minutes of exercise can last for 12 hours.[154]

Healthy Body + Healthy Mind = Happy Life.

People who exercise regularly have a better sense of wellbeing. They are more energetic during the day and sleep better at night. They have sharper memories and feel more relaxed and positive about their lives as well as themselves. People who exercise have better mental health and research has shown that exercising just three times per week works just as well as Zoloft for the recovery of depression.[155]

Perhaps, you still think exercise takes up too much time, that you don't have enough to make this ingredient a viable option for your wellbeing recipe. Think again. Exercise is critical to both your physical and mental health. The benefits listed above should more than compensate for the short amount of time you spend exercising and of course, there is nothing to stop you mixing it up and listening to some music or a podcast as you exercise. To keep you motivated, so you don't quit, exercise with a friend. If walking, it is someone to chat to. If you are working, do a walking meeting with your colleagues or walk with a colleague at lunchtime. It is easy to put into your schedule if you really want to.

Michael Mosley[156] of intermittent fasting fame, did research into the most time effective exercises that could be done and still be effective and produce measurable benefits, and came up with the following options.

1. Ten minutes of brisk walking, three times a day, three days per week. We have all been led to believe that doing 10,000 steps a day is what we should be aiming for. Unfortunately, there is no science behind this. With the advent of fitness trackers, it has never been easier to do, so its popularity has increased. What has been found, however, is that it when most people are doing their 10,000 steps, they are just meandering, wandering, not actually pushing themselves, and that is the key. The important thing is to get the heart rate up, so walking briskly for ten minutes, three times a day is the way to go.

2. Twenty seconds of full-on cycling, three times a day, three days a week. This is so easy it almost seems ridiculous that it could work. It works best if you have an exercise bike as opposed to a real bike as the object is to cycle as fast as you can for twenty seconds, have a breather for a couple of minutes, and then cycle for all you are worth for a further twenty seconds. Do it again a third time and you have done one minute in all of intense cycling activity. Do this three times per week. In other words, intensive exercise for three minutes a week! This exercise should improve your aerobic fitness as well as reduce the amount of glycogen (sugar) in your muscles, which will trigger other

beneficial changes, such as improved cardiovascular health.

3. Lifting weights until you cannot lift them any longer, three times a week.
Instead of lifting heavy weights in sets, lift both heavy and light weights but until you can no longer lift them. Curl a heavy weight with your right arm until you can no longer do so, then do the same with your left arm. Do the same with the light weights on both arms. You only have to do this once per session. You can also do this with your legs. If you don't have any heavy weights, don't worry, light weights mean you will be able to curl them for longer. You should see an increase in arm strength on both sides (and leg strength too). In a study, arm strength was increased by 18% and leg strength by 25%.

These are high intensity interval training (HIIT) exercises and in as little as six weeks, you should see improvements in your health. As with any exercise, you need to listen to your body. When exercising, you should feel mild tension but not pain. Pain is your body telling you that it is at risk of being damaged so listen to your body and stop. Also, with any pain or exercise, check with your doctor or GP first to make sure it is right for you.

Key Points

1. Exercise is one of those things we know we should do but many of us don't or don't do enough.
2. Our society is increasingly immobile with a study finding that more people in the UK spend time on the toilet than they do exercising.
3. The benefits of even just a little bit of exercise are phenomenal for both physical and mental good

health.
4. HIIT exercises don't take up a lot of time and can help maintain a healthy body.
5. People who exercise regularly have a better sense of wellbeing. They are more energetic during the day and sleep better at night.

SLEEP

There is a time for many words, and there is also a time for sleep.
— *Homer, The Odyssey*

Sleep is one of those things that you don't initially think of as something that can make you happy. After all, when you sleep, you aren't doing anything, and it is not a productive use of time. This is, of course, incorrect on both counts. Your body is doing many things while you sleep and sleeping can be some of the most productive time of your day.

So, what can sleep do for you? Here is a short list:

1. It improves memory.
2. It spurs creativity.
3. It can improve grades.
4. It can sharpen your attention.
5. It can help you lose weight.
6. It can lower stress.
7. It can help you steer clear of depression.
8. It can improve your mood.
9. It can strengthen your immune system.

Quite an impressive list and all of that will help in giving you wellbeing. Who wouldn't want a better immune system and lower weight? A better memory? Who else walks into a room and then immediately forgets what they walked in there for?[157]

The irony is, many of us know about these benefits but still choose to get less sleep than we know we need. We stay up late watching television, surfing online, studying, worrying, or working, when we can see from the list above that sleeping will aid us and make us more productive, less stressed, and improve our memory and attention to detail. We need to break the bad habits.

How much sleep should we get?

The ideal amount varies with each person and each age group. Between seven and nine hours of sleep per night are recommended with variations depending on such things as pregnancy and young children who will need more. It is estimated that a parent loses six years of sleep per child during the child's years living with their parents. That is a lot of lost sleep and explains why we look like ragged dolls most of the time. And this is on top of the lost sleep for the reasons mentioned above with many others that haven't been mentioned!

> *Sleep that knits up the ravell'd slave of care,*
> *The death of each day's life, sore labour's bath,*
> *Balm of hurt minds, great nature's second course,*
> *Chief nourished in life's feast.*
> *- William Shakespeare, Macbeth, II.ii.34-37*

How does sleep help?

Looking at it from the brain's point of view, the prefrontal cortex keeps the amygdala in check. That is the fight-or-flight trigger. When we rest, the prefrontal cortex is able to manage the amygdala, keeping control of our emotions. We are better able to process feelings and respond in a balanced way. When we don't rest, the amygdala is 60% more reactive, hence why you feel so moody and volatile and why your responses are unbalanced.

Our bodies have this thing called Adenosine. It is a molecule linked to the digestion process and it is in all of our cells. When you are awake, the sugars (glucose) in the foods you have eaten give you the energy to get through your day. This breaks down into glycolysis, which is broken down further into Adenosine Tri-Phosphate (ATP) but eventually decomposes into adenosine, which builds up in your bloodstream causing drowsiness. In other words, it is your body's way of saying you need to get some sleep. Of course, we have discovered this thing called caffeine, which is an adenosine blocker, but once that wears off, the adenosine kicks back in, and eventually we get some sleep. To cut a long story short, when you sleep, you clear the adenosine from your system and are ready to start again the next day, bright and cheery. When you don't, you feel fatigued and drowsy, dead on your feet.

Are you one of those people who start each morning with a cup of coffee? Is that the only thing that will get you up and alert, ready for the day? Fifty-two per cent of Americans over the age of eighteen start the day with a coffee. For many, that will be a habit, but for others it is to get their caffeine fix and wake them up for the day.

This may be doing more harm than good as the human body produces a chemical called cortisol, which helps you wake up each day. This is released into the body each morning. By drinking coffee, drinkers are double dipping and undermining the effect of cortisol and building a tolerance for both the hormone and the caffeine, therefore decreasing their effectiveness in the long-term. As the caffeine interferes with the production of the hormone, the drinker's body produces less, meaning the drinker must rely more and more on the caffeine in the coffee to wake them up. This is all an aside to the subject at hand, but if you are finding that your morning coffee isn't waking you up like it used to, it may be because the cortisol is no longer being produced within your body like it once was.

It's best to postpone the coffee until mid-morning when cortisol is not being released into your body and have some ice cold water when you first wake up. By all means, don't feel the need to stop drinking coffee but look at when and how often you do. In the United States, coffee is the number one source of antioxidants and can therefore prevent inflammation and oxidative damage of your brain cells, which basically means an imbalance between free radicals and antioxidants. Drinking coffee can also decrease your risk of depression and the caffeine in coffee and other drinks can also protect against cognitive decline, such as dementia.

Studies have shown a link between the brain's grey matter and sleep quality. Your brain's plasticity is improved with healthier structure and function. On the other hand, you could literally be losing your brain, studies showing you can lose brain tissue through lack of sleep.[158]

When dealing with other people, especially those we are closest with, a good night's sleep makes the world of difference. We are more patient and better at communicating. We have better energy levels. If you have children, you will know immediately the value of a good night's sleep on their mood. Surveys have shown that 88% of parents say their child's overall mood is impacted without quality sleep,[v] and 52% will yell at their kids when running on less than eight hours of sleep[vi]. Half of all adults surveyed lose their patience or yell at their partner and have less sex drive when tired. If nothing else, having sex is a good sleep inducer, releasing a hormone called prolactin in men, which causes sleepiness and drowsiness.

What happens when you don't get enough sleep?

We have seen what sleep can do for you and lack of sleep essentially does the opposite. Sleep and mood are closely connected. Much research has been done on this subject.

- If you're sleep deprived, an extra hour of sleep can do more for you than a $60,000 pay rise.[159]

- Lack of sleep has been shown to lead to depression and anxiety, with studies showing that 15 – 20 per cent of people diagnosed with insomnia going on to develop depression[160], more than five times more than the average person. When it comes to anxiety, someone with insomnia is twenty times more likely to develop panic disorder, a type of anxiety disorder.[161] To confirm the link, a study has shown that insomnia 'is a reliable predictor of depression and many other psychiatric disorders, including all types of anxiety disorders.'[162]

- Lack of sleep has been shown to increase your risk of having a stroke. A study done by the University of Alabama in Birmingham showed that if you are middle-aged or older, and you regularly get less than six hours of sleep per night, even if you don't have a history of stroke, aren't overweight or have an increased risk of obstructive sleep apnoea, you have an increased risk of having a stroke.

- Lack of sleep also increases your appetite, leaving you wanting less than ideal food choices. You increase your portion sizes in an effort to put off the tiredness caused by the increased production of the hunger hormone, ghrelin, and limited production of leptin, which balances your food intake. It is a recipe for obesity and coupled with less than ideal drink options as well, you also increase your risk of diabetes.

A study in 2012[163] found there was a link between poor sleep and insulin resistance, with teenagers who did not sleep as much having higher insulin resistance, and a second study in the same year found that cutting sleep increased insulin resistance in fat cells, even when diet and calorie intake was restricted.[164] It is recommended to stop eating at least one hour before bed in order to allow time for your body to digest what you have eaten and give you a better night's sleep.

- Lack of sleep also affects your memory and focus. This is quite common, but it can also lead to permanent cognitive issues especially in old age. We all associate older people as being a bit doddery and forgetful, but a study has shown that sleep deprivation may be behind memory loss in the elderly, preventing the brain from storing memories.[165]

- People who stay up late and lack sleep have an increased likelihood of repetitive and negative thoughts, according to another research study.[166] In fact, lack of sleep has been shown to lead to heart disease[167] and death.[168] A study in 2010 found that men were more likely to die over a 14 year period if they slept for less than six hours a night.

Sleep is great for your looks, being called a beauty product because your body creates new collagen when you sleep, which prevents sagging. The reason it is called 'beauty sleep' is because when you sleep, your body produces more growth hormones, which work to repair damaged skin and produce newer, younger skin cells.

Finally, with sleep, there is the option of napping. When it comes to napping, the consensus is that they are good. Power naps are especially good but not after 5pm, especially if you have trouble sleeping, as it will only make it worse. Naps are good for rest and unlocking your creativity. Famous nappers include Salvador Dali, Albert Einstein, Thomas Edison, and Napoleon Bonaparte.

Sleep Routine

If you can't sleep, then get up and do something instead of lying there and worrying. It's the worry that gets you, not the loss of sleep.

— Dale Carnegie

If you have trouble sleeping, the best thing to do is set up a bedtime routine. A routine will calm your mind, get your body and mind into a regular pattern associated with unwinding and going to sleep, and it will help you relax, ready for the pull of sleep to take you away for many hours.

Here are some things to try:

- Turn off electronic devices such as your television, phones, and tablets. The bright lights can affect your body clock, they can be addictive, and movement stimulates the brain. Don't check social media or emails as they can cause anxiety and worry and that is the last thing you need before going to sleep.

- When people struggle to sleep, a lot of the time it is because their mind is still buzzing. They are physically tired but not mentally tired. They may also have stress, anxiety or some other worry stopping them from sleeping. In these cases, relaxation exercises and meditation can help. As already discussed, meditation clears the mind and you focus on the now, which in turn helps you to relax and ultimately sleep.

- If you are lying in bed with worries, write them down. Similarly, if you think of things that you need to do the next day, write them down so that you can forget about them and get some sleep.

- Do you wake up at 3am, anxious and worrying? Do

you try counting sheep? Instead, try counting what you are grateful for. It will get you thinking, distracting. Even with the negatives in your life, the things that are keeping you awake, consider why you should be grateful for them.

- Before bed, reading or listening to music can help you relax and if you make it part of your routine, your body will use it as a cue or trigger to sleep once you have finished. If reading or listening to music, the idea is to do it somewhere other than your bedroom, simply because you need to associate places and spaces with themes. For example, your bedroom is for sleeping. It is not a workspace, a study or where you watch television or read; it is a place to sleep. By mixing your themes, you sully the association in your brain with the purpose for each space.

- Get into the habit of both going to bed and getting up at the same time. Remember the saying, 'Early to bed and early to rise, makes a man healthy, wealthy and wise.' Building this routine into your day will increase your ability to sleep better and more soundly on a regular basis.

- If you are unable to sleep, and find yourself lying in bed, tossing and turning, get up and read a book or do something. This will switch your brain off whatever it was focusing on, sometimes subconsciously, and after 20 – 30 minutes, you should be able to go back to bed and sleep.

Key Points

- Sleep offers many benefits, from increased immunity, to better memory and lower stress.
- If you're sleep deprived, an extra hour of sleep can do more for you than a $60,000 pay rise.
- People who stay up late and lack sleep have an increased

likelihood of repetitive and negative thoughts.
- Try to create a routine for sleeping and if you are lying in bed unable to sleep, get up and read or do something to reset then go back to bed.

FOOD AND DRINKS

I take a ridiculous pleasure in what I eat and drink.

- Ian Fleming, Casino Royale

It is funny how we do everything in our power to ensure that newborn babies and infants are provided with the most nutritious and beneficial foods and drinks because we know that if we provide them with the correct balance of nutrients, they will be healthier and grow up fit and strong. New mothers make sure they eat well when breastfeeding; they make sure the baby formula has the correct nutrients for growth and wellbeing. Everything is done for the wellbeing of the child, yet as parents and adults we don't give ourselves the same care and attention when it comes to what we eat and drink. When did we stop caring about ourselves and our own wellbeing, because much of it comes through what we eat and drink?

Food, exercise, and sleep are all closely related to each other. The way we live is largely defined by these basics. How much we eat, sleep and exercise has a huge effect on our wellbeing. Each of these can disrupt the brain, altering the chemical brothers' levels in our brain and body.

As discussed, depression is a major problem, especially in developed countries. Over 300 million people suffer from it and it is estimated that 75% of people will suffer some sort of depression in their lifetime. Exercise and the foods we eat are two great ways to alleviate or even remove symptoms of depression. You will recall that serotonin is found mostly in the digestive system (up to 90%!) and gets into your body through what you eat, primarily foods like nuts, cheese, and red meat.

As serotonin is known to help with depression, it would therefore make sense to eat the foods that give us the serotonin that helps our mental health, yet unfortunately this isn't what we do. When our bodies aren't making enough serotonin, what do we want? Carbs! If you aren't eating enough healthy foods to give your brain the serotonin it needs, you will desire the unhealthy alternatives to achieve the same thing.

The brain is a delicate machine. It needs the right balance of chemicals to make it work efficiently and effectively. Substituting the good fuels for alternatives can lead to a world of pain – and likely, you don't even realise it! We live a lifestyle designed to undermine our brain's chemistry. You feel tired so you get some caffeine through a coffee or energy drink. This keeps you awake and you can't sleep, so you get some sleeping pills to help you sleep. You then feel listless and drowsy and need more caffeine to stay awake and alert. You get quick sugar bursts of energy through snack foods like donuts and chocolate but start to feel moody, unable to focus, and highly stimulated. At the same time, you feel edgy and anxious, so you get anti-anxiety medication and perhaps some alcohol to calm down.

You start packing on the pounds and maybe even start losing your sex drive and becoming chemical dependent. You start to feel depressed so take anti-depressants and more sleeping pills and before you know it, you are in a loop trying to cure one thing with the other but ultimately spiralling out of control. What we eat and drink has a major effect on the way we feel. A change in diet can make a big difference in your brain's chemistry and ultimately how you feel and your overall mental and physical health. It is not easy to put into place for the long-term, yet even just doing a little of this can make a HUGE difference to the way you feel. Everything in moderation.

Things have changed. The foods have changed. Sure, meats, fruit and vegetables are the same and we have a wider variety of these available but much of what is left is now processed food with added salt, sugars, and preservatives. And this applies to not just snacks and takeaways but a lot of our meals. Even the way we rest in the evenings, in front of the television, has changed. Whereas our parents would sit with a cup of tea or coffee and have a single biscuit or, if they were feeling tempted, two, now we sit in front of the television and eat a whole packet of biscuits or bag of crisps, at the same time guzzling a bottle of soft drink or wine.

> *Our bodies are our gardens, to which*
> *our wills are our gardeners.*
>
> *- William Shakespeare, Othello*

So, what food and drink is making us unhappy and how? Here is a short list (prepare yourself):

- processed and takeaway foods
- processed meats
- fried food
- butter
- salt
- potatoes
- refined grains, such as those in white bread, pasta, cakes, and pastries
- sugary drinks and snacks.

If you are looking at that list and thinking, 'What other food groups are there?', you are not alone. A lot of people live on food like this and it can be addictive. The fact is, however, that foods like these are high in energy but low in nutrition. They give you a burst of energy but when that wears off, it leaves you feeling flat, tired, irritated, grumpy and mentally fatigued.

Sugary foods and drinks also release dopamine and serotonin, those feel-good hormones, throughout your body, which make you feel good and happy, much like you have been rewarded. These feelings hit quickly but also go away just as quickly and of course that makes your body want more so you drink and eat more of these drinks and foods only to fill your body with more nutritionally poor options, which in time, because your body cannot use the food you have consumed, makes you fat.

Not feeding your body with these foods, once it has had them, causes low levels of glucose, dopamine, and serotonin, and you then get withdrawal symptoms such as headaches, fatigue, lack of concentration and in some cases, depression. It is not a happy experience but necessary in order to feel happier over the long-term. Now, the goal is not to cut out all the foods you like to eat, far from it, and in today's society, it takes a very dedicated person to do so, with so much processed and sugar and salt laden food available, but with baby steps you can lessen the food and drinks you consume that fit into the list above.

If you need some more persuading, consider the following.[169]

- In the United States, almost 60% of the average daily energy intake is from ultra-processed foods.
- In Australia, about 40% of the calories children and adolescents have come from ultra-processed foods.
- Rates of obesity have tripled since the 1970's and more than doubled since the 1980's.
- Half of all mental disorders start before the age of 14.
- An adult's mental health is related to the quality of their diet.
- Higher rates of depression are consistently linked to

diets high in what we commonly call junk foods such as fried food, sugary drinks, packaged snacks and processed and refined breads and cereals whereas the opposite is true for foods such as vegetables, fruits, and fish.

- A diet high in junk foods quickly decreases your memory and cognitive function and ability to self-control your food intake, leaving you still feeling hungry and wanting to eat even when full.[170]

Have you ever had sore and bleeding gums even though you have good oral hygiene? These can be a sign of stress caused by the microbiotica in your mouth. Stress can cause neuro inflammation, which is inflammation of the brain and is one of the risk factors for depression. What has this got to do with diet? Other causes of inflammation of the brain include low vitamin D, insufficient sleep and exercise, bad dental health and gum disease, smoking, obesity *and* diet.

> *I think it could be plausibly argued that changes of diet are more important than changes of dynasty or even of religion… Yet it is curious how seldom the all-importance of food is recognised.*
>
> — George Orwell, The Road to Wigan Pier

So, what should you be eating and drinking?

The fact is, there are lots of nutritious and 'happy' foods out there and it would be surprising if you weren't already aware of most, if not all of them. It is that 'healthy stuff' that we see on TV and posters telling us to have our portions of per day, and based on untold amounts of research, they are correct. This stuff is good for you and makes you feel healthy, gives you a better sleep and ultimately, what we are aiming for, a better sense of wellbeing. On top of that, eating foods without preservatives has been shown to increase IQ by up to 14%!

So, what are the foods and drinks we should be consuming? Here they are:

- fruit (two serves per day)
- vegetables (five serves)
- whole grains
- nuts
- legumes
- oily fish
- dairy products
- small quantities of meat
- small quantities of olive oil
- water

These foods you will probably recognise from the food pyramid you learned about in school and to live solely on these would be great, but realistically, you just need to introduce these into your diet. Most of us already have, and perhaps just need to introduce a little more, while at the same time cutting back on the unhappy foods listed on the previous pages. If you are interested in weight loss, keeping your blood sugar low is the way to go and on top of that, it makes the brain work faster and stops brain fog.

> *A good cook is like a sorceress who dispenses happiness.*
>
> — Elsa Schiaparelli, Italian Fashion Designer

Foods like this will aid your goal to feel happier. There are five food types within a healthy diet that boost our mental wellbeing. We have all heard about carbs or carbohydrates, probably related to low-carb diets. There are two types of carbohydrates: complex carbohydrates and simple carbohydrates. You will find complex carbohydrates in vegetables, fruits, and wholegrains while you will find simple carbohydrates in sugary snack and drinks. Whereas simple carbohydrates release glucose into your body, which creates energy highs and lows through the day, complex carbohydrates release glucose slowly into your system, giving you a more even release of energy and decreased lows, which equals more feelings of happiness and positivity.

You may find when you are feeling down or low, you want food – you want carbs. Your body isn't making enough serotonin and knows that 'processed carbohydrates release big doses of serotonin in the brain in the same way that cocaine releases big doses of dopamine. If your brain isn't getting enough serotonin through healthy food, you will end up self-medicating with unhealthy food to achieve that same state.'[171]

Brightly coloured fruits and vegetables release antioxidants, which hunt down free radicals (unstable molecules that can cause damage to DNA or other parts of human cells), eliminate oxidative stress (an imbalance of antioxidants and free radicals in your body) and decrease inflammation on the brain. What does this all mean? An increase in the feel-good chemicals in your brain, which make you feel happy.

Only now are we truly starting to understand the importance of your gut health in our overall health and wellbeing. Pro- and prebiotics found in cheese and yoghurt as well as fermented products boost the bacteria living in your gut. Research indicates these pre- and pro-biotics may work in the same way as antidepressants, elevating happy emotions. This is through the bacteria producing 'chemical messengers from the gut to the brain that influence our emotions and reactions to stressful situations.'[172]

Oily fish produce Omega 3 and some fruits and vegetables contain Vitamin B, which both increases the production of the brain's happiness chemicals and are known to protect against both depression and dementia.

The facts are there, that a healthy diet can make you happy and give you better overall physical and mental health. Of course, you know this and would love to have an improved diet but that it is not that easy. You get started, do well for a few days, but don't see any difference or have a social gathering or 'a night off' and boom, you are back where you started. You know you should be doing something, but sometimes it isn't easy to change your diet, even just a little bit. Perhaps you can try cutting down the bad foods alone, which again can be difficult, but it is a start. Maybe you hate fruit or vegetables or both. Try using a blender to make it into a juice. There are many ways to get nutritious foods into your body. If you are taking or considering taking vitamins or other supplements, I suggest doing some research first as there is a body of research being done that suggests these products often do nothing for your health at all, and are consequently no substitute for the real thing.

If you are someone that goes on diets to lose weight, restricting your intake of food, carbs, fats, whatever, and yo-yoing back and forth trying to find a diet that works for you, have you considered where that fat goes once you lose it? The answer may be of interest to you and give you that bit of information you need to help you stick at losing that fat for good.

Most people, including professionals, believe that fat is turned into energy and lost that way. The fact is, you breathe out fat.[173] For every ten kilograms of fat that you lose, 8.4 kilograms is breathed out and the remaining 1.6% is through water. How do we breathe ourselves thin? When you breathe, you inhale two atoms of oxygen – O_2 – and exhale three atoms, carbon dioxide - CO_2. That extra atom you exhale, the carbon atom, is you breathing out the fat. The carbon you are breathing out is the carbon that exists in the foods you eat through carbohydrates. The key is to simply eat less carbon – eat less, move more, for the more you move, the faster you will breathe and remove the carbon from your body. Instead of thinking of calories in, calories out, think in terms of atoms in, atoms out. Look at swapping food and drink options with carbon in them for those that don't. For example, instead of a soft drink, have some water. Doing so will decrease the number of hours of breathing required to remove the carbon in the soft drink from your body.

How do you change the habits of a lifetime? Some of you probably scoff at the thought of being able to do a week, let alone ten days or even longer of cutting sugar from your diet. But hey, it's not about giving it up all together, it is about moderation and the way to change your habits is to build new habits.

Your brain, as we know, doesn't like change. When you start to lose weight, your body will do all it can to get you back to your previous body weight. It will release a torrent of chemicals and hormones in response to the drop in food intake and weight, and slow down your metabolism in order to preserve the status quo. The key is consistency and perseverance. You just have to keep going, riding it out until your body accepts the new norm and adjusts accordingly. As hard as that may sound, it isn't – if you really want to change.

Know this: dieting makes you fat. Not many people are able to stick to a diet and if they do it, it is no longer a diet but a lifestyle choice. People generally stick to a diet for a period of time, either to achieve a goal or because they give up. The problem comes with doing another diet and then another diet. Your body recognises the 'symptoms' of a diet and prepares the body to store fat and slow metabolism as described above. The more you diet, the more your body works against you. To truly succeed at improving your diet requires a change of mindset before you have a change of diet.

Remember, earlier in the book we talked about expensive restaurants and how they only gave small portions of food in order for you, the diner, to savour the flavours and experience? The same goes for all food. Junk foods make us want to keep eating when we are already full. We don't appreciate or savour what we are eating but keep doing so anyway. Learning to savour what we eat and the experience of doing so can help us in our journey to better living. Keep reading this book, for later we discuss ways to motivate you and build habits to commit to your goals and achieve what you ultimately want: lifelong wellbeing.

Key Points

- Exercise and the foods we eat are two great ways to alleviate or even remove symptoms of depression.
- A change in diet can make a big difference in your brain's chemistry and ultimately how you feel and your overall mental and physical health.
- Eating foods without preservatives has been shown to increase IQ by up to 14%.
- There two types of carbohydrates: complex carbohydrates and simple carbohydrates. You will find complex carbohydrates in vegetables, fruits, and wholegrains while you will find simple carbohydrates in sugary snack and drinks.
- Brightly coloured fruits and vegetables release antioxidants.
- Pro- and prebiotics are good for your gut health, and it is also through your gut that up to 90% of serotonin is created.
- To change your diet, do so in moderation, slowly over

time and stick at it so your body adapts and doesn't put up defences such as slowing your metabolism.

- Learning to savour what we eat and the experience of doing so can help us in our journey to better living.

SETTING AND COMMITING TO GOALS

Do or do not. There is no try.
- Yoda, The Empire Strikes Back (1980)

Do you find that despite countless failures in the past, at the start of each year, you set goals for the year ahead? Despite your best efforts, which may last from a few days to a few weeks, maybe even a few months, your resolution becomes the latest to be added to the pile of failures you have accumulated over the years. Why is it we set goals we almost invariably know we will not achieve, and how can we set goals that are achievable?

The idea of a goal is to have an end or result for the effort you have put in. Goals are good as they give us something to look forward to and strive towards. By having a goal, we focus our attention, actively working towards what we want to achieve.

Goals can bring a sense of accomplishment when they are achieved. They can give us a sense of meaning and purpose, as well as build our confidence and belief in what we can accomplish in the future. For all of these reasons, goals play an important role in giving us a sense of wellbeing. When we set goals for ourselves, something we truly desire to achieve and not imposed by someone else, they become a powerful motivational tool.

What makes a good goal?

Goals can be big or small, long-term or short-term. They can be easy or hard, completed individually, or in tandem with other people and groups, but whatever they are, they need to be achievable. If a goal is not achievable, you won't succeed, you won't feel any accomplishment, and you won't commit to other goals. Achievable doesn't mean a dead person could do it, either.

Dr Russ Harris, author of *The Happiness Trap*[174], noted that we need to set a live person's goals, not a dead person's goals. What this means is that if you have set a goal and a dead person could do it better than you, then you have set a dead person's goal. For example, if your goal is to stop smoking – that is something a dead person will always be able to do better than you. Whatever happens, they will never smoke again. Let's say you want to stop dating arseholes, or drinking every night, or watching too much television, or shouting at your kids, or obsessing over your weight, or feeling like crap, or whatever, it doesn't matter what it is, if you are setting goals to stop doing, or not to do something, you are setting a dead person's goal. You will never, ever, ever be able to do it better than a dead person will.

You need to flip your dead person's goal to a live person's goal, that is, something a living person can do better than a dead person. In other words, if you are not doing or feeling whatever it is you want to stop, what would you be doing instead? Again, as an example, you want to stop watching too much television, so instead you decide to do a night class on a subject that interests you, say medieval quilting; therefore, your goal is to do a medieval quilting night class. A medieval quilting night class is a live person's goal as no dead person could do it. Many living people probably wouldn't want to do it either, but that is beside the point. They could do it if they wanted to.

Goals don't have to be big to be worthwhile. Sure, you may have a goal to get a degree, or buy a house and compared to that, smaller goals may seem unimportant, but it is these goals that boost wellbeing, especially those that matter to you, are manageable and supported by other people. What works really well is to link smaller goals back to bigger goals and priorities.

A good goal is a SMART goal, that is Specific, Meaningful, Adaptive, Realistic, and Time-bound. It is likely you have heard this acronym before and for good reason. It is very common in the workplace and a succinct way of making sure your goal is achievable and well thought out. Of course, as time passes, people have altered what the letters stand for and depending on the context or purpose, you may decide to as well. For those that don't know, here is a quick summary of what SMART means for setting your goals.

- Specific

Be clear about what you want to achieve. As we discussed, be specific about what you are aiming for. 'I will watch less television' is too vague and ill defined. What does less mean? What will you do instead? Specify exactly what you will do.

Other 'S' options include: Simple; Sensible: Significant.

- Meaningful

Make sure your goal aligns with your values.

Other 'M' options include: Measurable (so you will know when you have achieved your goal); Motivating.

- Achievable

Make sure you are able to complete the goal. Will you be able to do it? Make sure it is not too airy-fairy. Other 'A' options include: Adaptability (Will your goal improve your life in some way?)

- Realistic

Make sure your goal is realistic. Do you have what you need to achieve the goal? For example, you may need money, time, support, certain skills, or knowledge. If you need any of these and you don't or cannot obtain them, you need to reset your goal. Other 'R' options include: Relevant; Reasonable; Resourced; Results-based.

- Time-bound

You need to have an end date in order to achieve your goal or it will go on and on and probably never be achieved.

SMART goals are good goals but (and there is always a but) they do have limitations, especially within the context we are discussing: personal growth. Being SMART is good for setting concise and clear goals that remove ambiguity and irrelevance, which is why they work well for businesses, but you are not a business. SMART goals focus on results, whereas you work in a universe of emotions that change from minute to minute and day-to-day where saying you will not watch television works one night but not the next. You may have had a bad day and just want to blob in front of the television and eat chocolate, but if this happens again and again, not only are you watching too much television, but you are also fat! Goals need to be as much about the journey as the destination. We go into this a lot more in Part III. Suffice to say, starting anything is a goal unto itself.

Another way to ensure your goal is both good and achievable is to make it CLEAR. This stands for: Collaborative, Limited, Emotional, Appreciable, Refinable.

This acronym is again taken from a business context but still works for individuals. Achieving goals is easier when they are:

- Collaborative:

Trying to lose weight alone is harder than doing it with someone. You keep each other accountable. So get a friend or partner to do it with you. Including others in your goals makes them much more achievable.

- Limited:

Goals should be limited in duration and scope to ensure that again they are achievable.

- Emotional:

Your goals should have meaning to you and something you are emotionally invested in, to tap into your passion and energy to achieve your goals.

- Appreciable:

Breaking down your goal into smaller goals in order to make them more accomplishable can give your quick wins, and keep you on track to your bigger goal.

- Refinable:

Importantly, have flexibility in your goals. Things change, such as your priorities, emotions, and drive. Allow yourself to make changes, refine, and modify what you want to achieve.

But what is still missing from this equation is a foundation of wellbeing: learning. A goal is easier to achieve if we are invested in it. We need to be challenged and to learn from the experience as we work towards the goal. Learning gives us the opportunity to improve ourselves and importantly, it forces us to leave our comfort zone while giving us the opportunity to enter a state of flow, therefore it needs to be part of the equation for successful goal setting. With that in mind, there is yet another acronym: LEAF.

- Learning
- Emotional

- Achievable
- Flexible

This can be expanded to include Time-bound, therefore making the acronym T-LEAF, although just working towards a goal is usually more than sufficient in achieving desired results in a personal situation. For example, watching less television, although a dead person's goal, is a goal achievable immediately, you simply watch less television. The goal is ongoing: to keep watching less television. The destination has been reached immediately and it is now the journey that is the primary focus. Therefore, Time becomes an infinite proposition, only relevant when a goal actually has a deadline such as travel overseas before the end of the year.

Goal vs Value Focus

See, in your life, everybody has a turn back moment. You have a moment when you can go forward or you can give up. But the thing you have to keep in mind before you give up is that, if you give up, the guarantee is that it will never happen, no way under the sun. The only way the possibility remains that it can happen is if you never give up, no matter what.

- Steve Harvey, American Entertainer

Do you find yourself failing to achieve goal after goal and not understanding why? The world in which we live is goal-focused. Think about it. The majority of goals are based on achievement and success, usually built on power, status, or wealth. These are all subjective and hedonic, subject to habituation. If not, our goals are focused on avoidance - avoidance of painful feelings, thoughts, and emotions. How many of your goals are based on these? These goals can be destructive, leading to suffering and misery in the form of addiction, self-inflicted sabotage of your wellbeing and life in general, pulling you further and further away from what you really want.

When you set goals based solely on extrinsic reward, you fail to achieve your true potential; for as much as achieving goals is commendable, achieving goals that align with who you are as a person, what you believe, and what you value is of tantamount importance. It is for this reason that you fail to achieve goals. You are not truly invested in them. They have no meaning to you. You have to set it for yourself.

Look at a goal you want to achieve. Examine the underlying values of that goal and see if they match your values. Are there any? If there are, then take action consistent with those values. If not, either give up the goal or be flexible and amend it so that it fits with your values. When you set goals, set them guided by your values and what is meaningful to you. The value in setting goals that have value to you is that you are more invested in them, you enjoy the journey towards achieving your goal because you appreciate where you are going; you live more in the present, appreciating what you have, and with a greater satisfaction of life as it is. Value-based goals become an opportunity to better yourself as you align with them, and a values-based goal is more likely to be achieved because you are more motivated to achieve it.

Studies[vii] have shown that when you are not strongly committed to a goal, seeing indifference and apathy in others only triggers and reinforces the same feelings in yourself. However, when you are strongly committed to a goal, as you are with one that includes your values, seeing apathy in others fuels your commitment to achieving your goal. Consider those who are strongly committed to a belief or opinion. If you try to have a discussion with them about it and offer different interpretations or opinions about what they believe, instead of them being open to a different point of view, they become even more entrenched in their beliefs. Your doubt and conflict in their belief only fuels their conviction because you are challenging values they hold dear; values that they identify with; values that define them. When put in an external locus of control, you can begin to see why people exhibit such strong conviction to their beliefs, no matter how ill-founded they are. You need to have that commitment, so you need to have strong values that support your goal.

Goals and motivation

Let me tell you the secret that led me to my goal. My sole strength is in my tenacity.

— Louis Pasteur

According to psychologists Richard Ryan and Edward Deci's Intrinsic Motivation and Self-Determination in Human Behaviour[175], when pursuing goals, it is making sure three basic human needs are met, which is important to our wellbeing and self-motivation as opposed to the goal itself. These are control, competence, and connection.

- Control

We are already familiar with control. When it relates to goals, setting your own goals is key. We want to be in control of what we will do and to choose how we will act. No-one is making us do it. What we do is our own decision and the consequences are from our own actions. Conversely, when you are told what to do or pressured to achieve a goal that you have little or no choice in, your self-motivation and wellbeing drops. Goals at our workplace can feel like this.

They are not yours, and if you cannot find value in what you are doing, then your motivation and desire to achieve the goal will decrease over time. Remember, when it comes to control, there is very little that you can control.

Apart from your actions, reactions, and your attention, you don't have much control over anything else, so focus on what you can control, not what you cannot. The more intense you let your feelings and emotions become, the less control you have over them.

- Competence

Everyone wants to feel competent, and this comes with time and practice. We all naturally feel inferior and incompetent from time to time but when we feel confident and effective in whatever it is we do, we are more likely to continue pursuing and ultimately achieving our goals.

- Connection

Goals can be very individual but our need to have relationships and connections with other people, our families, friends, and communities, those people we associate and identify with, are important. These connections we form through goal setting gives us the security and bonds we need, while providing the freedom to be ourselves and make our own choices.

When looking at your goals, consider their connection to one another as well. To increase your chances of success, setting goals that are intrinsically simple, work in harmony, and are consistent with one another are more likely to succeed.

Knowing why you are doing what you are doing is crucial to motivating you into action. Knowing why starts a change in our thinking, because we pause to examine what is going on. If your goal is to lose weight, ask yourself why? Are you doing it for yourself, someone else, society, or do you have no idea? If you don't know why or are doing so for reasons other than for yourself, you don't have a vested interest or don't want to do it truly for yourself, you are likely to never see your goal achieved especially over the long-term.

Nothing motivates like success and seeing your goal being achieved, or on the way to being achieved. It is a great motivational tool. This means coming out of your comfort zone for many people and average people never try to come out from their comfort zone. It isn't easy. Your brain is wired to make you as boring and static as possible in order to protect you, but the only way to achieve growth is to leave that cocoon. There is no magic tool for leaving your comfort zone but once you are out and on your way to achieving a goal or experiencing the opportunities and excitement outside the zone and the freedom it offers you, it becomes easier to stay out, but is all too easy to slide back inside. Such is the make-up of our brains.

The Journey

You don't have to be great to start
But you need to start to be great.
- Zig Zigler

Starting a goal is hard, but keeping the course once you have started is ultimately harder. Linking your goal to your values makes a world of difference, but sometimes we have to complete goals that don't match our values. Motivational tools that generally come into play in this scenario are the carrot and stick. You can be rewarded for achieving the goal or you can be punished for failing. Sticking at it is important, not just in goal setting, but in everything you do. That is why Part III focuses specifically on why we procrastinate, motivation, self-discipline, and building good habits.

You can't go back and change the beginning, but
you start where you are and change the ending.

- C S Lewis.

How we perceive our goals and how far away we are from reaching them can either enhance or detract from our ability to achieve them. The farther away a goal appears to be, the more likely your thinking is to change from 'I can do this' to 'Forget it' and you take a break, affording yourself the opportunity to stop for a period of time.

The problem is that once you stop, the voice in your head tells you that you have failed and starting again is just cheating, that you may as well quit because you have shown you don't want to go on anyway, and so, what do we do? We listen to that voice in our head and give up on achieving the goal.

With goals, the journey is about riding the highs and lows and figuratively getting back on the horse again (and again), building up our story and the experience of the journey on the way to the destination – the goal. The voice in your head will always want you to quit and have you believing that having to start over is a bad thing. No, you simply pick up where you left off.

The journey towards the goal is the key to success, not the goal itself. You will appreciate the journey more than the goal as that is just the end point. Once a goal has been achieved, then what? It is nothing, an anticlimax of epic proportions and what do you do next but find another goal to fulfil the desires you had for the first goal. Many goals, such as those where we want to stop doing something like eating or smoking or drinking, have no end date, so you need to appreciate and revel in the journey. Focus on what you have done, not what you still need to do. If you look at a goal as a destination at which you arrive, you are constantly looking at your here and now and using it as a snapshot of your entire life to see if you can be happy yet.

Of course, this one instant in time is not representative of your life. Everything is fleeting, passing through space and time, so no-one point in time can be representative of the whole. Success is not somewhere we arrive, it is the journey itself. It is not what we have finished, it is what we are doing, the actions we are taking, and the experiences we are having right here, right now.

The accomplishment of goals is not success. It is how much we expand, learn, and grow in the process that really matters. What is the point of accomplishing a degree if you remember none of what you have learned or put none of it into practice? It just becomes a framed piece of paper on the wall. It is what we do in the process of accomplishing a goal that matters.

> *Whatever you do will be insignificant,*
> *but it is very important that you do it.*
> *- Mahatma Gandhi*

Maybe you don't have any goals. Maybe there is nothing you want to achieve. It is worth keeping in mind Mark Twain's quote from the chapter on the WEALTH Mindset and adapting it to help determine your goals. 'Twenty years from now, what will you regret not having done?' It may be hard to answer that question, maybe even uncomfortable. Perhaps you can look at it from the point of view of 'what interests me the most?' 'What keeps pulling me in a specific direction?'

Once you have identified that, determine what platform or channel will help you develop the skills you need to achieve that goal. Once you know these things, you will start to shape your ambitions and desires and feel intrinsically motivated to achieve them. Don't be too concerned if your aspiration is only half developed. The truth is that goals don't have to be specific with a desired outcome. Goals ultimately help us achieve things and inspire and motivate us.

Do you ever pass houses and see the owner in the garden busy doing whatever, and wonder what could they possibly be doing? They are in the garden all the time, how much more could they possibly do? Research[viii] shows that staying busy, doing something, anything, is a goal itself. Staying busy inspires us. All things being equal, doing something is better than doing nothing, no matter how trivial, insignificant, or a waste of time it may seem to others. The person continually gardening is busy being busy, giving meaning to their life.

In answer to the initial question posed at the start of this chapter – why do your New Year resolutions fail? Now you can take something from what you have read and are now able to formulate and set realistic and achievable goals. Alternatively, instead of looking forward to what you want to achieve, however fanciful or unrealistic, perhaps the best strategy is to look back at the previous year and see what worked well for you, what you were good at, and what made you feel happy? What did you achieve? Use the answers to these questions as a basis for your goals for the coming year. Not only will they sync more with what you want and are good at, but they will be more achievable and give you a greater chance of success.

Key Points

- By having a goal, we focus our attention, actively working towards what we want to achieve.
- Goals are a great motivational tool.
- Don't set a dead person's goals. These are goals that a dead person could do better than you.
- Goals don't have to be big to be worthwhile; it is the small goals that boost our wellbeing, especially those that matter to us.
- Link smaller goals back to bigger goals and priorities.
- Many of our goals are based on achievement and success or avoidance.
- Goals that match your values are more likely to be

achieved.

- The accomplishment of goals is not success. It is how much we expand, learn, and grow in the process that really matters.

PRACTICING SPIRTIUALITY AND RELIGION

Let the measure of time be spiritual, not mechanical.
- Ralph Waldo Emerson

Faith is the belief in something beyond proof. It is trusting in something that cannot be seen, measured, or fully explained. For some people, faith is central to their life. For others, it feels unnecessary or difficult to accept. In modern Western society, where science and evidence are prioritised, religion does not hold the same influence it once did. However, despite this shift, both religion and spirituality continue to offer something that many people are still searching for. That something is meaning, connection, and a sense of wellbeing.

At its core, religion is a structured system of beliefs and practices that centres on a higher power or a greater purpose. This higher power may be referred to as God, Allah, or something else entirely, depending on the religion. Spirituality, on the other hand, is broader and more personal. It does not require adherence to a specific doctrine or institution. It is more about how you connect with yourself, others, and the world around you. Religion can be seen as one path within spirituality, but spirituality can exist without religion.

Understanding this distinction is important because it gives you options. You do not have to fully commit to organised religion to explore what faith or spirituality might offer you. Equally, you may find that structured religion provides exactly what you are looking for. The key is to understand what each offer and how you might engage with it in a way that supports your wellbeing.

Religion offers a framework. It provides answers, or at least guidance, to life's biggest questions. Why are we here. What happens after we die. What is the purpose of life. These are questions that science can explore but not always answer in a way that satisfies us emotionally. Religion steps into that space and provides meaning. It suggests that life is not random, but part of something larger. For many people, this belief alone brings comfort.

There is also the concept of hope. Many religions teach that there is something beyond this life. This might be an afterlife, enlightenment, or another form of existence. Believing that there is something more can change how you experience your current life. Difficult times may feel more manageable if you believe they serve a purpose or that something better lies ahead. This is one of the reasons religion has been such a powerful force throughout history. It has helped people endure hardship by providing a sense of meaning.

Religion also provides community. It brings people together through shared beliefs and shared practices. This sense of belonging can be incredibly powerful. Most of us, whether we admit it or not, want to feel part of something. Religion offers that. It creates groups of people who support each other, who gather regularly, and who share a common understanding of the world. This social connection is one of the strongest contributors to wellbeing.

Spirituality offers many of the same benefits, but in a different way. It is less structured and more flexible. It allows you to explore your beliefs without needing to follow a specific set of rules. You might believe in a higher power, or you might simply believe that there is a deeper connection between all things. You might not label it at all. Spirituality allows for that ambiguity.

The key difference is that spirituality is self-defined. It is shaped by your experiences, your thoughts, and what resonates with you. It does not require you to accept a fixed set of beliefs. Instead, it encourages exploration.

So, what are your options when it comes to religion and spirituality?

One option is to engage in organised religion. This involves participating in a structured belief system such as Christianity, Islam, Judaism, Buddhism, Hinduism, or others. Each of these has its own teachings, rituals, and community. Engaging in religion typically involves attending services, participating in rituals, and following certain principles or guidelines. The benefit of this approach is that it provides structure, clarity, and community. You are not figuring everything out on your own. There is a path to follow.

Another option is to practise spirituality without religion. This is a more individual approach. It may involve meditation, reflection, spending time in nature, or engaging in activities that help you feel connected and grounded. You may still believe in something greater than yourself, but you define what that is. There is no requirement to follow doctrine or attend services. This approach offers freedom and flexibility.

A third option is to combine the two. You might engage with aspects of religion that resonate with you, while also developing your own spiritual practices. Many people take this approach. They attend religious services occasionally, but also practise meditation, mindfulness, or other forms of personal reflection.

Once you understand the options, the next step is to consider how to practise them.

If you are interested in religion, one of the simplest ways to begin is through exposure. Visit a place of worship. This could be a church, mosque, synagogue, temple, or any other religious space. You do not need to participate. Simply being there is enough. Observe what happens. Listen to what is said. Pay attention to how people interact and what they seem to gain from the experience.

You may choose to speak to others who practise the religion. Ask them what it means to them. Why do they believe. What do they get out of it. These conversations can provide insight that you cannot get from reading alone.

Another step is to explore religious texts or teachings. You do not need to read everything or fully understand it. The goal is to become familiar with the ideas. Over time, you may find that certain concepts resonate with you.

Prayer is another way to practise religion. It does not need to be formal. It can be as simple as speaking your thoughts, expressing gratitude, or asking for guidance. Many people already do this without realising it. Moments where you hope things will work out, or wish for someone's wellbeing, are forms of prayer. Making this a more intentional practice can help you feel more connected and reflective.

Ritual is also an important part of religion. Rituals create structure and predictability. They provide regular moments of reflection and connection. This might be attending a weekly service, saying a daily prayer, or observing religious holidays. These practices create rhythm in life and can help reduce stress by providing consistency.

If you are more drawn to spirituality, the approach is different but equally accessible.

Meditation is one of the most common spiritual practices. It involves sitting quietly and focusing your attention. This might be on your breath, your thoughts, or simply being present. Meditation helps calm the mind and increases awareness. It allows you to step back from the constant noise of daily life.

Spending time in nature is another way to connect with your spiritual self. Being in natural environments can create a sense of perspective. It reminds you that you are part of something larger. Whether it is walking in a park, sitting by the ocean, or hiking in the bush, nature has a way of grounding you.

Reflection is also a key part of spirituality. This can be done through journaling, thinking, or simply sitting with your thoughts. It is about understanding yourself and your place in the world. Asking questions such as what matters to you, what gives your life meaning, and what you value can be part of this process.

Creative expression can also be a form of spirituality. Activities such as music, art, writing, or cooking can help you connect with yourself in a deeper way. These activities allow you to express thoughts and emotions that may not be easily put into words.

The important thing with spirituality is that it is personal. There is no right or wrong way to practise it. What matters is that it supports your wellbeing and helps you feel connected.

There are clear benefits to both religion and spirituality. Research has shown that people who engage in these practices often report higher levels of wellbeing, lower levels of stress, and a greater sense of purpose. Being part of a community, having a belief system, and engaging in regular reflective practices all contribute to this.

However, it is also important to recognise that religion is not without its challenges. For some people, religious beliefs can create feelings of guilt or pressure. In certain cases, religious institutions have caused harm, which has led people to distance themselves from organised religion. If you have had negative experiences, it is important to acknowledge that and choose a path that feels safe and supportive for you.

Spirituality, while more flexible, can also be challenging in a different way. Without structure, it can feel unclear or directionless. You are responsible for defining your own beliefs and practices, which can be difficult without guidance. Some people prefer the clarity that religion provides.

> *Having faith in God did not mean sitting back and doing nothing. It meant believing that you would find success if you did your best honesty and energetically.*
> - Ken Follett, The Pillars of the Earth

At a deeper level, both religion and spirituality address the same fundamental human need. The need for meaning. The need to understand our place in the world. The need to feel connected to something beyond ourselves.

We all seek belonging in different ways. For some, that belonging comes from family, community, or shared experiences. Religion offers another form of belonging. It provides a collective identity and a shared purpose. Spirituality offers a more individual sense of belonging, one that is internal rather than external.

> *Our scientific power has outrun our spiritual power. We have guided missiles and misguided men.*
> – Martin Luther King, Jr.

In recent times, science has provided explanations for many things that were once attributed to religion. This has changed how people view faith. However, science does not remove the human desire for meaning. It does not replace the need to feel connected or to understand why we are here.

This is why religion and spirituality continue to exist. They fulfil needs that go beyond logic and evidence. They speak to the emotional and psychological aspects of being human.

> *At this moment it seems as though science will never be able to raise the curtain on the mystery of creation. For the scientist who has lived by his faith in the power of reason, the story ends like a bad dream. He has scaled the mountains of ignorance; he is about to conquer the highest peak; as he pulls himself over the final rock, he is greeted by a band of theologians who have been sitting there for centuries.*
> — Robert Jastrow

Ultimately, whether you choose religion, spirituality, both, or neither, the choice is personal. What matters is finding something that supports your wellbeing. Something that helps you feel connected, grounded, and purposeful.

You do not need to have all the answers. In many ways, the process of exploring these questions is where the value lies. Being open to the possibility that there is something more, whatever that may be, can be enough.

Key Points

- Religion provides structure, community, and a framework for meaning.
- Spirituality offers a flexible, personal approach to con-

nection and purpose.

- You can choose religion, spirituality, or a combination of both.
- Practicing religion can involve attending services, prayer, and ritual.
- Practicing spirituality can involve meditation, reflection, and connection with nature.
- Both approaches can improve wellbeing, reduce stress, and increase a sense of purpose.
- Neither approach is right for everyone and the choice is personal.

AVOID OVERTHINKING AND SOCIAL COMPARISON

It never ceases to amaze me: we all love ourselves more than other people, but care more about their opinion than our own.

- *Marcus Aurelius*

For people today, it is so much easier to compare and despair. This is especially true of youth who have grown up with social media and are so much more aware and conscious of what is happening around them. A teenager these days can see where their friends are at any time of the day or night. They can see them out with other friends whilst they are struck at home with their parents, left out. When I was fifteen, I had no idea what my friends were doing if they weren't with me. There were no smart phones or apps and no Internet so they could have been having a great night out and I would have been oblivious, sitting at home with my family watching one of only two channels on the only TV we had in house. No idea, no compare.

Social media, or as some may see it, 'me' media because more and more people are using the channels not so much for engagement purposes but for marketing of themselves and their agendas, is pervasive. We are exposed to the ideals and ideas of those we follow or are shown to us based on algorithms developed by those behind the channels. Because a lot of the content we are exposed to is from people we know, it is content we take an interest in and are influenced by, as it is to our peers that we compare ourselves and therefore content we can use as a basis for comparison. We are all subject to overthinking, after all, we have thousands of thoughts per day[177] so filtering is very important.

The problem is that we are flooded repeatedly with images and other media (and this is not just referring to social media but all media, including television and publications) telling us what everyone else is doing and how they are 'winning' at life. Subsequently, we believe we should to be at that level of success and happiness and have accomplished what our peers have, especially when we may have felt we were ahead of them in the game of life earlier. We start wondering why we haven't moved forward and begin to feel stagnant and a failure. It can become obsessive, especially when we are bombarded with images of the life and social connections we feel and believe we should have, but don't.

Overthinking goes into overdrive. Did I make a mistake choosing my career? Why don't I know what I want to do with my life? How do they afford to do all these things? Am I doing something wrong? Why wasn't I invited to that party? Do they not like me anymore? The questioning and re-questioning inside our heads goes on and on in the loop we have already discussed. Our overthinking becomes detrimental to our daily performance, judgement, and decision-making,[178] and entices anxiety into our life. We all have that internal voice that doubts our skills and abilities, our value to the community and society as a whole, which is an important part of our survival instinct so we can be part of the tribe, but which can be detrimental to us in the modern age.

Comparison is the thief of joy.

- Theodore Roosevelt.

Overthinking and social comparison can make a real dent in our self-esteem. We tend to use social comparison to determine where we are in life, how we sit compared to those we compare ourselves against, usually our peers, basing our self-value and consequently, our self-esteem on this measurement. The stupid thing is that we base our self-esteem on things that are beyond our control. They have an external locus of control. Good looks, wealth, stuff – these things don't last, yet we use them as a guide to determine our value.

We all have different skills and talents in life, so using these as a basis for comparison is ridiculous as well. We may feel like a failure when we compare, feel that our lives are going nowhere as we struggle to make ends meet, week to week, but the mere fact that you are struggling, that life is a constant challenge, and that you continue to persevere and work hard, be a father, mother, friend, brother or sister, the fact that you do this and still weather the storm that is your life, shows you are a strong, determined and accomplished person, not because of it, but despite it.

If you can look at your life this way, you will see that your accomplishments, no matter how small, make you a success and someone to be admired. You have set your own standards, not those dictated to you by society. Sure, it is hard not to compare, in fact, it is very natural to do so, but when you place your value based on your own values and measure yourself by what you do and not by what you have, you are winning at life.

Jordan Peterson, in his book, *12 Rules for Life*, said you should compare yourself to who you were yesterday, not to who someone else is today. If you are doing better today than you were yesterday, that is an accomplishment. Own it. Take that self-esteem and revel in it, for no matter how much you compare yourself to others, how good you think you are at something, there is always – always – someone better than you. You may be one in a million, but that means there are still over 8,000 people just as good and probably better than you are, and that number is growing.

It is one thing to be trying to keep up with the Joneses, but it is another to be the Joneses and trying to stay ahead. There is always another Joneses ahead of you, so it is a losing game. It is not easy being the Evil Queen in *Snow White and the Seven Dwarfs*, pretty and the best but always on the lookout for that someone who will come along, be prettier and better, and take it all away. Social comparison from any angle is a mug's game, so how do we remove it from our lives?

The truth is, you never will be able to remove it. All we can do is identify it when it happens and learn to deal with it in practical and efficient ways. The first thing to realise is that social comparison is usually an illusion of your own mind because the people that you are comparing yourself to, you don't really know. You may think you do, but you really don't.

How many people really know you, the real you, the one you don't tell anyone about and probably don't even understand or acknowledge yourself much of the time? For the same reason, you don't really know anybody else. You may think they have life sorted; they are like a shiny new Ferrari, whereas you are a beat-up old hatchback. What you don't see is the inside of that car, ripped and torn to shreds, barely able to be driven, engine shot, and going nowhere. Moreover, just as many people are like a Ferrari, a lot are like a balloon, fun, bright and shiny on the outside but with nothing on the inside. In other words, they are just all air with nothing of substance, yet we emulate and desire to be just like them. The house may look picture perfect but you don't see the crushing, soul destroying debt being paid to maintain the mirage. Maybe their marriage looks Instagram-perfect, but at night they sleep in separate rooms. You just don't know. Don't judge a book by its cover. We are all unique and we all have issues and problems we are dealing with.

Social comparison is good for us in a way that it is a competitive motivator. We are forever competing against others and do so from the moment we start comparing ourselves to others. It doesn't matter if the prize at the end of the rainbow is big or small, we are driven to compete and measure ourselves against others. Winning activates the reward centre of the brain and releases the thrill that dopamine gives us. As much as we envy the super-rich and their mega mansions, super cars, and super yachts, we don't relate to them. They are at another level and we intrinsically know that to compare and compete with them is useless. When we compare, it is with people we relate to and only a small number as well.

Research done by Professor Stephen Garcia at the University of Michigan showed that the number of people we are competing against has a direct effect on the motivation we have to compete, and that we won't jump into competing with too many people, our brain instead opting for the steady as she goes, non-competitive state of mind. What does this mean? When we compare with too many people, we don't try to compete. We see that our chances of being the best are low, so we quit. Usually this is a bad thing, but in the game of social comparison, it's the right thing to do. The same goes when we widen our circle of influence. As discussed, we are influenced and compare with those we associate with, so if they drive BMWs and Mercedes Benz cars, we want one too. If they get a new phone every year, we want one too. When you broaden your network or circle of influence and include those who perhaps drive a Nissan or a Toyota, and keep the same phone for several years, you get a broader appreciation and perspective for what you already have.

The effects of social comparison on your wellbeing can be damaging, including anxiety, blame, apathy, and depression. These psychological contagions are like the coronavirus: easy to catch and with long-lasting effects. Becoming aware of these feelings and emotions early can prevent the negative outcomes later on. In a group setting especially, it easy to catch the comparison bug, so knowing what sets it off for you is important.

For example, the things that you hate about other people are things you cannot see in yourself, just as the things you love about others are the things you love about yourself. Most negative emotional reactions you have are you identifying a disassociated aspect of yourself. For example, when you are angry and bitch and complain or get upset about someone or try to change him or her or the situation, it is because it is an aspect of your life that you have isolated and detached yourself from. Once you know this, you can work to identify it, work on it, and own it as your own.

> *A dog finds a big, juicy bone. On his way home, he comes to a river and sees his reflection in the water. Upon looking into the water, the dog thinks he sees another dog with a bigger, better bone than the one he has. He barks at the 'other' dog to try and get his bone too, but when he barks, his bone falls out of his mouth and floats away down the river. The dog goes home with no bone at all.*
> *- Aesop*

The above story about a dog and his reflection has the moral of being content with what you have. Yet for many of us, keeping up appearances and wanting the bigger, better version has become a way of life. We consciously or not try to keep up with the proverbial Joneses and attain the façade of happiness through material gain. The truth is, it is a losing game and to see how might help in determining how far you go to keep up and when you have gone too far. We don't want to compare and despair but compare with care. The Joneses are in debt, a lot up to their eyeballs. You are trying to keep up and they are trying to do the same.

Australians spend $8.6 million on credit card debt every day with a total debt of $17.73 billion[179], which pays for the things you become envious of. On top of that, the things that most people buy are depreciating assets, meaning they do not go up in value; they go down, so when you invest in a new pair of shoes, a phone, a car, or furniture, you are losing money as soon as it leaves the shop. The more you spend keeping up or staying ahead, the more you get stuck in a financial trap, especially when outspending your income. Buy-now pay-later schemes, which have surged in popularity over the past few years, promise financial freedom in simple, affordable repayments however the facts show a different story with a survey amongst financial councillors showing their clients are in a worse financial position[180] with the average debt being $2,200[181]. With debt, you leave yourself with little wiggle room for the future, you become stressed, your credit rating can be affected, you lose and have no savings, and the living for now mentality cripples your future and ability to survive should you actually need money urgently. It is then that the house of cards can come tumbling down.

It is important to remember that people are selfish. They don't really care or even notice what you don't have. They become wrapped up in their own little worlds, their own problems and whether you have a new phone or car doesn't really register, let alone the fact that you have gone into debt to impress. The hardest part of keeping up with the Joneses is the misery it makes you feel for all the previous reasons, but also because it stifles you from being you.

In pursuing the Joneses, you are failing to pursue your dreams and goals. You become less content with the more that you buy, dissatisfied with yourself as you can never (and never will) catch up. It doesn't make you happy beyond that short period immediately after purchase, and it is exhausting trying to be someone you know in yourself that you are not.

This goes for all pursuits, whether it is spending on stuff, the job you have, the partner you have chosen, it doesn't matter. Doing things to impress others for social standing is inherent but ultimately destructive to your self-worth and self-esteem. Do you ever wonder why people feel pressured to be successful but no-one is ever pressured to be happy? There is something to be considered in that. The next time you recognise yourself comparing yourself to someone and wishing you had what they have, whatever it may be, acknowledge your admiration for what they have and then ask yourself this question – yes, but are they happy?

Key Points

- In many cases, we base our self-esteem on things that are beyond our control, like good looks, wealth, and stuff, things that don't last yet we use them as a guide to determine our value.

- Compare yourself to who you were yesterday, not someone else today.

- Keeping up with the Joneses is a fool's cause. They are indebted up to their eyeballs and doing the same as you with some other Joneses, if not you yourself.

- You cannot remove social comparison from your life. It is part of your DNA, but you can identify it when it happens and learn to deal with it in practical and efficient ways.

- Social comparison is good for us in a way that it is a competitive motivator.

- Social comparison doesn't make you happy and can make you feel anxious, depressed, stressed, and apathetic.

ACTING LIKE A HAPPY PERSON

Do you know someone who just exudes confidence, someone that can walk into a room full of strangers and talk to anyone, has a ready smile and a charm that draws everyone in? It has nothing to do with extroversion versus introversion; it's about believing the best in yourself and portraying it for the world to see.

The mind is an incredibly powerful thing, perhaps more powerful than we give it credit for. As discussed in Part I, humans have a tendency towards negativity. We are quick to criticise others as well as ourselves for how bad things are before we see the good and compliment others as well as ourselves. We convince ourselves that everyone else has it all together and knows exactly where they are going in their lives. What's worse is when you are older and you see younger people who seem to have their lives sorted while you, maybe twenty years older, still live from month to month, pay cheque to pay cheque. Inside, you know it's not that simple, that everyone has their own demons and issues to deal with and God knows what else, but we are negatively inclined creatures. It is easier to see the negatives in you than the reality of what is the essence of you. We refuse to see the good in ourselves, celebrate our achievements, believe in our abilities, or see the many ways in which we have it pretty good.

So, as the title of this ingredient says, you need to act like a happy person to become a happy person or more simply, fake it 'til you make it. Sounds simple, but how do you pretend to be happy and how will that actually make you happy?

Sometimes, pretending to be happy when you aren't can make you feel even worse, so how can it make you feel happy? Quite simply, it can't. Replacing one emotion with another doesn't work. You simply repress one emotion, letting it build up inside you until at some point it comes out, either explosively or by disabling you physically, emotionally, and mentally. This is something you don't want to happen. You need to express your emotions. We are emotional beings and therefore need to express these feelings.

The point of this book is to guide you to find and express happiness, but all emotions are valid and consequently, all emotions need to be allowed to be felt and expressed. This is Psychology 101 but how many of us repress our negative emotions and soldier on, becoming one of the increasingly silent majority, who go through the day with a smile on our face for the public to see but feeling miserable on the inside – and some of us cannot even manage that!

Our negative emotions and thoughts send our brains into fight-or-flight mode. Continued repression can create chronic stress and anxiety and ultimately depression. Depression is the result of excessive thinking, where your problem becomes the centre of everything. You can become a negative person, criticising others, expecting the worst, dwelling on bad things, taking things personally, complaining a lot, blaming others and never accepting blame yourself, and worst of all, you don't always see it yourself.[182]

In order to fake happiness and have it work, you need to address your negative emotions first. First, you need to identify what the emotion is and once you know (you can do this by talking to someone, venting your frustrations and emotions), remove yourself from whatever it is having a negative effect on you. This could be a person, maybe your job or something else completely, such as social media. If you can't remove it or them from your life, try limiting your time. Keep away from other negative people, as they will drag you into their drama. Unlike in mathematics, two negatives do not make a positive. You can write down your negative emotions, say 'no' if you are feeling like too many people are relying on you and spreading you too thin, and choose to live your life and not that of someone else.

Ultimately, the reason this is the last ingredient listed is because even if you don't feel like using any of the ingredients, by trying to address your emotions, even though you don't want to, with time, you will start to remove the negative emotions clogging up your mind and blocking you from feeling better and happier. You won't be able to get rid of your negative thoughts with the click of your fingers, but in order to start acting like a happy person, you can check your negative attitude at the door or put it on hold. It sounds ridiculous and just the same as repression, but there is a difference. Repression is bottling up the negative emotion inside whereas putting it on hold is leaving it where it is but focusing on something else, something positive and taking action from there. You may believe there is nothing positive in your life and yes, we all have bad days, but there is always some good, even in bad days. Focus on that then smile.

The Facial Feedback Hypothesis[183] says that our emotions can be influenced by our facial expressions. Yes, a simple smile can make you feel happy. There are tonnes of studies to support this. Dale Carnegie, back in the 1920s, knew it when he wrote *How to Win Friends and Influence People*. In it, he said a simple way to feel happy is to smile. It boosts your psychological state. It sends non-verbal messages that we are sociable and therefore would be a good friend. Our brain automatically associates smiling and happiness. If we force ourselves to smile, our brain will assume that we are happy.

Be Positive

Positivity is all around us. It is a veritable industry!

I am awesome!

I have the power to create change.

I am in charge of how I feel and today I am choosing to be happy.

I radiate success.

I am enthusiastic about every second of my life.

Happiness is my choice.

...the list goes on and on.

A lot of happiness and positivity books, websites and millions of memes promote the idea of thinking and talking yourself to happiness and success. You can't go through a day without seeing one. In many ways, they are sugar-coated gaslighting. Beware of people who are overly positive and optimistic as they are not the kind of person you need in your life when you aren't feeling overly positive. Their positively will just piss you off and make you feel even worse. You don't need someone telling you to 'just get over it', 'she'll be right', 'be positive', 'think happy thoughts', or simply 'be happy'. You need someone to support you, listen to you, be there for you, not rub salt into the wounds by minimising your feelings. You cannot be happy all the time.

Rhonda Byrne's book *The Secret* is based on the idea of the law of attraction where, when you truly want something and you truly believe you will have it, the universe will make it happen. Basically, what you think about and focus on, you attract. Therefore, if you focus on negative things, then that is what you will get, and if you focus on positive things, then that is what you will get. For example, I really want to own a million dollar house with a pool. It encourages you to focus on what you want and of course, when you do, what happens? You start seeing things that reinforce what you want. Does this sound familiar? It should, as it is a form of confirmation bias and that is concerning as that bias ignores other information in front of you because it doesn't match your bias. As a result, you may end up doing something regrettable such as getting a loan you cannot afford to buy the house you have visualised and convinced yourself you are entitled to, in the meantime ignoring all the other information out there that was contrary to your bias.

For example, interest rates have just gone up and you have bought in a down market or during a recession when you could lose your job etc. Another problem with 'the secret' is that if you are simply required to think yourself happy or successful, you generally aren't going to get what you want despite the fact that $e=mc2$[184]. At some point, you are actually going to have to do something to make it happen. You need to take action. James Altucher, in his book, *Choose Yourself*,[185] said 'It's one thing to know 'The Secret' or take whatever life-affirming steps you've read about in order to bring positivity into your life, but it's something else altogether to actually create opportunities for yourself. You're definitely not going to find them reading a book. It's a moment by moment effort in your daily life.'

The Secret is also very unrealistic in that it requires you to be positive all the time and never to doubt yourself or have negative thoughts, something that we have learned, as human beings, is not possible because we are negatively geared so overcoming that is near impossible. Despite this, having sold over thirty million copies, people love the idea of it, and why not? It sounds awesome. It is not an original idea though.

Before *The Secret,* we had many other books, most notably bestsellers like Napoleon Hill's *Think and Grow Rich* in 1936 and Norman Vincent Peale's *The Power of Positive Thinking* in 1952. These books and many others do offer some good advice and

The Secret is the next evolution of these self-help books. In fact, since its release, the number of places where you can get people offering you motivational messaging and positive affirmations has exploded with the Internet offering a tonne of channels for people to do so. Just look at any social media platform such as Facebook or Instagram and depending on the algorithm in your feed, there will be at least one motivational meme or positive affirmation. Before using them as a basis for your personal development, let's stop and take a look and see if they actually work.

The answer depends on you. If you go around telling yourself 'I am a good person' and you already have good self-esteem then yes, statements like this will reinforce what you already believe, even if only marginally. However, if you go around saying 'I am a good person' and you don't believe that you are, no matter how many times you say it, ultimately, if you have low self-esteem, the affirmation can be detrimental to you and seem like a cruel joke[186]. Your brain knows what you believe about yourself. You are basically arguing with your brain about how you feel and your brain, like anyone when someone argues with them, gets defensive and won't back down. If anything, you are just going to convince yourself that you are the exact opposite of what you want yourself to be, maybe even worse, so what was the point of trying to convince yourself otherwise?

Ironically, positive affirmations can have the opposite effect on many people. They do not improve your mood and can in fact make your mood worse. A study done at Lingnan University[187] supported other work published[188] showing that positive thinking can be harmful as it focuses on unrealistic positive thinking, leading to higher levels of depression. If you keep telling yourself that you are happy, when you know that you are not, you won't change and seeing a positive affirmation written down saying 'Be happy!' will not make you happy. If anything, it may reinforce the feeling that you are miserable and make you feel even worse. It found that listening to positive affirmations was more effective than reading them, as readers have more time to process what they are reading and align it with their existing self-beliefs.

From that, you can see why people get so worked up and excited when they go to a seminar or conference and hear someone telling them they are good people, a magnet for money, a success waiting to happen, pretty and desirable etc., etc. This couples with another way positive affirmations work and that is in a space where there is social pressure. An example is at a seminar or church or other social gathering where you are buoyed up to be positive by those around you because you are being watched[189] and caught up in the experience of those around you.

Although it seems contradictory to believe so, as we have seen, when you engage in positive thinking, the outcome can actually be worse. This is where you believe something will happen, but without any effort. For example, doing well in an exam but not studying for it beforehand. The same goes for job interviews or driving tests[190] and expecting to do well and then don't. The reason is because we put in less effort and feel less motivated because we feel it is something we have already accomplished. A little anxiety and uncertainty can certainly help motivate you to do your best.

Positive thinking and self-affirmations can be of benefit when they affirm your existing values. If you already believe in something, then affirmations that focus on them can lead to increased acceptance[191].

Positive affirmations can also work best when dealing with effort as opposed to ability. For example, saying, 'I am good at mathematics' is focused on an ability, an ability you may not have, and saying it as many times as you can doesn't change that fact. Saying 'I will do my best in mathematics' is an affirmation focused on effort and with effort, you can do your best at mathematics, and with more effort, you can continually improve to the point where maybe you can say 'I am good at mathematics.'

Using this method, you are not affirming something that is false (and your brain knows it to be) but affirming that you will give your best effort. Another way to look at it is to reconstruct the way you talk to yourself to focus on questions instead of predetermined answers. Asking yourself the question, 'Can I do better in mathematics?' sets the mind to thinking and building motivation and a solution to the question. Research[ix] conducted by University of Illinois professor Dolores Albarracin and her team has shown that those who ask themselves whether they will perform a task generally do better than those who tell themselves that they will.

Several studies[192] have shown that reminding yourself to do things that make you feel happy can make you happier than not reminding yourself. This doesn't mean, however, that the more you remind yourself to do things that make you happy will make you even happier. This is simply because when you actively monitor or chase happiness, you become less so.

> *Ask yourself whether you are happy and you cease to be so.*
>
> *- John Stuart Mill, Philosopher*

This is because when you are consciously monitoring your happiness or the pursuit of it, you are monitoring how you actually feel, and if that is not happy, then your pursuit of happiness will make you feel even more unhappy than you already were. This highlights the already mentioned pursuit of happiness as being counterproductive, that happiness comes as by-product of doing things. Ironically, chasing happiness only results in catching more of what you are trying to avoid.

More research[193] shows that being asked to be happy makes you less happy than just allowing happiness to happen as a fortuitous consequence of what you are doing. As an example, in yet another study[194], participants who simply listened to music enjoyed it more than those who were asked to make themselves as happy as possible when listening to music or at least monitor how they were feeling when listening to music. This is not really that surprising especially when you consider that, in much the same way, if you tell yourself to go to sleep, the chances are you are going to lie there for hours on end, doing the exact opposite. Much like saying, don't think of a tree, the chances are that is the first thing that you are going to do.

Telling yourself to do or not to do something can be counter-productive but at the same time, by giving it some importance, can make the achievement greater – think of achieving goals. To put it into context, let's say your goal is to get better sleep. Telling yourself to have a better sleep is not going to cut it. As mentioned, you will more likely lie there, tossing and turning, wondering why you can't do the simple thing you want to do. Instead by having a better sleep as a goal you can look at other aspects of your life that will aid this such as not eating foods or having drinks that will keep you awake, exercising, and winding down for the night.

In the same vein, when you give higher priority to being happier, you will make more choices that aid that goal. Just remember the Serenity Prayer, have strong emotional health, and choose to be active instead of reactive – take control of how you feel instead of letting events dictate how you feel. Go into life with the intention of being happier, practicing control of your emotions so that they do not control you. There is a principle called the Pareto Principle, also known as the 80:20 rule, which basically states that 80% of the result comes from 20% of the effort. You can relate it to nearly anything: work, activities, relationships, and so on. When it comes to acting happy, like all of the ingredients mentioned, start small and build up. Once you start, you will start to get more.

Positive affirmations will work with certain people in certain situations however, if you have low self-esteem, positive affirmations likely won't help. They are likely to make you feel worse, reminding you that you are not living up to the affirmation. Instead, you should look at the thoughts and emotions you have, learn to build realistic self-concepts of who you are and identify discrepancies between the reality and ideal, learning to build a bridge between them.

When you are in the right head space, stand tall, shoulders back, chest out, and smile. People will see a confident, happy, and positive person, someone likeable and attractive. People will respond to you, so step forward, speak your mind, have an opinion, and start to believe what you are portraying to the world is real, all the while feeling the serotonin flowing through you.

Always end the day on a positive thought
No matter how bad the day was
Tomorrow can always be better
Tomorrow can always be great
– I Am Fearless Soul

Key Points

- Overthinking and social comparison can have a real dent on our self-esteem.
- You can't be happy when you aren't. Pretending to be so will only make you feel worse. You need to address your issues first by expressing and acknowledging them.
- Our emotions can be influenced by our facial expressions.

- Positive affirmations can work, but you need believe in what you are saying. If you don't, they can seem like a cruel joke.
- Positive affirmations work best when dealing with effort, as opposed to ability.
- Studies have shown that reminding yourself to do things that make you feel happy can make you happier than not reminding yourself.
- Go into life with the intention of being happier, practicing control of your emotions so that they do not control you.

PART III

IT IS TIME TO GO FROM WELL NOW TO WELL ALWAYS

Goose, I've had about enough of this shit!
- Maverick, Top Gun (1986)

If you have come this far, then you are ready to start putting some of the ingredients together and making your own recipe for a life of positive wellbeing. It is time to say goodbye to the shit you have accepted as your life up until now and to make the life you want for yourself. It is likely that part of the problem to date has been that you know a lot of what you need to do already, but it never sticks. You feel motivated to change your life for the better but then something, anything, gets in the way of your progress, to the point where it is months or even years later and you are no further forward than you were the first time. In fact, you are even further back because the life you could and should be leading is getting shorter and shorter with every passing day.

Do not finish this book and file it away. True wellbeing is made up of the pillars contained in WEALTH. We have touched on all of them and made reference to the linchpin of them all, the one tenet that will ensure success, and that is habit. The secret ingredient to living a life of wellbeing, as opposed to having wellbeing in your life, is Habit. Why? Because habit ensures that you action your recommended ingredients on a consistent and regular basis. It is that simple, no gimmicks or secret sauce. Of course, it wouldn't be right to leave it at that. Habits are a simple yet complex thing to master. This next section of the book deals specifically with moving you from having the ingredients of wellbeing, to living a life of wellbeing, addressing all the issues, blocks, and excuses along the way, giving you a pathway to success. When you are done, you will be the master of your own destiny, able to build a future that works for you and living a life of overall positive wellbeing.

Self-help books are usually anything but. They sell you a vision of what you could do, what you could achieve, and the person you could become.

Could have, would have, should have.

They get you excited and you finish the book with great enthusiasm and optimism, motivated to achieve that vision. What they don't do, however, is give you a plan and if they do, it is flimsy with no incentive to commit because ultimately, they are *self*-help books, reliant totally on you to help yourself. Consequently, they become self-defeating and bring self-loathing because they expect you to be a certain way and do certain things, which you may be very motivated to do at first, but then don't for whatever reasons. The things they were meant to help you with are then worse than ever. You can be told all the ingredients you need to lead a life of positive wellbeing, but until you actually do something with those ingredients, this has just been a reading exercise.

For that reason, Part III will show you how to take what you have learned and actually apply it to your life. This should be a living book, one you refer to for years to come, not one you read once and it then sits on your bookcase forever more, taunting you for having done nothing yet again.

At the beginning of this book, you were asked to look at happiness as if it was a verb, an action as that is what is required to be happy – action. Now it is time to get you to pick the ingredients you want to work on and start using them.

To get us under way, consider the following joke: how many psychologists does it take to change a light bulb?

The answer? One, but the lightbulb has to want to change.

This joke is a great play on words and gets to the heart of wellbeing. Assuming you have read this book this far (and good on you for that!), you are motivated to make a better life for yourself and have not just a sense of, but an outpouring of positive wellbeing. You are the lightbulb and you want to change; you are ready to be the person you want to be.

This section of the book will show you how to start and then maintain the changes you want to make by looking at what is stopping you, why you procrastinate, what motivates you, and how to build good and long-lasting habits.

PROCRASTINATION

There is a fabled time and place called Weneim. It is somewhere people sought and to this day still do to make all of their dreams, goals and ambitions come true. To get there the seeker is told to head due west and follow their dreams. They will come to a place called Gonnadoo. This place is filled with many distractions and temptations and the seeker is told to leave this place as soon as possible but many are enamoured by what Gonnadoo has to offer and never leave. If the seeker is able to resist the allure of Gonnadoo they must continue due west following their dreams. They will come to a time, one day, when they must decide not just where they want to go next but when they want to go. The seeker has to be sure they are in the right place, literally and figuratively, for them to move forward. Are their life circumstances good enough for them to proceed? There are many things to consider. This decision can literally take an age to make. If they don't wait long enough, they will never find Weneim. If they wait for too long, they will eventually find Weneim, but it will be too late to achieve anything.

Like many of us, you get stuck in Gonnadoo (going to do) and Weneim (when I'm) a lot.

'I'm *gonna do* a marathon, start a business, write a book (you chose a goal) *when I'm* rich, have more time, the children are grown up, the cows come home (you choose the circumstance).' With that mindset, nothing gets done. Instead, if you are like many of us, you fall into a hole, intending to do one thing but end up doing another, simpler, less taxing thing.

Take for example, the YouTube hole. You go online intending to look at one thing, maybe a music video, which then links to a video on the tapestry of Elizabethan England (surprisingly interesting), a video on Elizabeth Shue's greatest movies and then, wait, did you know you that if you hold a sliced piece of bread in your mouth while cutting an onion, you won't cry? Interesting, but before you know it, it is 2 am and you have to be up at 6 am to go to work.

We are all constantly distracted and lack the self-discipline to do the things we really want to do. If there is a deadline on achieving something, then we will probably get it done, such as an assignment or project at work (even if it is because of rushing and cramming at the last moment). This is extrinsic motivation, the discipline to do it coming from the possible consequences of not doing it. When it comes to the important stuff, like our own self-improvement, where there is no deadline, then self-discipline, which requires intrinsic motivation, is well and truly lacking. For many of us, there has always been tomorrow or someday.

Tim Ferris in his book, *The Four Hour Work Week*, says it quite clearly: "Someday' is a disease that will take your dreams to the grave with you.'

That there is the crux. One day, there won't be a 'someday'.

So, what can we do?

First, let's define what procrastination is. In a nutshell, it is putting off things until later, whether that is tomorrow or someday. The word 'procrastination' comes from the Latin word, Pro-crastnis, which means 'belonging to tomorrow', which sums it up neatly – it will probably never be done. Procrastination can also be seen as a fear-based tool designed to protect us from the possibility of failure, embarrassment, shame or guilt, maybe all. But at what cost? In a nutshell, procrastination is a tool designed by your primitive brain that works to stop us from leaving our comfort zone.

> *Think of your many years of procrastination; how the gods have repeatedly granted you further periods of grace of which you have taken no advantage. It is time now to realise the nature of the universe to which you belong, and of that controlling power whose offspring you are; and to understand that your time has a limit set to it. Use it, then, to advance your enlightenment; or it will be gone, and never in your power again.*
>
> *– Marcus Aurelius*

Why do we procrastinate? It is an inability to self-regulate, that is, give yourself orders and then follow them. Again, it is all to do with the brain. Your neocortex decides you want to make a change, but your emotional limbic system doesn't want a bar of it. It does not want to act because, as we have discussed, your brain sees change as bad. Your emotional limbic system wants to stick to the status quo and stay in your comfort zone. It is not just a fear of failure that pushes us to procrastinate. As we have discussed, it is also a fear of success and a multitude of other things. Either way the brain doesn't want change. Each is a threat. It will tell you that you aren't ready yet. What if someone else is doing this and doing it better than you ever could? What if you fail? You'll be ridiculed, the laughing-stock. Geez, this sounds like hard work. Let's just take a step back, have a breather, and think about it for a while.

> *How long are you going to wait before you demand the best of yourself?*

– Epictetus

In many ways, your brain is right – it is hard work. That is why we procrastinate, feel disorganised and are unable to focus long enough to get anything done. We are easily distracted and then blame anything other than ourselves, such as friends and family or circumstances, before finally turning the blame on ourselves and feeling like abject failures. This is where we admit that we have a problem.

Next would be accepting you need to take responsibility for that problem but Dr Michael Bennett and Sarah Bennett in their book, *F*cK Feelings*, say no, you cannot be responsible for having a problem; it is hardwired into your brain. However, they say, you are responsible 'for working with it and finding ways around it, and (this) often requires you to overcome deeply ingrained bad habits and attitudes,'[195] something we will discuss later. 'It's impossible,' they continue, 'to change your instincts or make distractedness, impulsivity, and scattered thinking go away; you can, however, become a good manager of the impulses to procrastinate, avoid, lie, and cover up.'

> *You change your life by doing, not by thinking about doing.*
>
> *– Gary John Bishop, Unfuck Yourself*

To delve deeper, we can see procrastination not as a problem but as a symptom of another, bigger problem, that of willpower or self-discipline – the first of our WEALTH principles. Therefore, you shouldn't berate yourself for being a procrastinator. You just need to work on your willpower. You have to find a way to make yourself do things you don't want to do.

Motivation seems like the most obvious solution and in most cases, it will help you do this, but in reality, it is a work around. It amplifies the attraction of the goal but doesn't address or resolve your lack of willpower and self-discipline and consequently, when you come to do something else you don't like, you will likely procrastinate again.

> *It's a trap!*
> *– Admiral Akbar, Return of the Jedi (1983)*

Motivation subsequently becomes a trap for procrastination. But it is a hard one to come to terms with. How many of us have the willpower and self-discipline to do anything we aren't motivated to do? It's not laziness if you want to do something but cannot make yourself start. If you are a true procrastinator and not just lazy, putting things off by doing 'nothing' like watching TV, looking at Facebook, eating, sleeping, or playing video games, makes you feel bad and frustrated afterwards, because you have wasted your time again.

Mindset has a lot to do with why we procrastinate. Our beliefs influence our feelings. We need to identify what our limiting beliefs are and change them with empowering beliefs. Identifying what our beliefs are will allow us to recognise thoughts that put a stop to us moving forward, so-called handbrake thoughts. We need to move from *I can't do this* to *I can do this*, focusing on the now, not when some predetermined conditions are met, and focusing on the progress being made, not the outcome. Focus on the journey, not the destination.

> *Action will destroy your procrastination.*
> *-   Og Mandino*

To overcome procrastination and make sure you engage with the actions required to have positive wellbeing on a regular and consistent basis, we need to look at and better under-

stand the following:
1. Self-discipline
2. Motivation
3. Habits

SELF-DISCIPLINE

Distraction is like an addiction. Consciously or even subconsciously, you are doing it (procrastination through distraction) to avoid doing what you really want or need to do. You do it so much, the thought of doing anything else becomes abhorrent and pushes you even further into distraction. Your brain is designed to take pleasure and reward now, it has not been developed to plan for the future. Saying you will do any of the suggested ingredients for a life of wellbeing is planning whereas your brain wants to be distracted, play games, watch TV and eat chocolate now, hence why you never do what needs to be done.

Do you find that the only things that make you feel good are the things you know you shouldn't be doing? You try to do what needs to be done, but you get no feel-good factor or buzz from them. If you get a high dopamine fix through watching TV, Facebook, video games, junk food etc., and really want to improve your self-discipline, you need to have a dopamine detox. This means not doing some or all of the high dopamine things you distract yourself with.

To do so, set up a calendar of days to avoid stimulating activities that flood your brain with high amounts of dopamine. Doing this will allow your dopamine receptors to recover and make it easier for you to do the things you normally wouldn't like to do like study, exercise, or work. As these activities release low amounts of dopamine and because your dopamine levels will be low after your detox, you will feel a dopamine hit. Bingo! Don't think a detox is easy, it is not, but if you do it gradually and consistently, like everything, it gets easier. If you need to, you can reward yourself afterwards with a high dopamine hit but limit the amount, e.g only fifteen minutes of Facebook time or one episode of our favourite TV show.

Remember, dopamine is a pleasure chemical, but it is more than that, it is a desire chemical. Remove the desires from your life, even just for one day and yes you will feel bored but that is good, it means you dopamine receptors are recovering then select some of the ingredients for a life of wellbeing and give them a try, it is after all, that is what the intention is.

It is always your choice where you get your dopamine from: things that benefit you or things that don't. You choose.

Self-discipline comes with a healthy dose of perseverance. There is the story of the crow and the pitcher in which a crow is looking for water to drink on a very hot day. It comes across a pitcher of water, but when it tries to drink the water, its beak cannot reach far enough into the pitcher to get the water. The crow tries in vain to get the water and is on the verge of dehydration, ready to give up and die, when it sees some pebbles on the ground. One by one it drops the pebbles into the pitcher, raising the water level until it can reach in with its beak and drink. The moral of this story is not to give up when things look bad – where there's a will, there's a way. To solve problems, persistence is the key. Your ideas may seem bad but may simply need a little more work and amending or someone else to take a look at them.

Self-discipline is like a muscle; it needs to be exercised in order to get stronger. Petr Ludwig, in his book, *The End of Procrastination*, describes self-regulation as your imaginary willpower muscle, a cognitive resource that expresses the current energy of your neocortex. Remember, your neocortex wants to make changes, but your emotional limbic system puts a hold on it. To overpower this, you need to flex your 'muscle' and to do this, you need to strengthen your cognitive resources. Ways to do this include the following:

- Replenish your cognitive resources through regular scheduled breaks, for example take a walk, have a healthy drink.
- Gradually learn new habits.
- Make less decisions (too many choices can lead to decision paralysis and doing nothing) during the days, so you have more energy for completing tasks.

Self-discipline gives you the ability to get yourself to take action – to do what needs to be done.

> *It's impossible to change your instincts but you can become a good manager of your impulses to procrastinate.*
>
> *- Dr Michael Bennett and Sarah Bennett, F**K Feelings*

Like a job, you need to show up every day. You need to commit to action towards your vision or goal. Every day you commit is another day closer to what you want.

> *You must build up your life action by action and be content if each one achieves its goal as far as possible – and no-one can keep you from this.*
>
> *- Marcus Aurelius*

If you wait to feel motivated before doing anything, you will get nothing done. Those who wait to be inspired to do something are screwed. They are the ones who end up sitting on the couch every night watching television, surfing the Internet, or playing video games. Motivation and inspiration are unsustainable. You need to learn to work without them and exercise your self-discipline muscles in order to strengthen your purpose and passion, which come from the actions done through discipline.

Even if there is a purpose and a plan, 95% of people will still fail. That is why the first pillar of WEALTH is Will. You have to really want this and you need to be consistent every day and put in the work. You now know who you are and know that failure doesn't define your character. And let's face it, you will fail at times, maybe even most of the time, but it is your ability to keep going, your will, that moulds you into a disciplined and strong person.

Don't be defined by a bad day or a bad week. Each day is a new day and a new beginning. Each failure is a new learning. Focus on what is happening now and into the future (your goal), not the past and what you haven't done.

The first step in breaking your habit of procrastinating and exercising your self-discipline is simply to stand up. When we sit, we are settled. We may be reading, watching TV, or surfing the Internet. Whatever it is, it is usually done sitting down. Now, you can still do these things standing, but they are not as comfortable and at some point you will need to make a decision about what to do. Standing gets you ready for action, ready to do something. Simply standing gives you the motivation to take a step towards doing what you have procrastinated doing, to exercising your self-discipline.

Self-discipline usually comes with a healthy dose of self-judgement. You need to get rid of that. Using your emotions against yourself is detrimental to success. Self-discipline is not self-denial. Feeling guilty or shamed by yourself into doing something is not really self-discipline. Well, it is but it is the kind that doesn't last. Like a diet, it won't work. You are denying yourself, guilting yourself into sticking with a diet you don't really want to do but need to because you are getting fat or need to do it for whatever health reason. You stick it out, proud of your ability to deny yourself what you want, until the 'screw it, I'll start again next week,' sets in and then you feel even worse because you have let yourself down and feel shame and guilt all at once. Forgive yourself. Doing so prevents you from continuing to blame yourself and putting things off. Think about what you did well so you can repeat it again tomorrow. Be grateful for the good that happened today. To really achieve self-discipline, you have to *really* want to achieve your goal otherwise it will be stop-start affair that never really takes off. Focusing on what you are doing as opposed to what you aren't can be a real help. Again, this is looking at the perception of an issue. 'Exercise each day is keeping me active' as opposed to 'Exercise each day is stopping me from watching television.' You are doing things because they are good for you; they get you to where you want to be, but you do have to want it, and if you want it, you are working with the reasons instead of against them.

But don't fool yourself. Don't confuse motion with action. James Clear in his book, *Atomic Habits*, defined it very well when he said that motion is planning, strategising, and learning.
Action is doing something. You can plan and talk about doing your desired behaviour as long as you want, but until you take action and actually do something towards it, it is all for nothing. Motion is just another form of procrastination. You may think that you are doing something, but you aren't. Don't think your action has to be perfect either. Most of the time, it is best just to start and work out what is working for you along the way. Don't keep planning, just get doing.

> *If it's important to you and you want to do it 'eventually,' just do it and correct course along the way.*
>
> *- Tim Ferris, The 4 Hour Work Week*

Let's also consider task and achievement. A task is the doing of something but not necessarily achieving anything, even if you think you are. Take, for example, teaching. The teacher is doing something, but if no-one is learning, which is the goal of teaching, then teaching has just become a task, not something that has been achieved. This can be expanded to all sorts of tasks. When reading this, are you taking it in and learning from it or are you just doing the task of reading? The same goes for almost any situation. Remember, one of the key pillars of wellbeing is experience. When you go to work, are you there to do a task or there to achieve?

Discipline is overall a skill that helps you to take steps towards fulfilling your personal vision and goals. Thus, discipline is the opposite of procrastination.

MOTIVATION

Motivation is sweat and pushing. Inspiration is sweat and pulling. Motivation is what you do until you are inspired.

- Bradley Charbonneau

Action creates motivation. This could be dressed it up and given some anecdotes and stories, but when it comes down to it, it is as simple as that. To get motivated, you need to do something towards your goal or whatever it is you want to achieve. Doing something, even something small, miniscule even, is still something and that bit of action, that doing, can be the seed that inspires you to do a bit more and then a little bit more again.

If you look online for motivational quotes and to see what people think will inspire them, many quotes have the power to stop you doing what you always do, to break those habits that you hate, but are unable to change you. Often these are framed in a poster with some guy rock climbing or accomplishing some grandiose feat, accompanied with works like, 'A walk of a thousand miles begins with a single step.', 'The only place where success comes before work is in the dictionary.', 'Whether You Think You Can Or Think You Can't, You're Right.'

The list goes on and on. Now, this book is peppered with quotes and so on from things that have hopefully motivated and inspired you, giving you that briefest of dopamine hits, making you excited. However, let's face it, as much as words can excite you and resonate with what you are feeling, they have the same power to make you feel just as bad, if not worse, about yourself. Take the three examples above. They can be just as demoralising as they can be motivating. As discussed in the chapter *Acting Like A Happy Person*, if you are not in the right frame of mind, no positive affirmations are going to change the way you feel inside.

A thousand miles? Man, that is a lot of steps. I think I'll pass.

Work? I do that all day and I am exhausted when I get home. I don't have the energy. Now, where's the TV remote?

I can't, you're right.

And who's kidding who? Half of what has been written in this book is designed to get you inspired. The hope is that beyond inspiring you with some words, you get enough information and how-to, to get started in achieving a better version of yourself, to move from motion into action and trigger your motivation. Quotes and posters say it, but this book aims to show you how to do it too.

The greatest motivator you should have is time. This is why it is one of the pillars of wellbeing. However relative time may be, for you it is finite. You only have a limited amount of time to achieve your dreams, ambitions, and goals. You are born and one day you will die and there won't be a tomorrow, the next day or 'someday'. For some, that is enough to flip the coin and motivate them into action but for others, even when it is obvious that time is ticking away faster every day, there is still always a tomorrow in their mind, however fewer those are fast becoming. How then can someone be motivated into action?

How do you achieve your goals and things that need to be done, such as going to your job? Are you motivated by what will give you pleasure or what will save you from pain? If you are like most people, you are motivated to avoid pain rather than chase pleasure. You work to keep what you have rather than work to get something better. There is no right or wrong with this either. None of us want to be worse off, but find it hard to go for something that is aspirational over protecting what we already have. As we have discussed, we are negatively geared, and we focus on negative consequences rather than possibilities. What if I fail? What if something goes wrong?

Extrinsic motivation pushes us to achieve what needs to be done. This is the old carrot and stick form of motivation. I'll give you money (the carrot) if you do this, or if you don't do this by such-and-such a time, you will be punished (the stick).

This kind of motivation, although effective for many people, is temporal and doesn't lead to a positive sense of wellbeing. How many people go to work each day primarily because of this form of motivation? A job is needed to pay the bills and to support yourself and your family. In these circumstances you are pressured to do things that in ordinary circumstances you would have no desire to do. You come home tired and unhappy, which causes your brain to release less dopamine, which leads to lesser brain function, lower creativity, bad memory, and a decreased ability to learn.

The level of motivation we have, can affect how likely we are to achieve our goal. Of course, if we don't have enough, we are less likely to achieve our goal but conversely, if we have too much motivation, we are also unlikely to achieve our goal. This is because, according to the Yerkes-Dodson law,[196] if you are too motivated, your productivity drops.

As an example, a golf professional motivated by the prize money of a tournament, may do a bad job during the competition as the stress and high tension make it hard to achieve the intended results. According to the law, the optimal level of motivation for different tasks has been calculated as follows:

Difficult tasks: 2 – 3 / 10

Average tasks: 5 / 10

Easy tasks: 7 – 8 / 10

When we are driven by extrinsic motivators, what do we do with the rest of our time? If you are like most people, you do nothing, or more specifically, you do minor things. You need a mental break, to escape from reality. The 21st century has you well and truly covered for that.

Media is all around us, from television and streaming services to social media and gaming, you can spend hours distracting yourself from 'real life' (let's remember, what you see on your screens isn't always real life). The news always focuses on the negative because it knows your brain is programmed to react to it more than positive news, and television and social media especially, sell you a vision of what you could have but don't.

People post the best parts of their life, and between that and television, you are sold a desire for purchasing a way to keep up with the Joneses. The problem is, the Joneses don't really exist. They are most likely doing it for likes, indebted up to their eyeballs or both! You do this for too long and the minor activities in your life start to look like majors. Did you know that Americans watch television for an average of five hours and eleven minutes each day? That is nine years of their lives watching television, not to mention the amount of time spent using their phones or on social media. That is a lot of time to be spent doing nothing. Is it any wonder we aren't motivated to do anything else? As mentioned, distraction is like an addiction.

Let's not forget that minor activities aren't always things that you necessarily enjoy. Minors can be things that seem major and important, like study, and watching self-help videos or reading self-help books (Hello!) but unless we apply what we have learned and act, they are mere motion and minors. Coupled with this are things like housework, gardening, maintenance, and other tasks such as grocery shopping. Yes, these things need to be done, but they can also become a procrastination technique. Focus on these and what do you know, the day has come and gone and there is no time to work on achieving your goals.

> *Motivation doesn't cause action.*
> *Action causes motivation.*
> -   *Neil Pasricha*

A great way to stay motivated is to complete tasks – finish what you start. If you chronically fail to finish tasks, then you are more likely to fail to achieve goals in the future. This is because you have it in your head that you will fail before you even start. Your brain, however, doesn't like things to be incomplete. To the brain, this represents instability.

To illustrate this, draw a circle on a piece of paper but leave a small gap so that the circle isn't finished. Now look at it for a couple of minutes. Your brain will want to complete the circle and for some, the urge to do so will be overwhelming. As with the open-circle experiment, you can do the same with a task. Just start what is in front of you, start anywhere. This is called the Zeigarnik effect, and in summary, it states that if you are faced with a goal and are procrastinating as a result, getting started anywhere, even if it is just the smallest part, will give you the motivation to keep going; drawing that line in small increments until you have completed the circle. The only requirement for the effect to work is that you have to be motivated to complete the project in the first place. Once you start, the Zeigarnik effect kicks in.

Another consideration is to be aware of why you are doing what you are doing. If you don't know why you are doing what you are doing, your motivation seeps away. This is an issue with many work-based projects; people do them without any understanding as to why. Knowing why is a crucial step towards action as it makes us examine what is going on and what we are doing, and this starts a change in thinking.

According to Mark Twain, the first thing you should do each morning is to eat a live frog. You can then go through the rest of the day with the satisfaction of knowing that is probably the worst thing that is going to happen to you all day. The 'frog', of course, is your biggest, most important task, the one you are most likely to procrastinate on. Achieving your biggest task removes the burden that sits on you for the rest of the day. The sense of accomplishment alone is priceless.

If goals are being set, then let's look at goal-based motivation. After all, we went through this in the setting goals section of the book. Goals prompt us into action and action motivates us. This is called intrinsic goal-based motivation. It is intrinsic because it is being driven from within us and not external drivers. We are motivated by the desire for pleasure at the attainment of the goal. Seems like a brilliant motivator so why do we still fail to achieve many of our goals? Surely, as we have discussed, if we set SMART, LEARN or T-LEAF goals, then we will achieve them.

Do we need to introduce a little extrinsic motivation to make this happen? As we have set the goal for ourselves, we shouldn't need a carrot, the goal in itself should be enough, and introducing a stick makes the whole task just that, a task, not something we want to do. It can work though. The stick could be a deadline you impose on yourself or perhaps you could tell others about your goal and they hold you accountable for achieving it. It all depends on what your threshold is for taking action. Mixing both pleasure and pain motivators can work.

The other thing about intrinsic goal-based motivation is that you are driven by the goal; it is only part of the process that will bring you pleasure. It is all about the outcome. How you got there becomes just a means to an end. Due to hedonic adaptation, achieving goals only produces a temporary state of happiness before returning to normal levels. This can then lead to wanting to achieve an even bigger goal to achieve that feeling again. We have talked about this previously. If your goal is to get a new mobile phone, once you achieve it, you love it, it is the greatest thing, you are so happy; but hedonic adaptation ensures that feeling doesn't last long. You get used to it, it becomes the new normal and soon you are looking for an even newer phone. If this continues unabated, it can lead to addiction, and addiction, in any form, is not a good thing for your positive wellbeing.

> *A man's worth is no greater than his ambition.*
> *- Marcus Aurelius*

So, what is the solution? What can motivate us? The answer comes from what we have spent the first part of Part II discussing. You can look at who you are and how you identify yourself, what your strengths, passion, meaning, and vision is for yourself. Identify your ikigai – your reason for getting up in the morning. It is your sweet spot of four primary elements:

- What you Love (your passion)
- What the World Needs (your mission)
- What you are Good at (your vocation)
- What you can get Paid for (your profession)

In his book, *The End of Procrastination*, Petr Ludwig called it Intrinsic Journey-Based Motivation. There is no focus on a goal as the reward is the activity itself. That becomes the focal point. This motivates us as activities you want to do (as opposed to need to do or have to do) release dopamine more frequently in your brain. You do it because it is fun, enjoyable, and satisfying. You do it because you love it; it is your passion. Thanks to this, hedonic adaptation is overcome, allowing you to experience happiness more often. It is that simple. By focusing on activities you want to do that have meaning for you and incorporate your strengths, vision, and values, you will reach a state of flow. 'Your brain will constantly release more dopamine, resulting in higher levels of creativity and more effective learning abilities.'[197]

What's more, if you team up with people who share similar values and personal visions, a powerful group vision may arise. This results in an intense form of group motivation. Another form of group motivation is called body-doubling. This is simply having someone else in the same room with you or wherever you are. They can be doing the same thing, something similar or something completely different. Just having them there can be a great motivator for you to achieve your goals, as they act as a form of accountability. Limiting your time with them adds to the motivation as the limited amount of time pushes you to do what you want to do. Your body-doublers don't even need to be in the same location as you. Virtual body-doubling has been shown to be nearly as effective, acting as an anchor to motivate you.

Examples of Intrinsic Motivation

1. Playing sport because you enjoy it rather than because you want to win.
2. Volunteering because it matches with your values and because it makes you feel good.
3. Learning new skills, such as studying or learning a new language.
4. Playing games and spending time with friends and family.
5. Taking on more responsibility because you like the challenge and being slightly outside your comfort zone; you want to grow.

Remember, you can motivate yourself intrinsically by:

- Doing things that are meaningful to you by focusing on your values.
- Challenging yourself to do things that are a challenge to you but not so much that they become too hard and you quit.
- Looking for ways to make work fun and more engaging for yourself.
- Doing things because you want to be better, not for the extrinsic reward.
- Being nice, being kind, being the kind of friend you want people to be to you.
- Creating a list of activities you enjoy doing or have always wanted to do and then referring to it and choosing an activity when you want something to do.
- Taking part in activities such as sports because you want to be with friends and to socialise as opposed to because you have to be the best or to win.

Snags along the way

Through intrinsic motivation, fulfilling your vision and passions, you will be internally rewarded and satisfy your basic psychological needs. You will be happy and receive emotional and material results. Tick! There will, however, still be times when things happen, things that may be beyond your control, that pull you off track and consequently cause you to lose momentum, resulting in less happiness and feelings of defeat and failure. We all have off days and sometimes off weeks or months. Your brain is always looking for danger and will pick up on your negative thoughts faster than it will any positive, so you need to realise this and get out of the funk as soon as possible.

Think about procrastination and what gets you into that state. Maybe you have tried to start an activity, but something has happened that has caused you to stop or simply, you had no passion for the activity. Either way, the negative response from having failed repeatedly can induce a feeling that everything is hard, nothing ever works out for you and no matter what you do, there is nothing you can do about it. You feel trapped and do nothing, which leads to feelings of guilt and doubt. Your self-esteem and confidence are shot and you feel helpless.

In the late 1960s and early 1970s, psychologists Martin Seligman and Steven Maier conducted experiments that showed animals and people can fall into a state of learned helplessness. The experiment was first done with dogs and then rats and involved splitting the animals into three groups and putting them in cages. One group received escapable shocks, one received inescapable shocks, and one received no shocks at all. For the groups that received shocks, in one group the animals could press a lever to avoid getting a shock and get out of the cage and in the other group, the animals could also press a lever but would still get a shock that is they could not avoid being shocked. After a period of time the animals were moved to different cages but even though they were in cages that would not shock them and allow them to escape the cage, the animals that were unavoidably shocked in the previous cages, didn't even try to escape. The animals were convinced they were trapped and had fallen into a state of learned helplessness. The same can be seen with elephants that are kept in captivity. As babies they are chained with big chains but as they grow, the chain doesn't change and even though they could break it, they are trained to be helpless and don't try. Humans can be cruel.

As with the animals, humans can also be afflicted by the same behaviour. It is reactive depression symptoms caused by a reaction to a stressor such as rejection, lose, or failure where people get a mindset that there is nothing they can do to overcome their situation. Loss of motivation, self-belief and even hope are consequences of learned helplessness.

Why is this important? Because it happens and as much as we don't want to admit it, we need to know how we can get out of it as soon as we can. If you are at the point where you are feeling depressed because of helplessness or for any reason, you are best to contact your local health professional and speak with them. This is a self-help book and sometimes we need other help too!

Petr Ludwig said there are four things to realise when you deal with failure. The first is to flip what Ludwig calls your inner switch, what we have called perspective, where you look at your failure from a different point of view. This is critical for everything, not just failure, and it is recommended you re-read the Perspective section of this book if you need further clarification. Ask yourself, is it really a failure? Can it be seen in another light? Don't focus on the negative of what you have done, but the positive. The past is done and gone and there is nothing you can do about it. All you can do is change your attitude towards it. This opens us up to the second, which is to see your failure as something to learn from.

Soichiro Honda, founder of the Honda Motor Company, said about failure, 'My biggest thrill is when I plan something and it fails. My mind is then filled with ideas on how I can improve it.' We can always learn from our mistakes. Trying to write a book with the television on in the background is not going to aid you in completing your task. The learning is to move to a location where you are away from distractions. If we don't learn from the mistakes of the past, we are destined to repeat them. The third thing to realise when dealing with failure is not that you have failed, but that you have tried to do something, to move forward. That is not failure, that is commendable because you have moved out of your comfort zone, which leads to the fourth realisation - it doesn't matter what results you get but that you tried, you put in your maximum effort to do something of value to you.

There will be examples of learned helplessness in your life that you cannot get rid of or that keep recurring. The key is to identify them when they happen and work on them, turn negative into positive where you can and when you can't, realise this and accept you cannot do anything about it. Acceptance can be turned into a positive attribute and over time, your feelings of helplessness will disappear as you accept there are certain things you can change and things that are beyond your control. Taking small steps can lead to big changes and that leads us nicely into the next section: building habits.

You've got to accentuate the positive
Eliminate the negative
Latch onto the affirmative
And don't mess with Mr In-between.

- Sung by Bing Crosby

BUILDING GOOD HABITS AND BREAKING BAD

We are what we repeatedly do. Excellence, then, is not an act, but a habit.

– Aristotle

You see them everywhere; the dirt path across a lawn or field when you should be following the concrete pathway around the lawn or field. This well-trodden pathway created by people as they take a shortcut from A – C instead of following the official pathway: A – B – C. The repeated use of the shortcut makes it more obvious until it becomes the main thoroughfare itself, the pathway created through repeated use, a well-worn shortcut embedded into the landscape.

Much like the example above, you brain builds new neural pathways through repetition. What does that mean? Habits are formed in your brain by doing the same thing repeatedly. Whether it is a task, thoughts, actions or whatever, the more you do it, the more it becomes a habit. A habit is something you do without thinking; it is that engrained into your brain. It is simple to determine what a habit is but they can also be frustrating as they don't care or know good from bad, just what is done repeatedly, so building good habits is difficult and bad habits easy whereas breaking good habits is easy and breaking bad habits is difficult. In what follows, we will better understand habits, how they are formed, how to make them stick and how to get rid of them – the bad ones, at least.

We all have habits. The good, the bad, and the ugly. Generally speaking, according to Charles Duhigg in his book, *The Power of Habit*, people are prone to routine, which is a form of habit.

Our brains follow a three-step loop.
1. The **trigger** or **cue** that tells the brain which habit to use.
2. The **routine**, which can be physical, mental, or emotional.
3. The **reward**, which reinforces the behaviour.

As an example, you might put the children to bed, (the trigger) then come downstairs, get something to eat and drink (the routine) and then relax with sweet, serotonin releasing foods and drinks, watching mindless shows on the television (the reward).

To see what habits you have, you need to take a step back and try to see yourself as others see you as we did in the exercise in the *Know Yourself* section. So, if you know how people see you, you can then work on identifying what you do as a habit, and there will be many, and then determine for yourself if the things you are doing are the things that you – the you, you want to be – want to keep doing. Yes? Great. No? Then you need to change them. Much like an alcoholic admitting they have a problem, identifying the habits you want to change is the first step.

Our brains are predictors; they like to make life easy so base a lot of what we do on expected outcomes based on certain cues or triggers as demonstrated in the example above. Once we do it automatically, we stop paying attention to it. If you are doing something without thinking about it, you have adopted a habit. Using another perspective and seeing what you do helps you become aware and can help in determining your habits, good and bad. As Stephen R Covey says in his book, *The 7 Habits of Highly Effective People*, the way we see the world is entirely based on our own perceptions. In order to change a given situation, we must change ourselves and in order to change ourselves, we must be able to change our perceptions.

> *You'll never change your life until you change something you do daily. The secret of your success is found in your daily routine.*
>
> - John C. Maxwell, Falling Forward

Habits are learned and built into us when we are young, usually up to the age of about seven years old. This is why it is really important to teach young children good habits such as brushing their teeth, reading, and good manners, because they stick. The neural pathways created in youth are incredibly strong. It is very hard to build new pathways in adulthood, so don't feel bad that you find it hard to create new habits and don't be surprised when you fail at so many things that require long-term commitment such as going on a diet and going to the gym.

The odds are against you from the start, but you can beat them with some good information and a bit of commitment. Building good habits isn't easy or immediately rewarding and your brain will not make neural pathways for this reason. It wants to feel positive emotions now as these create neural pathways very quickly, which is why it is easy to eat junk food or watch television. Your brain is using your emotions against you. It's like learning your times table, boring and hard work, but with perseverance it pays off and is worth it.

With the likes of trying to stop watching so much television or eating junk food at night, you need to come up with a distraction, something to do, perhaps a new hobby. Your brain keeps wanting a drink or something bad to eat and will pray on your mind saying, 'Just one, what's the harm?' It is miserable to keep ignoring what your brain wants and your hobby can seem boring but eventually you will start to feel better and not have the need to feed. You will start to see new advantages and options open up such as having more money because you are not buying junk food or finding you have more time because you are not watching television.

What is consistent across all the literature about building and breaking habits is this: make it easy. Human behaviour follows the law of least effort. The less your brain has to think and the less you have to do, the easier it is to do. We have discussed self-discipline as a requirement to break out of procrastination. Doing something like learning your times table is boring and hard work. It requires repetition, doing something over and over, but with perseverance, it pays off. But and this is the big but, it isn't easy. We discussed a dopamine detox and lowering your dopamine levels, so the learning has it rewards, but again a detox isn't easy. The key is to take it easy to make it easy.

What does that mean? As Stephen Guise, says in his book, *Elastic Habits*, build better habits by designing them to suit you. Have flexibility in your approach as things change and we need to stay motivated and moving forward. Don't overburden yourself and be rigid with habits. You don't have to learn the whole nine times table in one session or cut all sugar from your diet. Sometimes you can do more, sometimes you need to do less. The point is to make starting the habit as easy as possible. When what you are doing becomes a chore, boring or a hassle, stop. There is no point continuing as this will just put you off and remove the desire to build a habit at all. That doesn't mean you stop completely, just at that point in time. Go back to it later. To make it super easy, start out small, go slow and be easy on yourself. How easy? Two minutes. You may be a busy person with no time to do anything, but you have two minutes. What you want to do is get into the routine of starting a routine. You want the idea of starting a routine to be as easy as possible.

The Kaizen approach, taken from the Japanese word for continuous improvement, was developed in Depression-era America by business management theorists. As the word suggests, it is about improving things all the time as opposed to making radical and drastic changes. So, instead of planning a whole new department layout or a big installation of new equipment, the idea is to look for lots of small things that can be improved on existing jobs with existing equipment. Obviously, it was developed to assist with business management processes but has been adapted with the intention of building habits. Instead of trying to make major changes, it suggests making small improvements every day that will gradually lead to the change you want. What it suggests is focusing on getting one per cent better in whatever it is you are trying to improve.

What difference will one per cent make? A lot. Think about compound interest on the money you have invested in the bank. It's not much, maybe four or five per cent if you are lucky, but over time it builds up. Let's look at brain teaser as a bit of an example. If you were offered one million dollars now or one cent that would double every day for thirty days, which would you choose? Most would choose the one million dollars for obvious reasons as it satisfies your brain's need for immediate reward; it's a lot of money, and because one cent doubled daily surely cannot add up to much money after only thirty days. Yet, if you work it out, after thirty days, one cent would be worth a staggering \$5,368,709.12! Yes, that is over five million dollars! The same thing happens with the effort you put into building habits.

Your brain wants to choose the immediate reward of sitting in front of the television eating chocolate and drinking, but making the effort to build up your habits doing whatever it is you want to do, pays off in dividends in the long-term. Small steps. Big reward. Many of us believe that to make a big difference, we need to make a big change, but that is also the problem. Big changes require big sacrifices. Big change requires you to come out of your comfort zone and your brain doesn't like that. It prefers the status quo. It's for this reason that diets don't work over the long-term and why going to the gym seems like a good idea at the time, but not so much after a while. We don't think we can do much to change the future, let alone small things, but do you ever watch time travel movies or just think about time travel and going back into the past and how just one small change can have a massive impact on the present, the old butterfly effect? You would be very cautious about what you did because by simply being at a certain place at a certain time or doing one small thing can massively change what is to come. The same thing happens with building habits. You don't think about it, but this present moment will very soon be the past and one small change now can have a massive impact in the future. Quite a mind-blowing concept and it shows the power of now and how small actions now can make big changes later.

Habits, routines, and rituals
are like anchors in our lives.

– *Michelle Bridges, Lifestyle and Fitness Coach*

Making small changes makes changing easier. Eat some fruit, go for a short run, or even just walk and build from there to joining a gym. Let's say you want to get into the habit of reading before bedtime. Instead of saying you are going to read each night, be more specific and say I will read a page. One page, two minutes. Easy. The power of the Kaizen Approach is not in the one per cent but thousands of them. Like building

LEGO or doing a jigsaw puzzle, nothing much seems to have happened after a few pieces have been put together but over time you have built something amazing.

It is important to standardise what you are doing before you optimise. Stick to the two minutes or whatever you choose to get into the routine. Don't jump too far ahead. If you exceed your goal, don't increase it, as having a good day doesn't mean every day will be a good day. Resist changing to save yourself from failure. Once you are consistently doing whatever it is you want to do, then it is time to take your foot off the brakes but only a little and increase your expectations slowly. You are now using your willpower and self-discipline and as mentioned earlier, it is like a muscle, the more you use it, the stronger it becomes.

> *People do not decide their futures, they decide their habits and their habits decide their futures.*
> *– F M Alexander*

To make building your habits even easier, track your progress. Write down how you are doing. Goals gain power the moment you write them down. The simple act of tracking a habit can help to change it.

James Clear in his book, *Atomic Habits*, recommends recording what you do for a habit each day. He talks about creating a chain using a diary or calendar where you cross off each day you have done something towards building your habit and achieving your goal. Doing so encourages you not to 'break the chain' and stay on track, as well as it being a visual cue. Progress is the most effective form of motivation. It can become quite an addictive form of motivation as well and this is where you need to be careful that you aren't falling into the trap of intrinsic goal-based motivation where your primary goal is to build the chain as opposed to building the habit of whatever it is you want to do. Building the chain has wonderful effects as each small piece of the chain gives you the impetus to keep going, which is especially helpful on your off days when you can't be bothered but don't want to break the chain. As an example, consider apps like Duolingo, the language learning app, which uses streaks to measure how frequently someone is using the app. After reaching goals you get badges and if consistent every day for s specific period of time you go up a tier. People are motivated to keep the streak running and doing their language lessons without breaking the chain. Much like your to-do list at work or in your everyday home life, your goals gain power from the moment you write them down and you can look at the list and see how far you have come. Crossing things of the list makes you feel good, keeps you focused on the process and not just the result. You are in the present moment and as we have discussed, consequently you are happier.

If you miss a day, don't fret, just get back on track as soon as possible otherwise breaking the chain becomes your new habit.

> *I was giving up. I would have given up – if a voice hadn't made itself heard in my heart. The voice said, 'I will not die. I refuse it. I will make it through this nightmare. I will beat the odds, as great as they are. I have survived so far, miraculously. Now I will turn miracle into a routine.*
>
> *- Yann Martel, Life of Pi*

Another important factor to make building a habit easy is your environment. Consider how your immediate environment influences what you do and your motivation and self-discipline. Consider how it is stifling your ability to stop bad habits as well as build good habits. Think how easy it is to watch television when there is one in the room or how easy it is to have a drink when you in a bar. Consider about how many times you have gone to the supermarket to buy one thing and come back with a dozen.

How items are placed within a supermarket is no accident. Just think about how many things you buy off the end isles. It is the environment that drives purchases, and more than that, it is the context in which these things are associated. Shops are associated with buying, bars with drinking, and televisions with relaxing. The environment in which you are trying to either build or break your habits may be influencing your ability to succeed. How can this be overcome? Build an environment that suits your needs.

As an example, someone who has to work from home. Immediately there is an issue. Home is a not a working environment. They may have a computer on a desk in the open plan living area, which includes the kitchen and dining area.

The environment, both physically and mentally, is not conducive to working. The house doesn't have the space to change the environment, but it could be redefined or rearranged. For example, the desk and computer could be moved into a spare bedroom, removing the bed and storing it away, therefore creating a dedicated workspace. As James Clear says in *Atomic Habits*, 'One space. One use.' Doing this creates a more disciplined working environment. Now they know this is where work is done. When they are in this room, it is to work and when they are not, they are at home and can turn off work mode.

When trying to stop watching television by reading a book, do so in a room where there is no television or to add more context, go to a library and read there, surrounded by like-minded people. When trying to eat better, shop somewhere different. At your usual supermarket, you have a higher chance of buying the same foods as it is all too familiar. Go to a new store, somewhere you have not been before and are unfamiliar with its layout; it will lessen the likelihood of you buying the same foods. Wanting to exercise more? Go to a gym with like-minded people or out onto the streets. Set up your environment to make it easy to start your habit. Remove friction points and if you are trying to get rid of bad habits, add friction points. Remember, your brain wants things easy.

Remove yourself from tempting situations; they are usually the cue to your bad habits. It is the cue or trigger that tells the brain what habit to do and the trigger could easily be your environment so where you can, change your negative environment into a positive one and where you can't, redefine your environment to suit your requirements.

Stephen Guise, in his book, *Elastic Habits*, says it is not just the physical environment that needs to be considered but how you are feeling mentally and emotionally – in the environment of your mind. We aren't always 'on' and there are always things happening that will be beyond our control that fog up the roadmap of our mind. Sometimes you do just need to turn off and take a break. We have discussed understanding what you can and cannot control and finding acceptance and peace in that. If your mind's environment is cluttered, unconducive and your ability to get things done is weakened, pause, take a break, but never stop. When the environment of your mind is on and firing on all cylinders again, you can use it to fly higher again.

Also consider the social environment and its influence on the formation of habits. Our culture and society are especially important to us and we all want to fit in, to be loved, wanted, and appreciated. To do so, we adhere to social customs. Think of the chaos that would ensue if we didn't. Yes, there are laws that ensure we act in a certain way but consider the impact COVID-19 had on habits in society. We all washed our hands often and practiced social distancing when in public. As a society on the macro scale, we have our social norms and customs, but what of the smaller social environments or groups we are all a part of? Your friends, workplace, sports team, or the religious or social groups and clubs you belong to? What social environments are you a part of? Does the culture of these environments accept your desired behaviour as normal?

Think of the social dynamics and groups represented in John Hughes' movie, *The Breakfast Club*. The film had the brain, the athlete, the princess, the basket case, and the criminal (in their words), all different and with different backgrounds, goals, and aspirations but very much alike as well. As the character Andrew says in the movie, 'We're all pretty bizarre. Some of us are just better at hiding it, that's all.' Being around people who have the same habits as you want, who share the same passions as you have, increases exponentially your likelihood of success in building and maintaining your habits. So, if you like books, join a book club; cycling, join a cycling group; being anti-social, join an anti-social social club (it is written on a t-shirt so there must be one!). We have discussed this idea already, but socialising is important for your future happiness and wellbeing.

It is difficult, but you need to take stock of your current social groups. Are they the right fit for the person you want to become? Are the people like-minded to your ideals, vision, and goals? It is especially hard, as we all want to fit in, and with your current social groups you may very well do that, but the group may not be where you desire to be any longer. It not that the people in the group are necessarily bad, but they may be preventing you from growing into the person you are destined to be. You can stay as you are and with your current social circle, or you can choose to go against the crowd to find a social group that will support your desired behaviours and aspirations.

Neither option is attractive, but staying as you are prevents you from growing and ultimately sets you back. You will grow miserable as more time passes and ultimately will need to move on. Sometimes these things happen organically as time passes.

Think of your mates, always together, drinking, at parties, inseparable. The good times will last forever. Then, one by one, they start getting partners and slowly spending more time with them, getting married or having children, perhaps both. You drift apart as priorities change. No-one has said anything, it has just happened. Moving on sees little reward as it is not attractive and hard to do, but changing your social group to change your habits to fit in is attractive and will see a lot of reward, so although it may seem hard, it is better to move on. You are more likely to regret something you haven't done, than something you have.

You can use your social groups to aid and motivate you to achieve your desired goals and habits. Tell your like-minded friends about your goals and the habits you want to form. Tell them you would like their support. Have them follow up on you to see how you are doing. People of a similar mindset are a great asset and motivator to help you be the best version of yourself.

Another option is to use people you trust and money as a motivator. Give someone, such as your partner or a close friend, an amount of money that you would miss, such as $1,000 or $5,000. You then use that as a tool to motivate and push yourself to build your desired habits or achieve your goals. The motivation being that if you don't achieve your goal within a predetermined timeframe, your partner or friend gets to keep the money and do with it as they wish.

If you're considering this, make sure you put it all down in writing so that a) you cannot back out and say you were only joking, and b) they don't go off and spend the money before the timeframe is up.

Great things are not done by impulse, but by
a series of small things brought together.

– Vincent Van Gogh

Habits are an entry point, not an end point. They come from the first action. Writing a book? Sitting in front of the computer away from distraction, not the actual writing, is the start of the routine. Going for a run? Putting on your running shoes, not leaving the house and running, is the entry point. If we have an entry point, it becomes our cue and the formation of the habit. Once we have started the entry point action, we are more likely to follow through with the next step and so on.

It is not the *amount* of time you have been doing your habits but the *number of times* you have participated in it. At the start of this section, you were asked to consider how other people see you and the habits you have. As you will have seen, some of the habits you have weren't obvious to you and not surprisingly either. They are after all an unconscious action on your behalf, all you need is the cue, but how many times have you done a routine only to find you have missed something because it was done on autopilot?

Consider this example: you are driving to work, intending to get some petrol on the way, and the next thing you know you are pulling into your work carpark. You took the same route you always take, listened to the same radio stations you always listen to and wonder where the time went, and yes, you forgot to stop and get petrol. It wasn't part of your routine.

Here's another example: you are going on an overseas holiday with your family. Before you leave for the airport you write a list to ensure you have everything. You make sure everything is packed, you double-check the weight of the suitcases and then do it a third time, just to be sure, because excess baggage is so expensive. You make sure you have your phone and charger, the kids have their iPads (and their chargers), money, the airline tickets, and your passports, which you again double-check to make sure they haven't expired. You are very aware of everything that needs to be done. You say it out loud to yourself as you mentally tick it off your list and then again to your partner so they can double-check what you have done. This is not a habit; you are very conscious about what you are doing, unlike driving to work or one of the multitudes of other habits you possess. To become conscious of your habits and what you are doing, saying what you are doing aloud gives you the ability to consciously be aware of and change what you are doing.

With bad habits, let's use the example of putting the kids to bed as the cue to watch television. Being conscious of the cue, you can work to change the habit but as Charles Duhigg, author of *The Power of Habit* says, 'You must keep the old cue, and deliver the old reward, but insert a new routine.' All of our habits are etched in our minds. We can stop doing them, but the neural pathways have been made and they are never forgotten. All that is needed is the cue to set off the temptation again. To change the habit, we have to make it easy, obvious, and according to James Clear's *Atomic Habits*, attractive and satisfying. How can we change the routine while keeping the cue and reward the same? It is likely that your desired habit doesn't offer immediate reward and isn't nearly as attractive as your bad habit.

Breaking bad habits is hard because our brains are wired for survival and reward, and bad habits generally give us rewards very quickly. You need to accept the bad feelings instead of the automatic response that tells you to make them go away. The first thing to do is nothing. Just stop. Your cortisol will insist on taking action, but doing nothing, no matter how hard it is, will teach your brain that nothing happens when you do nothing, there is no consequence to your lack of action, and this creates a new neural pathway.

If you want to increase your chance of success, be specific about what you want to do, when and where. Using the same example, you could say, 'I will go for a run around the block of my street after I have put the children to bed at 8:30.' There is more power in this statement than saying, 'I will go for a run.' Adding a time and place makes it more likely that the behaviour will be performed.

To make it attractive, you can pair the behaviour with something you want to do. 'After putting the children to bed at 8:30, I will go for a run around the block and then watch an episode of my favourite television show.'

Using a diary or calendar to make a chain makes the likelihood of success increase even more. To really put you in the driver's seat and take control of your life, you can then add another good habit you want to build onto the one you have started. Let's say you want to start reading more. After your run and the reward you have given yourself, you can then go to bed and read for thirty minutes before sleeping. Doing this is called Habit Stacking[198] or the Tiny Habits Recipe[199].

Use one good habit to start another and over time build in more good habits. To use an example of something you most likely already do, you brush your teeth before bed then after that, add the new habit of reading for thirty minutes before sleeping. You can then add more habits either before or after your current good habits bearing in mind you can add little rewards if required along the way. Using this formula, you now have a good habit loop.

You have:

1. made it obvious.
2. Created a positive environment.
3. made it easy.
4. made it attractive and satisfying; you can get that immediate pleasure and reward and consequently you are likely to repeat it.

If you find that you are still not able to make your habits stick, and that repeat, repeat, repeat has become repeat, repeat, return to old habits, don't feel too disheartened. Sometimes the biggest threat to forming successful habits is boredom. If your habit, for example, was to run, it can get pretty boring doing the same thing over and over again. You get sweaty, tired, and bored with the repetition. By being conscious of your desired habit, you can make changes, be flexible and realise that sometimes life happens.

Keep in mind the Serenity Prayer and accept what you can and cannot control and go from there. Stop and reflect on what you are doing. Review what you have achieved and see if there is something you can change to improve your routine. Run a different route, add a challenge such as hills, or mix it up by running the streets some days and running on a treadmill on others, or running with someone else, maybe even doing another exercise completely, such as cycling. The habit you want to form should be something you want, not something you feel you must have. You need to want the goal, not need it. Need turns to willpower and extrinsic motivation, whereas you want something that is intrinsic and brings you joy and flow. The habits you choose for yourself should match your personality and strengths. Don't pick something that you hope will improve your weaknesses.

To have a sense of positive wellbeing, you need to focus on your strengths and make them stronger. Focus on what you are good at. An uncoordinated person is never going to be the next Michael Jackson or Fred Astaire, but they may be good at piano or guitar and be the next Elton John or Eric Clapton. And remember, even though these are examples of people that were at the top of their game, you aren't aiming to be the best; that will only add undue stress, anxiety, and feelings of failure, you are simply aiming to be better than you were yesterday.

In regards to how long it takes to build a habit, there is no time frame, so don't listen to those that say it takes 30 days, or 45 days, or 80 days, for it to become automatic; it takes as long as you keep doing it.

> *It might take 30 days to create a habit, but that habit could change your life for the next 30 years.*
>
> *It might take 1 hour to complete a workout, but it will keep you in a good mood for 12 hours.*
>
> *It might take you 30 minutes to complete a morning routine, but it will build momentum for the rest of the day.*
>
> *It might take you 5 hours to read a book, but you'll keep the knowledge forever.*
>
> *It might take 3 months to learn a new skills, but that skill could make you millions.*
>
> *Long-term thinking is really key.*
>
> *- Richard Yuzee*

Finally, let's remember that habit building should be flexible. Habits aren't a chore or something to feel guilty about because you missed an action. Focus on the one percent and keep it simple. As per the seventh habit in Stephen R Covey's *Seven Habits of Highly Effective People*, 'sharpen the saw' and renew yourself spiritually, physically, socially, and mentally.

Always look to improve yourself – your greatest asset. Look for continuous improvement opportunities in what you are doing so you can progress along the upward spiral of growth and change. But above all, follow Newton's first law, which states that an object will remain at rest or in uniform motions in a straight line unless acted upon by an external force. Make your willpower the external force and then be that object forever moving forward. It is easier to keep going once you have started. Other external forces may throw you off track or stop you and when they do, just start again. Don't remain at rest. You can't keep starting over. You need to stick at it at some point or else the habit will never build. Inertia is a powerful mistress, but if you start, you will find it easier to keep going.

Keep it simple, start small; build the LEGO of mini habits and they will build up to bigger habits in no time and before you know it, the ingredients of your recipe for wellbeing will be habits that bring you ongoing wellbeing and the knowledge that you are being the best version of yourself that you can be.

NEXT STEPS

Now this is not the end. It is not even the beginning of the end. But it is, perhaps, the end of the beginning.

- Winston Churchill

And so, we come to the end of the beginning of your journey towards a life of wellbeing. The proverbial fly buzzing at the window is now dead on the windowsill. It died trying to break through the glass wall to somewhere it could see but never had a chance of reaching. You do!

A year from now you will wish you had started today.

– Karen Lamb, Author

You now need to go and create some neural pathways, cementing in your mind what you have learned by going out there, taking some sort of action and putting what you have learned into practice, having experiences and new learnings. Take this and apply it to your everyday life, building for yourself a life of wellbeing.

If you didn't learn these things in order to demonstrate them in practice, what did you learn them for?

- Epictetus

You are unique, and in fact, for lack of a better word, you are what they call 'normal.' Your brain just thinks you are living 12,000 years ago in a cave as a hunter-gatherer, fearing for your life every day, ready to be killed by some sabre-toothed tiger. Your brain is about as primal as they come and you are stuck with it as it is in the 21st century.

Accept that you can't be happy all of the time, in fact, rarely any of the time. You are on a sliding scale, so set realistic expectations. What you want is an overall feeling of positive wellbeing. There will be good days and bad days and one does not determine the other or the rest of your life. Don't see a glass as half full or half empty; it's a moot point. You just need to focus on putting something in the glass in the first place. You get out what you put in.

Select some of the ingredients, try them out, a dash of this, a dollop of that, and see what tastes good, what works for you. Bear in mind your brain will work to stop you moving forward. The creation of habits is what will pull you forward, so just do one percent and over time this will increase your wellbeing exponentially.

What you choose to do will vary depending on who you are, what your interests are, your values, your needs, and where you find happiness. Focus on your strengths, not your weaknesses. Accentuate the positive. Choose what will fit in with your lifestyle. Not all ingredients are going to taste good to everyone or anyone. Based on this, some ingredients will suit and others won't, so pick those that will and get started. You need to put in effort and commitment, but the pay-off will be a more consistent feeling of positive wellbeing and happiness.

Certain ingredients will work better after certain events, such as meditation or sleep after a stressful day. Don't fall into the trap of doing the same activities or using the same well-being recipe all the time. Using the same methods will become monotonous and a chore, causing the repeated routines to lose their effectiveness and ability to make you feel positive. Variety, as they say, is the spice of life.

Seek the support of family and friends. Be part of groups that share the same goals and view on life as you want for yourself. Find ways to feel intrinsically motivated; the more motivated you are, the more effort you will make and the more commitment you will have.

Remember, not all that glistens is gold. People may look like they have their lives together, but just like you, they have their demons to battle. Don't try to be like them or better than them, just try to be better than you were yesterday. You are the only person on this planet with whom you can fairly compare yourself.

> *You only live once, but if you*
> *do it right, once is enough.*
>
> *– Mae West*

You only live once? Well, maybe, but then again, perspective could say you live every day. You only die once! Time is your greatest asset and your worst enemy. You have no more and no less time than anyone else. Use it wisely to become the person you were always meant to be. Don't let fear stop you or regret despair you. Don't procrastinate, waiting for something better to come to you. Life is for living, as simple as that. Get out there, live, and be happy. Weep, laugh, mourn, dance, plant, pluck, get, lose, keep, cast away, harvest, sow, meditate, be silent, speak, scream, be kind, live in the moment, feel. Simply do what works for you and your wellbeing.

You have the mindset and you have the ingredients.

Now is the time to put them together.

*We are all given the ingredients of happiness,
but the mixing is left to ourselves.*
– Ethel M Dell

BIBLIOGRAPHY

Altucher, J (2013) *Choose Yourself!* Createspace Independent Publishing Platform.

Bayer, M (2019) *Best Self: Be You, Only Better.* HarperCollins US.

Becker, E (1997) *The Denial Of Death.* Free Press.

Bennett, M & Bennett, S (2015) *F8ck Feelings: One Shrink's Practical Advice for Managing All Life's Impossible Problems.* Simon & Schuster.

Bishop, M. (2015) *The Good Life: Unifying The Philosophy and Psychology of Well-being.* Oxford University Press.

Brooks, D (2019) *The Second Mountain: The Quest For A More Moral Life.* Penguin.

Bryson, B (2019) *The Body: A Guide For Occupants.* Doubleday Books.

Burnett, D (2018) *The Happy Brain: The Science of Where Happiness Comes From, and Why.* Guardian Faber Publishing.

Burton, N (2020) *Heaven and Hell: The Psychology of the Emotions.* Acheron Press.

Byrne, R (2006) *The Secret.* Simon & Shuster Australia.

Casals, P (1974) *Joys and Sorrows; Reflections.* Simon & Schuster.

Charbonneau, B (2017) *Every Single Day.* Independently published.

Clear, J (2018) *Atomic Habits.* Avery.

Coelho, P (1999) *The Alchemist*. HarperCollins Publishers.

Covey, S (2013) *The Seven Habits of Highly Effective People*. Simon & Schuster.

DiSalvo, D (2018) *What Makes Your Brain Happy and Why You Should Do The Opposite*. Prometheus Books.

Dow, M (2015) *The Brain Fog Fix – Reclaim Your Focus, Memory, and Joy In Just 3 Weeks*. Hay House.

Ferris, T (2011) *The 4 Hour Work Week: Escape the 9 – 5, Live Anywhere and Join the New Rich*. Vermilion.

Fromm, E (2013) *To Have or To Be*. Open Road Media.

Furness-Smith, P (2015) *Introducing Well-being: A Practical Guide*. Icon.

Gittens, R (1998) *The Happy Economist*. Allen & Unwin. Sydney.

Godin, S (2018) *This Is Marketing*. Portfolio.

Graziano Breuning, L (2015) *Habits of a Happy Brain: Retrain Your Brain to Boost Your Serotonin, Dopamine, Oxytocin, & Endorphin Levels*. Adams Media.

Greenville-Cleave, B (2012) *Introducing Positive Psychology: A Practical Guide*.

Guise, S (2019) *Elastic Habits*. Selective Entertainment LLC.

Harari, YN (2014) *Sapiens: A Brief History of Mankind*. Harvill Secker.

Hardy, Benjamin (2020) *Personality Isn't Permanent: Break Free from Self-Limiting Beliefs and Rewrite Your Story*. Portfolio

Harris, D (2017) *10% Happier: How I Tamed the Voice in My Head, Reduced Stress Without Losing My Edge, and Found Self-Help That Actually Works - A True Story*. Yellow Kite.

Harris, R (2007) *The Happiness Trap: Stop Struggling, Start Living*.

Hawking, S (2006) *The Theory of Everything*. Jaico Publishing House.

Inman, M (2017) *How to be Perfectly Unhappy.* Andrews McMeel Publishing

Jacka, F (2019) *Brain Changer: The Good Mental Health Diet.* Macmillan Australia.

Johnson, S (1999) *Who Moved My Cheese.* Vermilion.

Kiyosaki, R (2020) *Rich Dad Poor Dad: What the Rich Teach their Kids About Money That The Poor And Middle Class Do Not!* Bespoke Books.

Kwik, J (2020) *Limitless: Upgrade Your Brain, Learn Anything Faster, And Unlock Your Exceptional Life.* Hay House.

Lively, L (1999) *The Procrastinator's Guide to Success.* McGraw Hill.

Ludwig, P (2019) *The End of Procrastination: How to stop postponing and live a fulfilled life.* Murdoch Books

Lundin, S C & Paul, S & Christensen, J (2002) *Fish!: A remarkable way to boost morale and improve results.* Hodder & Stoughton.

Manson, M (2016) *The Subtle Art of Not Giving A Fck: A Counterintuitive Approach to Living a Good Life.* Macmillan Australia.

Meurisse, T (2019) *Master Your Focus. Independently published.* Exisle Publishing.

Pasricha, N (2016) *The Happiness Equation.* G.P. Putnam's Sons.

Peterson, J B, 12 *Rules For Life: An Antidote to Chaos.* Penguin Press.

Safran Foer, J (2018) *Extremely Loud and Incredibly Close.* Penguin.

Sachette, B (2018) *Get Out Of Your Head: A Toolkit for Living with and Overcoming Anxiety.* We Are The Change Publishing.

Salzgeber, j (2019) *The Little Book of Stoicism,* Jonas Salzgeber.

Scott Peck, M (1990) *The Road Less Travelled.* Arrow Ltd.

Seligman, M (2011) *Flourish*. Random House Australia.

Smith, B (2016) *Mindset – How Positive Thinking Will Set You Free & Help You Achieve Massive Success In Your Life*. Createspace Independent Publishing Platform.

Robbins, J (2014) *Live It!: Achieve Auccess by Living with Purpose*. Grand Harbor Press.

Rosling, H (2018) *Factfulness: Ten Reasons We're Wrong About The World – And Why Things Are Better Than You Think*. Sceptre.

Teja, V (2019) *YOLO: Essential Life Hacks for Happiness*. The Unapologetic Voice House LLC.

Watt, T (2012) *Introducing Mindfulness: A Practical Guide*. Icon Books Ltd.

Wiest, B (2018) *101 Essays That Will Change The Way You Think*. Thought Catalog Books.

Wiest, B (2020) *The Mountain is You – Transforming Self-Sabotage Into Self-Mastery*. Thought Catalog Books.

Wilson, S (2017) *First, We Make The Beast Beautiful*. Macmillan Australia.

ENDNOTES

[1] *Happiness, N.: Oxford english dictionary* (no date) *Oxford English Dictionary*. Available at: https://www.oed.com/viewdictionaryentry/Entry/84070 (Accessed: 28 January 2024).

[2] *Well-being, N.: Oxford English Dictionary* (no date) *Oxford English Dictionary*. Available at: https://www.oed.com/viewdictionaryentry/Entry/227050 (Accessed: 28 January 2024).

[3] Roy, E.A. (2019) New Zealand's world-first 'wellbeing' budget to focus on poverty and mental health, *The Guardian*. Available at: https://www.theguardian.com/world/2019/may/14/new-zealands-world-first-wellbeing-budget-to-focus-on-poverty-and-mental-health (Accessed: 29 January 2024).

[4] Bishop, M. (2015). *The Good Life: Unifying The Philosophy and Psychology of Well-being*, Oxford University Press.

[5] *Flourishing* (2024) Wikipedia. Available at: https://en.wikipedia.org/wiki/Flourishing (Accessed: 29 January 2024).

[6] *Six-factor model of psychological well-being* (2023) Wikipedia. Available at: https://en.wikipedia.org/wiki/Six-factor_Model_of_Psychological_Well-being (Accessed: 29 January 2024).

[7] *Nicomachean Ethics* (2024) Wikipedia. Available at: https://en.wikipedia.org/wiki/Nicomachean_Ethics (Accessed: 29 January 2024).

[8] Seligman, M. (2012) *Flourish*. William Heinemann Australia.

[9] Gittens, R (2010) *The Happy Economist: Happiness for the hard-headed*, Allen & Unwin, page 16.

[10] Gittens, R (2010) *The Happy Economist: Happiness for the hard-headed*, Allen & Unwin, page 16.

[11] Salzgeber, J, Salzgeber N, ((2019), *The Little Book of Stoicism: Timeless Wisdom to Gain Resilience, Confidence, and Calmness*, Jonas Salzgeber, page 38–40.

[12] *Experientia - Wiktionary, The free dictionary* (no date) *Wiktionary*. Available at: https://en-

.wiktionary.org/wiki/experientia#Latin (Accessed: 29 January 2024).

[13] *The time paradox* (no date) *The Time Paradox*. Available at: https://www.thetimeparadox.com/zimbardo-time-perspective-inventory/ (Accessed: 29 January 2024).

[14] Branson, R, (2011) Screw It, Let's Do It: Lessons In Life, Virgin Digital

https://www.amazon.co.uk/Screw-Lets-Do-Lessons-Quick-ebook/dp/B005F3GK92

[15] Schmich, M (June 1, 1997). Advice, like youth, probably just wasted on the young, Chicago Tribune. https://www.chicagotribune.com/columns/chi-schmich-sunscreen-column-column.html accessed: April 28, 2020.

[16] Manson, M, (2016), The Subtle Art of Not Giving a F*ck: A Counterintuitive Approach to Living a Good Life, Harper.

[17] Bryson, B, (2019) *The Body: A Guide for Occupants*, Transworld Digital, Page 63.

[18] Martin, P., & Smyer, M. A. (1990). The Experience of Micro- and Macro-events: A Life Span Analysis. *Research on Aging*, *12*(3), 294-310. https://doi.org/10.1177/0164027590123002

[19] Sedikides, C, Wildschut, T, Arndt, J, and Routledge, C, (2008) *Nostalgia. Past, Present, and Future*, University of Southampton, Association for Psychological Science, Volume 17 – Number 5. https://www.southampton.ac.uk/~crsi/Sedikides%20Wildschut%20Arndt%20%20Routledge%202008%20CDir.pdf

[20] *Back to the future: nostalgia increases optimism* (13th November 2013), University of Southampton., https://www.southampton.ac.uk/news/2013/11/13-nostalgia-increases-optimism.page.

[21] *Back to the future: nostalgia increases optimism* (13th November 2013), University of Southampton., https://www.southampton.ac.uk/news/2013/11/13-nostalgia-increases-optimism.page.

[22] Rossen, J (30th September 2019) *Retro Analysis: The Science of Nostalgia*, MentalFloss.com, https://www.mentalfloss.com/article/600055/science-behind-nostalgia-tv-shows-movies

[23] Kaiz, M, BS, Howard, K PhD, and Bennett, E MS, Journal of the American Academy of Child and Adolescent Psychiatry, *The altering of reported experiences by Daniel offer MD*.

[24] DiSalvo, David (2012), What makes your brain happy and why you should do the opposite, Prometheus Books.

[25] Eriksen Flanker Task (2023) Wikipedia. Available at: https://en.wikipedia.org/wiki/Eriksen_flanker_task (Accessed: 29 January 2024).

[26] *Stories* (no date) *Image*. Available at: https://bankofideas.com.au/stories/ (Accessed: 29 January 2024).

[27] Wilson, T. D., & Gilbert, D. T. (2013). The impact bias is alive and well. Journal

of Personality and Social Psychology, 105, 740-748. https://dtg.sites.fas.harvard.edu/WIlson_Gilbert_2013.pdf

[28] Santos, L. (no date) *Annoying feature #4 - why our expectations are so bad, Coursera*, Time stamp: 1:40 Available at: https://www.coursera.org/learn/the-science-of-well-being/lecture/MIqZv/annoying-feature-4 (Accessed: 29 January 2024).

[29] Gittens, R, *The Happy Economist*, page 15.

[30] Lucretius (2024) *Wikipedia*. Available at: https://en.wikipedia.org/wiki/Lucretius (Accessed: 29 January 2024).

[31] Johnson, S, (2015), Who Moved My Cheese: An Amazing Way to Deal with Change in Your Work and in Your Life, Ebury Digital.

[32] Breuning, L.G, (2015) Habits of a Happy Brain: Retrain Your Brain to Boost Your Serotonin, Dopamine, Oxytocin, & Endorphin Levels, Adams Media.

[33] Gračanin A, Bylsma LM, Vingerhoets AJ. (28th May 2014) *Is crying a self-soothing behavior?* Front Psychol.;5:502. Doi: 10.3389/fpsyg.2014.00502. PMID: 24904511; PMCID:

PMC4035568. https://www.ncbi.nlm.nih.gov/pmc/articles/PMC4035568/

[34] Inga D. Neumann, 'Oxytocin: The Neuropeptide of Love Reveals Some of Its Secrets', *Cell Metabolism*,

Volume 5, Issue 4, 2007, Pages 231-233,

ISSN 1550-4131, https://doi.org/10.1016/j.cmet.2007.03.008.

(https://www.sciencedirect.com/science/article/pii/S1550413107000691)

[35] Beazer, J (20th January 2022)*The 4 Most Effective Ways To Increase Your Serotonin,*. https://brainmd.com/blog/4-ways-to-boost-your-serotonin/

[36] Young SN. (2007 Nov) *How to increase serotonin in the human brain without drugs.*

Journal Psychiatry Neuroscience, ;32(6):394-9. PMID: 18043762; PMCID: PMC2077351. https://www.ncbi.nlm.nih.gov/pmc/articles/PMC2077351/

[37] Lyle, L (November 2016) *Serotonin and Conflict.* . Published by thepositivepsychologypeople.com. https://www.thepositivepsychologypeople.com/serotonin-and-conflict/

[38] *Habits of a Healthy Brain*, by Loretta Graziano Breuning, page 109.

[39] Plous, S. L. - Faculty, Wesleyan University

[40] *Emotion definition & meaning* (no date) *Merriam-Webster*. Available at: https://www.merriam-webster.com/dictionary/emotion (Accessed: 29 January 2024).

[41] *The difference between feelings and emotions:* WFU online (2020) WFU Online Counseling. Available at: https://counseling.online.wfu.edu/blog/difference-feelings-emotions/#:~:text=A%20fundamental%20difference%20between%20feelings,the%20depths%20of%20their%20emotions. (Accessed: 30 January 2024).

[42] Burton, N, (2020), *Heaven and Hell: The Psychology of Emotions*, Acheron Press, page 194.

[43] Disney Pixar (2015) *Inside Out*,

[44] Tromholt, Morten. (1 November 2016)*The Facebook Experiment: Quitting Facebook Leads to Higher Levels of Well-Being* https://www.liebertpub.com/doi/full/10.1089/cyber.2016.0259.

[45] Fottrel, Quentin, (10 October 2018), *Nearly half of Americans report feeling alone.* https://www.marketwatch.com/story/america-has-a-big-loneliness-problem-2018-05-02

[46] Dattani, S. et al. (2023) *Mental health, Our World in Data*. Available at: https://ourworldindata.org/mental-health (Accessed: 29 January 2024).

[47] (No date) *Depression and other common mental disorders - world health organization*. Available at: https://apps.who.int/iris/bitstream/handle/10665/254610/WHO-MSD-MER-2017.2-eng.pdf (Accessed: 29 January 2024).

[48] *Anxiety disorders* (no date) *NAMI*. Available at: https://nami.org/About-Mental-Illness/Mental-Health-Conditions/Anxiety-Disorders (Accessed: 29 January 2024).

[49] *Learn about mental health* (no date) *Beyond Blue*. Available at: https://www.beyondblue.org.au/the-facts (Accessed: 29 January 2024).

[50] *Depression: Statistics* (no date) *Mental Health Foundation*. Available at: https://www.mentalhealth.org.uk/statistics/mental-health-statistics-depression (Accessed: 29 January 2024).

[51] *Suicide statistics* (2024) *American Foundation for Suicide Prevention*. Available at: https://afsp.org/suicide-statistics/ (Accessed: 29 January 2024).

[52] National Institute on Drug Abuse (2023) *Drug overdose death rates, National Institute on Drug Abuse*. Available at: https://www.drugabuse.gov/related-topics/trends-statistics/overdose-death-rates (Accessed: 29 January 2024).

[53] Brooks, David. (2019) *The Second Mountain: The Quest for a Moral Life*, Penguin.

[54] Newswire, M.-P. (no date) *New cigna study reveals loneliness at epidemic levels in America, Multivu*. Available at: https://www.multivu.com/players/English/8294451-cigna-us-loneliness-survey/?mod=article_inline (Accessed: 29 January 2024).

[55] Newswire, M.-P. (no date a) *New cigna study reveals loneliness at epidemic levels in America, Multivu*. Available at: https://www.multivu.com/players/English/8294451-cigna-us-loneliness-survey/?mod=article_inline (Accessed: 29 January 2024).

[56] Brooks, David. (2019) *The Second Mountain: The Quest for a Moral Life*, Penguin.

[57] (No date) *A 'prozac generation': Dark truth about life in 'lucky country'*. Available at: https://www.news.com.au/lifestyle/health/mind/prozac-generation-dark-truth-about-life-in-lucky-country/news-story/bfca213b0fb16ffb76f200e17cb9f020 (Accessed: 29 January 2024).

[58] Byron Katie (2024) https://thework.com/

[59] Dr Michael Bennett and Sarah Bennett, (2016) *F*ck Feelings: Less Obsessing, More Living*, Harper Thorsons, page 24.

[60] Maltz, M, (2015), *Psycho-Cybernetics*, TarcherPerigee.

[61] Peck, M.S (2012), The Road Less Travelled: A New Psychology of Love, Traditional Values and Spiritual Growth, Ebury Digital

[62] Indiana Jones, Indiana Jones and the Last Crusade

[63] Becker, E, (1997)*The Denial of Death*, Free Press, https://www.amazon.com/Denial-Death-Ernest-Becker/dp/0684832402/

[64] Wilson, S, (2017) *First, We Make the Beast Beautiful: A New Journey Through Anxiety*, Macmillan, page 111.

[65] Sachetta, B, (2018) *Get out of your Head: A Toolkit for Living with and Overcoming Anxiety*, We Are The Change Publishing.

[66] Grenville-Cleave, B, (2012) A Practical Guide to Positive Psychology: Achieve Lasting Happiness, Icon Books.

[67] Mel Robbins, (uploaded: June 12, 2011) *How to stop screwing yourself over.* TEDxSF. https://www.youtube.com/watch?v=Lp7E973zozc

[68] (2024) *Encyclopedia.com*. Available at: https://www.encyclopedia.com/daily/is-it-true-that-99-9-of-all-species-are-extinct/ (Accessed: 29 January 2024).

[69] Hsu, J. (2021) *Estimate: Human brain 30 times faster than Best Supercomputers, IEEE Spectrum*. Available at: https://spectrum.ieee.org/tech-talk/computing/networks/estimate-human-brain-30-times-faster-than-best-supercomputers (Accessed: 29 January 2024).

[70] (No date a) *Nature news*. Available at: https://www.nature.com/scitable/blog/brain-metrics/are_there_really_as_many/ (Accessed: 29 January 2024).

[71] *How many thoughts do we have per minute?* (no date) *Reference*. Available at: https://www.reference.com/world-view/many-thoughts-per-minute-cb7fcf22ebbf8466 (Accessed: 29 January 2024).

[72] Finn, E.S. et al. (2015) *Functional connectome fingerprinting: Identifying individuals using patterns of brain connectivity, Nature News*. Available at: https://www.nature.com/articles/nn.4135 (Accessed: 29 January 2024).

[73] Casals, P (1974), *Joys and Sorrow: Reflections*, Simon & Schuster, page 295.

[74] Beauchamp, Z. (2014) *The World's victory over extreme poverty, in one chart, Vox*. Available at: https://www.vox.com/2014/12/14/7384515/extreme-poverty-decline (Accessed: 29 January 2024).

[75] Rosling, H, et al. (2018) *Factfulness: Ten Reasons We're Wrong About the World — and Why Things Are Better Than You Think*, Sceptre.

[76] Rosling, H, et al. (2018) *Factfulness: Ten Reasons We're Wrong About the World — and Why*

[77] *Things Are Better Than You Think*, Sceptre.

[77] Mr Miyagi, The Karate Kid

[78] Burnett, D (2018). The Happy Brain: The Science of Where Happiness Comes From, and Why, Guardian Faber Publishing.

[79] Jessica Elliott, A. (2022) How to get to know yourself: Self-discovery questions & more, WikiHow. Available at: https://www.wikihow.com/Get-To-Know-Yourself (Accessed: 29 January 2024).

[80] Courtney E. Ackerman, MA. (2023) *What is attachment theory? Bowlby's 4 stages explained*, PositivePsychology.com. Available at: https://positivepsychology.com/attachment-theory/ (Accessed: 29 January 2024).

[81] Hardy, B, (2020), Personality isn't Permanent: Break free from Self-Limiting Beliefs and Rewrite Your story, Penguin Publishing Group.

[82] *Know yourself? 6 specific ways to know who you are* (no date) *Psychology Today*. Available at: https://www.psychologytoday.com/us/blog/changepower/201603/know-yourself-6-specific-ways-know-who-you-are (Accessed: 29 January 2024).

[83] Kruger, J., & Dunning, D. (1999). Unskilled and unaware of it: how difficulties in recognizing one's own incompetence lead to inflated self-assessments. *Journal of personality and social psychology, 77 6*, 1121-34.

[84] Hawking, S, (2009) *The Theory of Everything: The Origin and Fate of the Universe*, Phoenix Books.

[85] byquoteresearch, P. (2018) *The fable of the lion and the gazelle*, Quote Investigator. Available at: https://quoteinvestigator.com/2011/08/05/lion-gazelle/ (Accessed: 29 January 2024).

[86] Generation Wealth, Netflix

[87] More recent studies have shown that this may in fact be incorrect based on analysis of more than 40,000 U.S. adults aged 30 and over, over a period of five decades between 1972 and 2016. The study run by the San Diego State University found the link between money and happiness changed as the years went by with more saying they were happier having more money. There is no plateau for an income happiness saturation point. People earning US$160,000 in 2020 reported they were happier than those earning between US$115,000 and US$160,000. The trend has been put down to an increase in income inequality over the time period, the so called 'haves' and 'have nots'.
Twenge, J. (2022) *Money buys even more happiness than it used to*, The Conversation. Available at: https://theconversation.com/money-buys-even-more-happiness-than-it-used-to-141766 (Accessed: 30 January 2024).

[88] Fromm, E, (2020). To Have or To Be, Upfront Books, page 72.

[89] Hershfield et al, (2016).

[90] Whillans et al, (2016).

[91] Mogilner, (2010).

[92] See the 'Living in the Moment' chapter

[93] Lundin, S, et al. (2014), Fish: A Remarkable Way to Boost Morale and Improve Results, Hodder & Stoughton, Page 37

[94] Boys, J, (1629), *The Workes of Iohn Boys: Doctor in Diuinitie and Deane of Canterburie*, Section: The first Sunday after the Epiphanie, Imprinted for W. Ashley, London, Page 129.

[95] (No date) *Totalmindtherapy.net*. Available at: http://www.totalmindtherapy.net/subconscious-mind-training/using-nlp-to-change-negative-self-talk-into-positive-self-talk/ (Accessed: 29 January 2024).

[96] NLP is too in depth a topic for this book but if you Google it you will find a lot of information on the topic.

[97] *A Theory of Human Motivation*, Psychological Review, (1943)

[98] See Renovating the Pyramid of Needs: Contemporary Extensions Built Upon Ancient Foundations as an example - https://www.ncbi.nlm.nih.gov/pmc/articles/PMC3161123/

[99] (No date) *Act randomized controlled trials (1986 to present)*. Available at: https://contextualscience.org/act_randomized_controlled_trials_1986_to_present (Accessed: 29 January 2024).

[100] Wilson, S, (2017)*First We Make the Beast Beautiful: a new conversation about anxiety*, Transworld Digital.

[101] (1924 August 14) Visalia Morning Delta, *Contemporaneous Opinions: You Cannot Control*, Page 2, Column 2, Visalia, California.

[102] *Choosing positive words improves mindset and performance* (no date) *Psychology Today*. Available at: https://www.psychologytoday.com/au/blog/the-athletes-way/201212/choosing-positive-words-improves-mindset-and-performance (Accessed: 29 January 2024).

[103] *Perception is not reality* (no date) *Psychology Today*. Available at: https://www.psychologytoday.com/au/blog/the-power-prime/201908/perception-is-not-reality (Accessed: 29 January 2024).

[104] Grenville-Cleave, B, (2018), *A Practical Guide to Positive Psychology: Achieve Lasting Happiness*, Icon Books, Chapter 6 Meaning and Purpose. Page 829 of 3042.

[105] Elizabeth Mostofsky, Malcolm Maclure, Jane B. Sherwood, Geoffrey H. Tofler, James E. Muller and Murray A. Mittleman. *The Determinants of Myocardial Infarction Onset Study* Originally published 9 Jan 2012 https://doi.org/10.1161/CIRCULATIONAHA.111.061770Circulation. 2012;125:491–496

[106] Sahlgren, G.H. (2013) *Work longer, live healthier* - institute of economic affairs. Available at: https://iea.org.uk/wp-content/uploads/2016/07/Work%20Longer,%20Live_Healthier.pdf (Accessed: 29 January 2024).

[107] Gardner, J (November 10, 1990), *Personal Renewal*, available at: http://www.pbs.org/johngardner/sections/writings_speech_1.html (last accessed 29th of January 2024).

[108] Emily Esfahani Smith, (April 2017), TED, available at: https://www.ted.com/talks/emily_esfahani_smith_there_s_more_to_life_than_being_happy, (last accessed 29th of January 2024).

[109] Dostoevsky, F, Translated by MacAndrew, A. (1981) (Translation Copyright 1970), *The Brothers Karamazov*, Bantam Books, New York, Book V: Pro and Contra, Chapter 5: The Grand Inquisitor, Quote Page 306 and 307.

[110] Jackson, E. (2011) *The steve jobs stanford commencement speech*, Forbes. Available at: https://www.forbes.com/sites/ericjackson/2011/08/24/the-steve-jobs-stanford-commencement-speech/#620360c5d071 (Accessed: 29 January 2024).

[111] Manson, M. (2023) *Screw finding your passion, Mark Manson*. Available at: https://markmanson.net/screw-finding-your-passion (Accessed: 29 January 2024).

[112] Manson, M. (2023) *Screw finding your passion, Mark Manson*. Available at: https://markmanson.net/screw-finding-your-passion (Accessed: 29 January 2024).

[113] Walton, G. (2018) *Psychological science*, available at: http://gregorywalton-stanford.weebly.com/uploads/4/9/4/4/49448111/okeefedweckwalton_2018.pdf (Accessed: 29 January 2024).

[114] We discuss more about fixed and growth mindsets later in the book.

[115] Walton, G. (2018) *Psychological science*, available at: http://gregorywalton-stanford.weebly.com/uploads/4/9/4/4/49448111/okeefedweckwalton_2018.pdf (Accessed: 29 January 2024).

[116] *It's what you can contribute* (2015) YouTube. Available at: https://www.youtube.com/watch?v=WRYRBGX4lVM (Accessed: 29 January 2024), timestamp 10:50.

[117] Jose, et al (2012).

[118] The Mind Explained, Netflix, Ep. 5: Meditation.

[119] It is actually 46.9%.

[120] DiSalvo, D, What makes our brain happy and why you should do the opposite, Page 84

[121] Matthew A. Killingsworth, Daniel T. Gilbert, (2010). A Wandering Mins is an Unhappy Mind. Science 330, 932-932 DOI: https://doi.org/10.1126/science.1192439

[122] Lazar SW, Kerr CE, Wasserman RH, Gray JR, Greve DN, Treadway MT, McGarvey M, Quinn BT, Dusek JA, Benson H, Rauch SL, Moore CI, Fischl B. Meditation experience is associated with increased cortical thickness. Neuroreport. 2005 Nov 28;16(17):1893-7. doi: 10.1097/01.wnr.0000186598.66243.19. PMID: 16272874; PMCID: PMC1361002.| Hölzel BK, Carmody J, Vangel M, Congleton C, Yerramsetti SM, Gard T, Lazar SW. Mindfulness practice leads to increases in regional brain gray matter density. Psychiatry Res. 2011 Jan 30;191(1):36-43. doi: 10.1016/j.pscychresns.2010.08.006. Epub 2010 Nov 10. PMID: 21071182; PMCID: PMC3004979.

[123] Mrazek, M.D. et al. (2013) *Mindfulness training improves working memory capacity*

[124] Shapiro, S. L., Astin, J. A., Bishop, S. R., & Cordova, M. (2005). Mindfulness-Based Stress Reduction for Health Care Professionals: Results From a Randomized Trial. *International Journal of Stress Management, 12*(2), 164–176. https://doi.org/10.1037/1072-5245.12.2.164 | Speca, Michael PsyD; Carlson, Linda E. PhD; Goodey, Eileen MSW; Angen, Maureen PhD. A Randomized, Wait-List Controlled Clinical Trial: The Effect of a Mindfulness Meditation-Based Stress Reduction Program on Mood and Symptoms of Stress in Cancer Outpatients. Psychosomatic Medicine 62(5):p 613-622, September 2000. | Davidson, Richard J. PhD; Kabat-Zinn, Jon PhD; Schumacher, Jessica MS; Rosenkranz, Melissa BA; Muller, Daniel MD, PhD; Santorelli, Saki F. EdD; Urbanowski, Ferris MA; Harrington, Anne PhD; Bonus, Katherine MA; Sheridan, John F. PhD. Alterations in Brain and Immune Function Produced by Mindfulness Meditation. Psychosomatic Medicine 65(4):p 564-570, July 2003. | DOI: 10.1097/01.PSY.0000077505.67574.E3

[125] Sutton, J. (2023) *20+ health benefits of meditation according to Science, PositivePsychology.com*. Available at: https://positivepsychology.com/benefits-of-meditation/ (Accessed: 29 January 2024).

[126] Goyal M, Singh S, Sibinga EMS, et al. Meditation Programs for Psychological Stress and Well-being: A Systematic Review and Meta-analysis. *JAMA Intern Med.* 2014;174(3):357–368. doi:10.1001/jamainternmed.2013.13018

[127] Chen KW, Berger CC, Manheimer E, Forde D, Magidson J, Dachman L, Lejuez CW. Meditative therapies for reducing anxiety: a systematic review and meta-analysis of randomized controlled trials. Depress Anxiety. 2012 Jul;29(7):545-62. doi: 10.1002/da.21964. Epub 2012 Jun 14. PMID: 22700446; PMCID: PMC3718554.

[128] Penman, D. (2015) *Can mindfulness meditation really reduce pain and suffering?, Psychology Today.* Available at: https://www.psychologytoday.com/au/blog/mindfulness-in-frantic-world/201501/can-mindfulness-meditation-really-reduce-pain-and-suffering (Accessed: 29 January 2024).

[129] Fadel Zeidan, Adrienne L. Adler-Neal, Rebecca E. Wells, Emily Stagnaro, Lisa M. May, James C. Eisenach, John G. McHaffie, Robert C. Coghill, *Mindfulness-Meditation-Based Pain Relief Is Not Mediated by Endogenous Opioids*, Journal of Neuroscience 16 March 2016, 36 (11) 3391-3397.

[130] Davidson RJ, Kabat-Zinn J, Schumacher J, Rosenkranz M, Muller D, Santorelli SF, Urbanowski F, Harrington A, Bonus K, Sheridan JF. *Alterations in brain and immune function produced by mindfulness meditation.* Psychosom Med. 2003 Jul-Aug;65(4):564-70. doi: 10.1097/01.psy.0000077505.67574.e3. PMID: 12883106.

[131] Davidson, Richard J. PhD; Kabat-Zinn, Jon PhD; Schumacher, Jessica MS; Rosenkranz, Melissa BA; Muller, Daniel MD, PhD; Santorelli, Saki F. EdD; Urbanowski, Ferris MA; Harrington, Anne PhD; Bonus, Katherine MA; Sheridan, John F. PhD. Alterations in Brain and Immune Function Produced by Mindfulness Meditation. Psychosomatic Medicine 65(4):p 564-570, July 2003. | DOI: 10.1097/01.PSY.0000077505.67574.E3

[132] Morgan N, Irwin MR, Chung M, Wang C (2014) The Effects of Mind-Body Therapies on the Immune System: Meta-Analysis. PLoS ONE 9(7): e100903. https://doi.org/10.1371/journal.pone.0100903

[133] Thorpe, M. (2023) *12 benefits of meditation, Healthline*. Available at: https://www.health-

[134] line.com/nutrition/12-benefits-of-meditation#section2 (Accessed: 29 January 2024).

[134] Van Edwards, V. (2024) *14 amazing benefits of meditation that can actually rewire your brain, Science of People.* Available at: https://www.scienceofpeople.com/meditation-benefits/ (Accessed: 29 January 2024).

[135] *The 24 character strengths* (no date) *VIA Institute On Character.* Available at: http://www.viacharacter.org/www/Character-Strengths (Accessed: 29 January 2024).

[136] Kiyosaki, R.T, (2017), *Rich Dad Poor Dad: What the Rich Teach Their Kids About Money That the Poor and Middle Class Do Not!,* Plata Publishing.

[137] This was just an example, but who doesn't love Agatha Christie movies and television series?

[138] Miller, K, (21st May 2019), *What is Kindness in Psychology?*, Positive Psychology, https://positivepsychology.com/character-strength-kindness/, (Accessed: 29th January 2024).

[139] (Hays translation) Marcus Aurelius

[140] Chesterton, G.K, (1936), *The Autobiography of G. K. Chesterton,* Chapter 16: The God with the Golden Key, Quote Page 341 and 342, Sheed & Ward, New York.

[141] *Home* (2022) *TRP@HOME.* Available at: https://theresilienceproject.com.au/at-home/everyone/gratitude/ (Accessed: 29 January 2024).

[142] Burnett, D (2018). The Happy Brain: The Science of Where Happiness Comes From, and Why, Guardian Faber Publishing.

[143] Brooks, David. (2019) *The Second Mountain: The Quest for a Moral Life,* Penguin.

[144] *Harvard Second Generation Study* (no date) harvardstudy. Available at: https://www.adultdevelopmentstudy.org/ (Accessed: 30 January 2024). And: Waldinger, R. and Schultz, M. (2023); *The good life book,* The Good Life. Available at: https://the-good-life-book.com/ (Accessed: 30 January 2024).

[145] Holt-Lunstad J, Smith TB, Baker M, Harris T, Stephenson D. Loneliness and social isolation as risk factors for mortality: a meta-analytic review. Perspect Psychol Sci. 2015 Mar;10(2):227-37. doi: 10.1177/1745691614568352. PMID: 25910392.

[146] Santos, L. (no date) *The science of well-being, Coursera.* Available at: https://www.coursera.org/learn/the-science-of-well-being (Accessed: 30 January 2024).

[147] NORC at the University of Chicago (no date) NORC at the University of Chicago | Research You Can Trust. Available at: https://www.norc.org/ (Accessed: 30 January 2024).

[148] Jo Cox, (2017), Commission on Loneliness.

[149] Interestingly at the same time, the 'loneliness epidemic' apparently does not exist.

'Surveys from rich countries do not suggest there has been an increase in loneliness over time. Today's adolescents in the US do not seem to be more likely to report feeling lonely than adolescents from a couple of decades ago; and similarly, today's older adults in the US do not report higher loneliness than did adults of their age in the past.'.

[150] *Home* (2024) *Framingham Heart Study*. Available at: https://www.framinghamheartstudy.org/ (Accessed: 30 January 2024).

[151] Richard L Moreland, Scott R Beach, (1992) *Exposure effects in the classroom: The development of affinity among students*, Journal of Experimental Social Psychology, Volume 28, Issue 3, Pages 255-276, ISSN 0022-1031, https://doi.org/10.1016/0022-1031(92)90055-O. (https://www.sciencedirect.com/science/article/pii/002210319290055O)

[152] Franco, M.G. (2019) *Science says people like you more than you know | psychology Today*, Psychology Today. Available at: https://www.psychologytoday.com/us/blog/platonic-love/201908/science-says-people-you-more-you-know (Accessed: 30 January 2024).

[153] ukactiveMore (2017) *Inactive Brits spend twice as long on toilet per week as they do exercising*, *ukactive*. Available at: https://www.ukactive.com/events/inactive-brits-spend-twice-as-long-on-toilet-per-week-as-they-do-exercising/ (Accessed: 30 January 2024).

[154] Sibold JS and Berg KM (2010) *Perceptual and Motor Skills*.

[155] Siri Kvam, Catrine Lykkedrang Kleppe, Inger Hilde Nordhus, Anders Hovland, (2016), *Exercise as a treatment for depression: A meta-analysis*, Journal of Affective Disorders, Volume 202, Pages 67-86, ISSN 0165-0327, https://doi.org/10.1016/j.jad.2016.03.063. (https://www.sciencedirect.com/science/article/pii/S0165032715314221)

[156] https://www.amazon.com/Fast-Exercise-Intensity-Training-Get-Stronger/dp/1780721986

[157] Interesting sidenote, if this does happen to you, the best thing to do is think of something completely different and because you are not trying to remember, it will pop back into your head.

[158] Neurology. (2014 Sep 9); 83(11): 967–973. doi: 10.1212/WNL.0000000000000774 PMCID: PMC4162301 PMID: 25186857 Poor sleep quality is associated with increased cortical atrophy in community-dwelling adults. Claire E. Sexton, DPhil, Andreas B. Storsve, MSc, Kristine B. Walhovd, PhD, Heidi Johansen-Berg, DPhil, and Anders M. Fjell, PhD

[159] Stroka, J. (2017) *An extra hour of sleep can do more for daily happiness than a $60,000 raise*, *HuffPost*. Available at: https://www.huffpost.com/entry/an-extra-hour-of-sleep-ca_b_8114998 (Accessed: 30 January 2024).

[160] Breslau, N. et al., *Sleep Disturbance and Psychiatric Disorders: A Longitudinal Epidemiological Study of Young Adults*, Biological Psychiatry. Mar 1996; 39(6): 411–418.

[161] Neckelmann, D. et al., (2007), *Chronic Insomnia as a Risk Factor for Developing Anxiety and Depression*, Sleep. 30 (7): 873-880

[162] *How to sleep better* (no date) *Harvard Health*. Available at: https://www.health.harvard.edu/topics/sleep (Accessed: 30 January 2024).

[163] *Could too little sleep put teens at risk for diabetes?* (2012) *HuffPost*. Available at: https://www.huffpost.com/entry/sleep-insulin-resistance-teens_n_1929374 (Accessed: 30 January 2024).

[164] Broussard, J. L., Ehrmann, D. A., Van Cauter, E., Tasali, E., & Brady, M. J. (2012). Impaired insulin signaling in human adipocytes after experimental sleep restriction: a randomized, crossover study. *Annals of internal medicine*, 157(8), 549–557. https://doi.org/10.7326/0003-4819-157-8-201210160-00005

[165] University of California - Berkeley. (2013, January 27). *Poor sleep in old age prevents the brain from storing memories.* ScienceDaily. Retrieved January 29, 2024 from www.sciencedaily.com/releases/2013/01/130127134212.htm

[166] Nota J and Coles M (2014) *Cognitive Therapy and Research*

[167] University of Warwick. (2011, February 8). *Sleep deprivation: Late nights can lead to higher risk of strokes and heart attacks, study finds.* ScienceDaily. (Accessed: January 29, 2024) from www.sciencedaily.com/releases/2011/02/110208091426.htm

[168] (No date) *Academic.oup.com*. Available at: https://academic.oup.com/sleep?pid=27894 (Accessed: 30 January 2024).

[169] Jacka, F, (2021), *Brain Changer: How diet can save your mental health – cutting-edge science from an expert,* Yellow Kite.

[170] Stevenson Richard J., Francis Heather M., Attuquayefio Tuki, Gupta Dolly, Yeomans Martin R., Oaten Megan J. and Davidson Terry, (2020), *Hippocampal-dependent appetitive control is impaired by experimental exposure to a Western-style diet,* R. Soc. Open Sci.7191338191338, (accessed: 30th January 2024), available at: https://royalsocietypublishing.org/doi/10.1098/rsos.191338

[171] Dow, M, (2015) *The Brain Fog Fix: Reclaim Your Focus, Memory, and Joy in Just 3 Weeks*, Hay House, page 35.

[172] Lee, M. (2023) *Want to improve your mood? it's time to ditch the junk food, The Conversation.* Available at: https://theconversation.com/want-to-improve-your-mood-its-time-to-ditch-the-junk-food-107358#:~:text=The%20review%20found%20that%20across,who%20ate%20more%20unhealthy%20foods. (Accessed: 30 January 2024).

[173] Meerman, R. (2019) *How breathing and metabolism are interconnected: Ruben Meerman: TEDxBundaberg, YouTube.* Available at: https://youtu.be/nM-ySWyID9o (Accessed: 30 January 2024).

[174] Harris, R, (2007), *The Happiness Trap: Stop Struggling*, Start Living, Exisle Publishing.

[175] Deci, E, (1985), *Intrinsic Motivation and Self-Determination in Human Behavior* (Perspectives in Social Psychology), Plenum Press.

[176] Mochon, D., Norton, M.L. and Ariely, D. (2010) *Who benefits from Religion*. Available at: https://www.hbs.edu/ris/Publication%20Files/mochon%20norton%20ariely%20who%20benefits%20from%20religion_e072e4b1-8c04-4698-9cdf-e2d27b1f237d.pdf (Accessed: 30 January 2024).

[177] Different sources tell of difference numbers, and they range from 12,000 through to 80,000 per day!

[178] Cohen, J. (2013) *Overthinking can be detrimental to human performance*, The Current. Available at: https://www.news.ucsb.edu/2013/013593/overthinking-can-be-detrimental-human-performance (Accessed: 30 January 2024).

[179] Bavin, E. (2023) *Aussies spend $8.6 million every day on avoidable cost*, Yahoo! Finance. Available at: https://au.finance.yahoo.com/news/aussies-spend-86-million-every-day-on-credit-card-debt-002458034.html (Accessed: 30 January 2024).

[180] *Small loans, big problems – insights on buy now pay later from more than 500 financial counsellors on the frontline* (2023) Financial Counselling Australia. Available at: https://www.financialcounsellingaustralia.org.au/docs/small-loans-big-problems-buy-now-pay-later/ (Accessed: 30 January 2024).

[181] *Research-buy-now-pay-later* (2023) Anglicare. Available at: https://www.anglicare-tas.org.au/research-buy-now-pay-later/ (Accessed: 30 January 2024).

[182]

[183] *Facial feedback hypothesis* (2024) Wikipedia. Available at: https://en.wikipedia.org/wiki/Facial_feedback_hypothesis (Accessed: 30 January 2024).

[184] The thought here is that your thoughts are energy (e) so using Einstein's theory (e=mc2), your thoughts should materialise into something real (m – mass) i.e. by thinking I really want a house, I will actually get one.

[185] Altucher, J, (2013), *Choose Yourself!*, James Altucher.

[186] Wood, J.V., Perunovic, E. and Lee, J.W. (2009) *Positive Self-Statements Power for Some, Peril for Others*. Available at: https://www.uni-muenster.de/imperia/md/content/psyifp/aeechterhoff/wintersemester2011-12/seminarthemenfelderdersozialpsychologie/04_wood_etal_selfstatements_psychscience2009.pdf (Accessed: 30 January 2024).

[187] Chun, J.Y. and Miu Chi, V.L. (2016) *When self-help materials help: examining the effects of selfdiscrepancy and modes of delivery of positive self-statements* . Available at: https://commons.ln.edu.hk/cgi/viewcontent.cgi?referer=https://scholar.google.ca/&httpsredir=1&article=3651&context=sw_master (Accessed: 30 January 2024).

[188] Killam, K. M., & Kim, Y.-H. (2014). Positive Psychological Interventions and Self-Perceptions: A Cautionary Tale. In A. C. Parks & S. M. Schueller (Eds.), *The Wiley-Blackwell*

[189] Irwin Rosenfarb, Steven C. Hayes, (1984), *Social standard setting: The achilles heel of informational accounts of therapeutic change*, Behavior Therapy, Volume 15, Issue 5, Pages 515-528, ISSN 0005-7894, https://doi.org/10.1016/S0005-7894(84)80053-2. (https://www.sciencedirect.com/science/article/pii/S0005789484800532)

[190] Kappes, H. B., & Oettingen, G. (2011). Positive fantasies about idealized futures sap energy. Journal of Experimental Social Psychology, 47(4), 719–729

[191] Sheeran, P. (2014) The impact of self-affirmation on health-behavior change: A meta-analysis, Health psychology: official journal of the Division of Health Psychology, American Psychological Association. Available at: https://www.academia.edu/13555803/The_Impact_of_Self-Affirmation_on_Health-Behavior_Change_A_Meta-Analysis (Accessed: 30 January 2024).

[192] Cheatham, Lauren and Goldsmith, Kelly and Gal, David and Raghunathan, Rajagopal, (October 29, 2018). The Pursuit of Happiness: Can It Make You Happy? Available at: SSRN: https://ssrn.com/abstract=1979829 or http://dx.doi.org/10.2139/ssrn.1979829

[193] Cupchic and Leventhal, (1974); Kashdan, Breen and Julian (2010); Mauss, Tamir, Anderson, and Savino (2011); Schooler, Ariely, and Loewenstein (2003); for review see Gruber, Mauss, and Tamir (2011).

[194] Schooler et al. (2003), study 1.

[195] Dr Michael Bennett and Sarah Bennett, (2016) *F*ck Feelings: Less Obsessing, More Living*, Harper Thorsons, page, page 27.

[196] *Yerkes–Dodson Law* (2024) *Wikipedia*. Available at: https://en.wikipedia.org/wiki/Yerkes%E2%80%93Dodson_law (Accessed: 30 January 2024).

[197] Ludwig, P; Schicker, A, (2019), The End of Procrastination: How to stop postponing and live a fulfilled life, Murdoch Books.

[198] Clear, J (2018), *Atomic Habits*, Avery.

[199] *Welcome* (2023) *Tiny Habits*. Available at: https://www.tinyhabits.com/welcome (Accessed: 30 January 2024).

---

[i] https://en.wiktionary.org/wiki/experientia#Latin

[ii] Harvard University. (2010, November 12). Mind is a frequent, but not happy, wanderer: People spend nearly half their waking hours thinking about what isn't going on around them. *ScienceDaily*. Retrieved January 10, 2024 from www.sciencedaily.com/releases/2010/11/101111141759.htm

[iii] The Bible. Acts 20 – 35. King James version

[iv] Healing through helping: an experimental investigation of kindness, social activities, and reappraisal as well-being interventions. Cregg ,David R. and Cheavens ,Jennifer S. The Journal of Positive Psychology. https://doi.org/10.1080/17439760.2022.2154695

[v] Brown, W., Wilkerson, A., Boyd, S., Dewey, D., Mesa, F. and Bunnell, B., 2017. A review of sleep disturbance in children and adolescents with anxiety. Journal of Sleep Research, 27(3), p.e12635.

[vi] GoodTherapy.org Therapy Blog. 2021. When Yelling is a Pattern – GoodTherapy.org Therapy Blog. [online] Available at: <https://www.goodtherapy.org/blog/yelling/> [Accessed 21 October 2021].

[vii] Leander NP, Shah JY, Sanders S. Indifferent reactions: regulatory responses to the apathy of others. J Pers Soc Psychol. 2014 Aug;107(2):229-47. doi: 10.1037/a0037073. PMID: 25090128.

[viii] Hsee, C. K., Yang, A. X., & Wang, L. (2010). Idleness Aversion and the Need for Justifiable Busyness. *Psychological Science*, *21*(7), 926-930. https://doi.org/10.1177/0956797610374738

[ix] "The Effects of Chronic Achievement Motivation and Achievement Primes on the Activation of Achievement and Fun Goals," by William Hart and Dolores Albarracín, Journal of Personality and Social Psychology © 2009 American Psychological Association. 2009, Vol. 97, No. 6, 1129–1141 0022-3514/09. DOI: 10.1037/a0017146

ABOUT THE AUTHOR

A R Arnold

A R Arnold is an accomplished author and digital strategist whose work spans across genres, from health and wellbeing to gripping mystery thrillers. His first book, Everything You Wanted To Know About Happiness And Wellbeing (previously published as WEALTH and Wellbeing), has become a cornerstone for readers seeking to enrich their lives, blending practical advice with inspiring insights into achieving balance and fulfillment.

A R Arnold's writing reflects a deep understanding of human psychology and life's pivotal transitions, as seen in his book, The Dawn Thread. Here, he dives into the life of a middle-aged man, exploring themes of nostalgia, financial pressures, and the quest for purpose.

Whether he's offering tools for personal growth or weaving tales of suspense, Andrew is passionate about connecting with readers and helping them explore life's possibilities.

www.ingramcontent.com/pod-product-compliance
Lightning Source LLC
Chambersburg PA
CBHW070135100426
42743CB00013B/2708